AN ARGUMENT FOR
SAME-SEX MARRIAGE

Religion and Politics Series
John C. Green, Ted Jelen, Mark Rozell, series editors

AN ARGUMENT FOR SAME-SEX MARRIAGE

Religious Freedom, Sexual Freedom, and Public Expressions of Civic Equality

EMILY R. GILL

Georgetown University Press
Washington, D.C.

Library of Congress Cataloging-in-Publication Data

Gill, Emily R., 1944-
An argument for same-sex marriage : religious freedom, sexual freedom,
and public expressions of civic equality / Emily R. Gill.
    pages cm — (Religion and politics series)
Includes bibliographical references and index.
ISBN 978-1-58901-920-1 (pbk. : alk. paper)
1. Same-sex marriage—United States—Religious aspects. 2. Same-sex
marriage—Law and legislation—United States. 3. Religion and politics—
United States. 4. Religion and state—United States. I. Title.
HQ1034.U5G55 2012
306.84'8—dc23
                                                    2011052058

15 14 13 12   9 8 7 6 5 4 3 2   First printing

To my family, with the hope that its younger members will see equal value accorded to all families

James Rountree Temples
Robert Oliver Temples and Carrie Elizabeth Temples
Emily Hannah Temples

CONTENTS

PREFACE

This book germinated in my thinking about United States Supreme Court decisions centering on Justice Sandra Day O'Connor's endorsement test, proposed in *Lynch v. Donnelly* (465 U.S. 668 [1984]). O'Connor's endorsement test says that when the government makes or allows policies that seemingly endorse some religious beliefs over others, it effectively classifies some citizens as insiders in the political community and marks others as outsiders. Public policies that include this kind of classification are public expressions of civic inequality. Such expressions have no place in a polity that should stand in the same relationship to all of its citizens.

The institution of civil marriage comprises public policies about who may marry and under what circumstances they may do so. Although the government does not need to allow religious or sexual practices deemed harmful to others, I believe it should not endorse the relationships of straight couples over same-sex couples. Both straight couples and same-sex couples who wish to marry desire to commit publicly to the same type of long-term relationship that civil marriage has upheld as a foundation of society. When the government recognizes the commitments of opposite-sex couples but ignores those of same-sex couples, it classifies same-sex couples as outsiders and regards their relationships as less valuable than those of traditional couples. This book is not a constitutional exegesis, because religion and sexuality cannot be treated in entirely parallel fashion; but I do argue from a jurisprudential viewpoint that the comparison induces us to think in new ways and is therefore instructive.

The government should attempt to be neutral among religions as well as between those who are religious and those who are not. Likewise, some have argued that the government should take a neutral stance between those who defend and those who condemn same-sex relationships. One theme throughout this book is that neutrality is a complex concept and that achieving neutrality is more difficult than it may first appear, in the realms of both religion and sexuality. In the first two chapters I make comparisons between religious belief and sexuality and then address the impossibility of achieving policies that are neutral on all levels. Chapter 3 analyzes four major but conflicting positions on same-sex marriage. Chapters 4 and 5 take up, respectively, the establishment clause and the free exercise clause of the First Amendment to the United States Constitution, arguing that the widespread ban on same-sex civil marriage can be regarded as a violation of both clauses. Finally, in chapter 6 I suggest that both religion and sexuality are goods that may be part of a full human life. The state should provide a framework for exercising these capabilities, one that sometimes requires noninterference but at other times requires positive, empowering action.

I have looked forward to writing this preface to thank many people whose input made this book possible. While developing my arguments, I have written several convention papers, articles, and book chapters on which fellow panelists, reviewers, and editors have made constructive comments. Several of my undergraduate students have collaborated on the research. I thank Dan Hatley, Andromeda McGregor, and Julie Mierzwa for stimulating conversations and intellectual interchange. Andromeda and Julie each copresented a paper with me at different meetings of the Midwest Political Science Association. I most want to thank Gordon Babst. We have served together on several convention panels over the past decade, and at his invitation I served in two capacities on the program of the 2006 Western Political Science Association meeting. Around this time I realized I had enough content to write a book on this topic. Ever since he liked my initial book proposal in 2007, Gordon has been my cheerleader-in-chief, commenting extensively after I wrote each chapter. After finishing the first draft, I revised both to shorten it and also to reflect his suggestions wherever my thinking was muddled or my expression unclear. Gordon then reread the entire manuscript, making a few more suggestions along the way. This project is a better book because of Gordon's willingness to participate in its improvement.

I also thank Richard Brown of Georgetown University Press for shepherding the manuscript through the review process, as well as Ted Jelen and an anonymous reviewer for their constructive suggestions. The staff of Georgetown University Press have helped me to improve the book in many ways; these individuals have my profound appreciation. Kathy Lundy, administrative support for the Department of Political Science at Bradley University, has been invaluable in figuring out how to get my computer to do what I want it to do, as well as helping with details on her own computer. I also benefited from a sabbatical leave from Bradley University in spring 2010. Finally, I thank my husband, James Temples, for supporting me throughout this project, as well as taking me away from it when I needed a break.

I conclude with a point about mechanics. Italics or emphases that appear within quotations are original unless otherwise indicated.

CHAPTER 1

Religion and Sexuality

Setting the Stage

The current controversy over the legitimacy of same-sex marriage reveals a number of fault lines both in our conception of citizenship and also in our thinking about the relationship of church and state in a modern liberal democracy. Marriage is in many ways a private, consensual relationship, yet its contours are defined by public policy. It is entered by a civil contract, yet it may also be religiously sanctioned by clergy invested with civil authority. In the United States the First Amendment prohibition against establishment of religion implies that the nature of the institution of marriage should not be dictated by religious beliefs. Yet the First Amendment guarantee of the free exercise of religion suggests that religious citizens, like nonreligious citizens with strong moral and ethical convictions, may seek to shape civil institutions so that these reflect their sincere beliefs.

This work was inspired by competing accounts regarding whether including same-sex couples in the institution of marriage constitutes approval or endorsement of same-sex relationships. Upon reflection, parallels appear between this controversy and two others: controversy over the establishment or endorsement of religious belief, as well as controversy over justifications offered for the free exercise of such beliefs. Although same-sex marriage is independently a popular topic of debate, I examine this subject through the prism of the religion clauses of the First Amendment because many debates over sexual orientation and the recognition of same-sex marriage mirror debates over the proper application of the religion clauses. Tension between these clauses is commonly acknowledged. Attempts to avoid the establishment of religion can increase the perceived secularity of the common culture, making the free exercise of religion more difficult for some. On the other hand, attempts to ease the free exercise of religion, as in equal access to forums or benefits by religious groups, can seem like an establishment of religion.

Like religious faith, sexual orientation is a central facet of one's identity. Even today many assume that most others are Christian and regard non-Christians as deviants from the true faith. Similarly, the assumption that most others are heterosexual has historically been the social and especially the legal norm, with sodomy laws representing a condemnation of homosexuality. Gays, lesbians, and bisexuals have in most cases been tolerated at best, expected to practice their "religions" discreetly so as not to disturb the equanimity of those of the dominant "faith" or consensus. The status quo could be described as establishing heterosexuality—until 2003, when the Supreme Court struck down all remaining antisodomy laws in *Lawrence v. Texas*. Only seventeen years before *Lawrence*, the court upheld the Georgia antisodomy law in *Bowers v. Hardwick* (478 U.S. 186 [1986]). Although such prosecutions were uncommon, until *Lawrence* individuals could be prosecuted where state antisodomy statutes existed. A criminal record and sometimes sex offender registration followed individuals convicted under these statutes, and the specter of such a record haunted countless others who knew they could be subject to conviction if apprehended and prosecuted. Moreover, before *Lawrence* individuals known to experience same-sex attraction could be objects of contempt, subject to discrimination for no other reason than the fact that they were breaking the law. However, exactly what the "disestablishment" represented by *Lawrence* means or should mean is still under discussion, to say the least.

Although disestablishment of a majority religion logically implies greater free exercise by followers of minority religions, traditionalists may believe that such a move disadvantages them when their own religious practice includes presenting their beliefs and moral teachings as superior to those of others. The same is true of sexual orientation. That is, the elevation of competing sexual orientations or "faiths" through equal access to jobs, housing, and perhaps marriage appears to traditionalists to be a hostile and competing way to establish a religion. Equal access means that the majority religion (broadly Judeo-Christian) or the majority sexual orientation (heterosexual) is no longer the one true faith—or at least, it is no longer the only one that is publicly recognized (leaving others to exist on the fringes of society). On the other hand, to those with nontraditional sexual orientations restricting state-sanctioned civil marriage to opposite-sex couples is also a type of establishment of religion. Although civil marriage does not require adherence to traditional religious beliefs, civil marriage in the West originated in such beliefs. Moreover restricting civil marriage to opposite-sex couples denies particular benefits to and imposes certain burdens on same-sex couples that traditional couples do not experience.

Sexual orientation and intimate life is a central constituent of identity, just as religious belief and practice are. As Martha Nussbaum (2010) explains, sexual orientation is like religion "in being intimately personal, connected to a sense of life's ultimate significance, and utterly nontrivial. Like religion, it [sexual orientation] appears to be something in which authenticity, or the involvement of conscience, is central. We understand that it goes to the heart of people's self-definition, their search for identity and self-expression" (39; see 36–41, 60–61). Likewise I believe that the denial of marriage to same-sex couples is equivalent to a denial of their free exercise of religion. This can be true in the narrow sense, in the case of same-sex couples who adhere to faith traditions that require a formal religious commitment as well as a civil one. A denial of the free exercise of religion may also apply more broadly, however, for couples who are not traditionally religious but for whom a formal civil commitment is central to and partly constitutive of what it means to them to be partners in a committed relationship.

A few commentators have drawn provocative comparisons between religious belief and practice and sexual orientation and practice (McConnell 1998; Jakobsen and Pellegrini 2004; Laycock 2008; Metz 2010; Nussbaum 2010). As far as I am aware, however, none have engaged in an extended comparison of religious belief and practice and same-sex marriage. Several initial parallels present themselves. First, the liberal polity has typically viewed sexuality as a private matter. Like cultural or religious affiliation, sexuality may be deemed of no concern to public authority; even more than culture or religion, it falls within the sphere of the intimate lives of individuals. Thus it seems doubly private. Yet public authority forbids some sexual practices, just as it forbids some religious practices. This parallel may go unnoticed because religion is generally associated primarily with belief, and the practices that flow from it are considered beneficial to society, without and sometimes despite evidence to the contrary. Sexuality, in contrast, connotes practice or action as well as diverse value judgments, and its nontraditional manifestations more readily raise the specter of harm. In both cases, however, the issue arises as to whether or when the state has a compelling interest in abrogating free exercise, and whether doing so constitutes or maintains an establishment of religion.

In a second parallel between religion and sexuality, the attribution of privacy to sexuality admirably suits people who want to preserve the traditionally dominant consensus that nonconformists can comfortably exist on the fringes of the polity. This view holds that those whose sexual orientation is nontraditional need not and should not be the subjects of public policy that appears to constitute approval of their practices. This state of affairs parallels that in some tolerant political entities that have an established state religion: Those of dissenting faiths are free to practice their religion as long as they do not disturb the appearance of consensus. However, even political entities without an official religion sometimes fear some unfamiliar religions and establish obstacles to their practice. In the United States, for example, Wiccans are often mistakenly classified as Satanists and are harassed, both socially and legally, as "a threat to God, Christianity, and/or American society" (Cookson 2003, 139). As a matter of formal policy, public authority takes notice of sexuality by confining civil marriage (in most states) to contracts between men and women and by prohibiting gays and lesbians from serving openly in the armed forces until 2010. Public authority also takes notice of religious faith or its equivalent by exempting conscientious objectors from military service, but this practice is one of accommodation rather than prohibition. Overall, the ostensibly private character of both religion and sexuality is belied by public attention that is both social and legal.

Finally, with respect to both religious faith and sexuality, I am committed to the value of personal autonomy. Autonomy comprises not only the freedom to pursue what one judges to be good and to define this good in one's own manner, but also the capacity to engage in rational scrutiny of and critical reflection on one's projects and goals. This focus on the capacity for autonomy may seem to accord poorly with the topic of sexuality. People who champion the right of gays and lesbians to equal recognition and citizenship typically base these claims on the unchosen nature of sexual orientation, arguing that individuals should not suffer disadvantages because of constituents of their identities that they did not choose. However, I believe that although sexual orientation, like initial religious identity, may be unchosen, how one handles or responds to that orientation is something that one chooses or affirms. Like religious affiliation, sexual orientation should therefore be respected in a liberal polity not because it is unchosen but rather because it is a central facet of personal identity (Gill 2001, 175–217; Jakobsen and Pellegrini 2004, 97–101). Such respect does not mean, however, that society should permit all sexual or religious practices simply because they fulfill, upon critical reflection, some individuals' conceptions of the good. For example, neither sexual abuse nor human sacrifice in the name of religious belief needs to be permitted. But because sexual orientation, like religious faith, is critically important to personal identity, individuals who engage in legally acceptable practices in both areas should be accorded the same measure of consideration and respect. However, although religious belief is often best served by public noninterference, living out one's sexual orientation may require not only noninterference—as in the deconstitutionalization of antisodomy laws—but also positive action through public policy, such as removing barriers preventing same-sex couples from committing to a civil marriage impelled by their conscientious beliefs. In this chapter I discuss religious belief, the history of marriage, and conceptions of national citizenship as they affect society's views of same-sex marriage.

The Claims of Religious Belief

Public attitudes toward sexual orientation provide an interesting contrast with attitudes toward religious belief. Most people, at least in theory, accord equal consideration and respect to all individuals who engage in religious practices legally acceptable in the liberal polity. Most agree that religious practice is a matter of personal obligation, desire, or choice, but that the expression of religious belief is open to all. They do not argue that respect for diversity requires public policies that privilege the convictions of those who dislike certain manifestations of religious belief over the convictions of those who simply wish to engage in their own religious practices without loss of respect or civic standing. Yet when it comes to issues of sexuality, many people move in the opposite direction. They suggest that although individuals with seemingly distasteful sexual practices should be accorded grudging toleration, they should adopt a low profile and not receive respect equal to that accorded to those who pursue more conventional practices. Many argue that although sexuality is a personal matter, its public expression, as in civil marriage, may be regulated, even to the detriment of those who simply desire equal access to a public institution freely available to other couples. Finally, many argue that liberal hospitality shown to diversity means that persons in the majority who dislike certain sexual practices possess an equal or even greater entitlement to shape public policy governing these practices than do those individuals who engage in these practices.

Those who frown on same-sex relationships often want public policy to reflect their disapproval, arguing that recognition of these relationships connotes approval of what they view as immoral sexual activity. Following the 2004 reelection of President George W. Bush, many commentators remarked that the balance of power in that election was held by the "values voters," those for whom moral values connected with abortion, same-sex marriage, and stem cell research outweighed other issues such as the economy and foreign policy. Although exit polls indicated that 22 percent of voters reported that "moral values" were paramount in their choice for president, the construction of this category was in some ways ambiguous. As journalist Peter Steinfels (2004) observed at the time, "If the polls of voters had constructed an equivalent catchall economic category adding concern about health care and taxes to that about jobs and growth, it would have been the top concern of 33 percent of the voters. If the poll findings had combined concern about terrorism with concern about Iraq, as apparently many voters did, the resulting category would have ranked first, with 34 percent of the voters." Steinfels noted that although stem cell research is supported by many, same-sex marriage is not, whereas opinions on legal access to abortion fall somewhat between these first two issues. In other words, when the category of moral issues is subdivided, people are not united in their opinions. Furthermore, he asked, "Are not moral values also at stake in decisions about war, in drawing lines against torture, in addressing poverty or in providing desperately needed housing and health care? . . . All of a nation's common life, not just sexual matters or personal behavior, is shot through with moral and ethical issues" (Steinfels 2004; see also Feldblum 2009, 212–14). Although he argued that people's specific concerns must be addressed regarding all of these issues, Steinfels implied not only that moral issues are legion, but also that people differ in the way they identify and define moral issues and that this difference is crucial. By 2009 the percentage of voters who said that moral values would matter most if they were voting then for president fell to merely 10 percent, whereas concern over the economy and jobs rose from 20 percent in 2004 to 50 percent in 2009 (Dionne 2009).

Recognition of diversity among moral issues has been growing among both evangelicals and Roman Catholics. A number of evangelical church pastors have spoken out about traditionally liberal issues such as HIV/AIDS and poverty (Luo and Goodstein 2007). In 2008 a large group of members of the conservative Southern Baptist Convention signed a declaration on climate change calling "all Christians to return to a biblical mandate to guard the world God created" (Banerjee 2008). Douglas Kmiec, a staunch Roman Catholic opponent of the Supreme Court's pro-choice abortion decision, *Roe v. Wade*, decided in 2008 to support Democratic presidential candidate Barack Obama because prohibiting abortion may be just one of many ways to promote a culture of life. "To think you have done a generous thing for your neighbor or that you have built up a culture of life just because you voted for a candidate who . . . wants to overturn Roe v. Wade is far too thin an understanding of the Catholic faith," explained Kmiec (Dionne 2008). Not only do all individuals have differing views on what counts as moral values, but those with seemingly traditional definitions may also expand their conceptions in some contexts.

The commentator George Will was therefore correct, I believe, when he observed in 2006 that liberals who promote a more equitable distribution of income, libertarians who oppose public attempts to inculcate morality, and social conservatives who believe that the public nurturing of morality is necessary to preserve liberty all vote according to their values. Thus, he noted, "by ratifying the social conservatives' monopoly of the label 'values voters,' the media are furthering the fiction that these voters are somehow more morally awake than others." In sum, aspiring presidential candidates "are and remain busy courting only values voters, because there is no other kind" (Will 2006). For the present purposes, I consider both opponents and proponents of same-sex marriage to be "values voters" who argue and act on their conscientious beliefs. It serves no purpose for each side to vilify the other as acting in bad faith. Nevertheless, each of us must still argue for our conviction that some constellations of values are superior to others as guides to our common life as citizens of a liberal democratic polity.

One way that the tension over the manifestation of moral values has become apparent is found in heightened sensitivity to the question of whether those with religious sensibilities are being treated fairly in the formation of public policy. Criticizing John Rawls's position that individuals should form their own conceptions of the good, William Galston argues that a public commitment to Enlightenment rationalism "tends to exclude individuals and groups that do not place a high value on personal autonomy and revisable plans of life" (Galston 1991, 153; see also 130, 276, 329n12). If liberal democracy is to be neutral with regard to rival conceptions of the good (Dworkin 1985, 191; Dworkin 1978, 272), Galston says, the state cannot promote personal autonomy "without throwing its weight behind a conception of the human good unrelated to the functional needs of its sociopolitical institutions and at odds with the deep beliefs of many of its loyal citizens. As a political matter, liberal freedom entails the right to live unexamined as well as examined lives" (Galston 1991, 254).

This tension is particularly acute when one interprets the practice of religious beliefs as requiring a context that permeates the whole of life. Galston explains, "If, to be fully effective, a religious doctrine requires control over the totality of individual life, including the formative social and political

environment, then the classic liberal demand that religion be practiced privately amounts to a substantive restriction on the free exercise of that religion" (Galston 1991, 277). Although a liberal society is pluralistic, the
range of its pluralism excludes some kinds of groups; and "for those who
are left out, it is hard to see how liberalism can be experienced as anything
other than an assault" (149; see 143–49). Alternatively, as Stephen Carter
describes, liberal pluralism accepts the moral opinions of individuals from
diverse belief systems—unless these opinions are grounded in religious convictions. Although the public square is formally open, he observes, "The
legal culture that guards the public square still seems most comfortable
thinking of religion as a hobby, something done in privacy, something that
mature, public-spirited adults do not use as the basis for politics" (Carter
1993, 54; see also 218).

A large body of literature addresses the legitimacy of using religious reasons
as possible justifications for public policy (e.g., Greenawalt 1995; Perry 1997;
Audi and Wolterstorff 1997; Audi 2000). Robert Audi, for example, argues
for governmental neutrality between religion and nonreligion, because even
state preference that favors religion in general tends to reflect the interests of
historically dominant religious groups. Therefore he advocates principles of
secular rationale, or the requirement of adequate secular reasons for advocacy,
and *secular motivation*, or the impetus to advocate a policy even in the absence
of religious reasons (Audi 1997, 25, 28–29). Governments may, however,
advocate or adopt policies that have the effect of advancing religion—as in
declaring state holidays when a majority of people want them, or establishing
an educational voucher system that includes religious schools—as long as the
justification is not intrinsically religious (Audi 2000, 128, 98; see also 117–18,
181). Nicholas Wolterstorff, on the other hand, also advocates neutrality but
interprets it as impartiality, under which a government that offers state aid to
any schools, for example, must offer equitable state aid to all schools, religious
or not (Wolterstorff 1997b, 75–76; see 115–16; Wolterstorff 1997a, 149).
Wolterstorff believes that theorists such as Rawls are mistaken to think that
reasonable and rational citizens, through the application of public reason, will
arrive at a consensus on which all can agree (Wolterstorff 1997b, 99–102).
Moreover it is not equitable to insist that citizens refrain from applying their
comprehensive perspectives, conventionally religious or not, to public policy.
Wolterstorff explains, "Their religion is not, for them, about *something other*
than their social and political existence; it is *also* about their social and political
existence. Accordingly, to require of them that they not base their decisions
and discussions concerning political issues on their religion is to infringe, in-

equitably, on the free exercise of their religion" (105). These religious believers exemplify the integralists, described by Nancy Rosenblum, who are alienated by living "the divided life of believer and citizen. Integralists want to be able to conduct themselves according to the injunctions of religious law and authority in every sphere of everyday life, and to see their faith mirrored in public life" (Rosenblum 2000a, 15).

The question of being fair to those with religious sensibilities as well as those without them is further complicated by historical changes in claims regarding what fairness entails. As Rosenblum explains, although marginalized groups have historically claimed religious exemptions from the effects of general laws, now all groups make these claims. "Religious associations want not only exemption from certain obligations but also a share of public benefits, and courts and legislatures are forced to articulate the grounds on which they extend or deny public funding for the activities of religious groups in specific areas" (Rosenblum 2000a, 13; see 13–14). Some interpret public support as constituting a forbidden establishment of religion, or at least an endorsement of religious belief. Others, however, argue that conditions attached to this support threaten the free exercise of religion, also forbidden under the First Amendment. Implicit in this challenge, furthermore, is the assumption not only that government is responsible for ensuring religious freedom, but also that "government is responsible for insuring the conditions of religious flourishing" (14).

Rosenblum's moral integralists, who want to reinvigorate faith to promote the public good, and civic integralists, who aim to reinforce democratic values by promoting greater pluralism, do not necessarily threaten the free exercise of others' beliefs and practices (Rosenblum 2000a, 15–19). Foundationalist integralism, however, seeks "a share of political as well as social power; its goal is to give religion a controlling place in public arenas and public law," holding that "because of its truths, religion is the sole carrier of value" (20). The most challenging version of this phenomenon, fundamentalist integralism, seeks to apply religious law and authority to every aspect of life, characterizes secular democracy as nihilistic, "conflates discipleship and citizenship," and "entails an outright rejection of voluntarism and separationism" (15). Citizens of this persuasion are most likely to argue that delegitimizing the claims of those experiencing same-sex attraction is a necessary extension of their free exercise of religion. In fact parts of Rosenblum's description of fundamentalist integralism could well apply to groups like the Taliban.

What matters most, therefore, is not whether religious or secular justifications are given in the course of public advocacy, but how these reasons affect the individual's free exercise of conscientious belief, or how they affect religion in general, broadly conceived as the search for core and transcendent meaning in life. I focus on religious justifications, however, because those with religious justifications are currently the ones most likely to express concern about perceived limits on the free exercise of their beliefs. Religious groups increasingly desire positive public benefits such as funding, as Rosenblum observes. However, the free exercise of religion or conscience is increasingly interpreted to require not simply the individual's right to freely exercise religious belief, but also the right of religious individuals and religiously based corporate bodies to shape broader aspects of public policy as an extension of their free exercise rights. Although these attempts may function as an expression of moral or civic integralism, some attempts, if successful, shade into Rosenblum's foundationalist integralism and adversely affect the rights of others.

This broader interpretation of the free exercise of religion or conscience conflates two distinct stances. First, the government may protect the individual's right to believe and worship as conscience dictates, as well as engage in practices flowing from these beliefs that do not affect others' rights. Second, the government, perhaps even as a matter of public policy, may protect the right of individuals and their faith communities to engage in and promote policies that essentially penalize those who do not share their beliefs. In this second scenario, for example, I may believe that God has called me to ensure that adherents of other beliefs and practices are marginalized, even when their thoughts and actions directly affect none but themselves. More importantly, my coreligionists and I may enlist the government's aid and may refute critics by suggesting that they wish to infringe upon my right of conscience.

The circumstances that led to *Romer v. Evans* (517 U.S. 620 [1996]), a key Supreme Court case concerning gay rights, provide an example of this second, broader position. In this case, the court struck down a Colorado constitutional amendment, passed by referendum, that not only repealed ordinances adopted by three political subdivisions to prevent discrimination based on sexual orientation, but also barred any state or local entity from enacting similar protections in the future. An additional amendment would therefore have been necessary to change this policy. In his majority opinion, Justice Anthony Kennedy wrote that the rights withheld under the amendment "are protections against exclusion from an almost limitless number of transactions and endeavors that constitute ordinary civic life in a free society" (631). The amendment imposed a broad disability on a particular group without any rational relationship to legitimate state interests, and "a State cannot so deem a class of persons a stranger to its laws" (635). Whether they were motivated by religious or secular reasons, those who wished to discriminate against individuals experiencing same-sex attraction apparently believed that it was not enough to eschew such relationships themselves. They sought additional control over the formative social and political environment, as Galston describes it (1991, 277), in which they lived their lives. The difficulty, of course, is that this desired context or environment permeated not only their own lives, but also the lives of those disadvantaged by the public policy that they formulated.

In the view of David A. J. Richards, such legislation embodies "political homophobia" and is "a constitutionally illegitimate expression of religious intolerance." Selective enforcement of traditional moral values against particular groups' claims to equal protection under the law suggests that their identity is equivalent to that of individuals of traditionally despised religions, whose their adherents are expected to either convert or remain silent (D. Richards 1998, 357, 360; see also D. Richards 1999, 70, 90, 92, 126–27; D. Richards 2005, 107–8). *Romer* exemplifies a foundationalist integralist interpretation of the right of conscience because the Colorado amendment represented the co-optation of the machinery of government by supporters of traditional values, many animated by religious commitments. But even in cases where religiously based organizations merely influence political bodies not to pass antidiscrimination legislation, they may claim the moral high ground because, after all, their free exercise of religion and the status of their conscientious beliefs are at stake. Because of the First Amendment guarantee of religious free exercise, religious organizations are more likely to claim point of privilege than secular organizations. As columnist Neil Steinberg colorfully explains, religious organizations may act like the proverbial bully in eyeglasses. When someone stands up and challenges his pushing around smaller kids on the playground, "he cringes, raising an arm, saying, 'You wouldn't hit a man in glasses, would you?'" (Steinberg 2007). That is, religious organizations want to compete for influence in the marketplace of ideas, but then they may claim their religious status to insulate themselves from criticism.

This point is put well by Karen Struening, who suggests that freedom in intimate association is analogous to freedom of religion and expression; the process of forming one's own judgment in these areas is a central constituent of self-definition. For her, "The regulation and expression of non-coercive and consensual sexual practices between adults is a direct assault on moral pluralism" (Struening 1996, 509)—often intentionally so. The dominance of social convention hinders one's ability to form and develop one's own identity. Although admitting the legitimacy of competing understandings of the good can complicate the traditionalist's effort to perpetuate his or her own mode of life, Struening observes, "We do not take from him what he needs to live *his life*," whereas we do take the necessities of life from the dissident when we censor practices concerning his or her own life. "Sexuality," she concludes, "like religious and moral beliefs, is our own in the sense that without it our ability to be self-determining and self-defining is seriously compromised" (512). Private sexual conduct between consenting adults constitutes neither harm nor direct offense to others; it is merely what John Stuart Mill called a contingent or constructive injury. As Nussbaum explains, "people imagine how offended they would be if they were present at those acts, and . . . they get all worked up and feel disgust and indignation" (Nussbaum 2010, 58; see 57–60, 171–75)—a reaction that may also attend disapproval of others' religious practices. As Mill argued, however, "there is no parity between the feeling of a person for his own opinion, and the feeling of another who is offended at his holding it, no more than between the desire of a thief to take a purse, and the desire of the right owner to keep it" (Mill 1859, 84; see 82–84, 89–90).

The larger point here is that whether it is justified on the basis of conventionally religious or secular reasons, the ability of individuals to develop and expend their own internal resources in their search for fundamental and transcendent truths is the crucial value. Too often this search is threatened by those who believe they already have the answers. From this perspective the problem in a liberal polity with those who wish to fit individuals into a procrustean bed of convention is not that their reasons are often grounded on conventional religious views, or that they offer religious reasons for their positions. Instead the difficulty is that the reasons they offer go beyond what they need to live their own individual lives according to their conscientious beliefs and attempt to impose them on others who do not subscribe to these beliefs. If the practice of one's religious beliefs requires, in Galston's terms (1991, 277), control over the whole of life, including the sociopolitical environment, this demand may work in communities set off from the larger society, membership in which is voluntary in some way, such as the Old Order Amish or various Hasidic communities (Feldman 2003, 123–34, 162–71). Although such groups resemble Rosenblum's foundationalist integralists because they do want to give religion a controlling place in their communities, they seek this control only among their own committed believers. If a precondition for the full practice of religious belief requires control over the whole of life, this precondition cannot work in liberal democracies, where the free exercise of religion by some overlaps with the freedom of others to live their own lives as they see fit.

Writing in 1993 about the dangers of the Christian right, Carter observed, "If the Christian Coalition is wrong for America, it must be because its message is wrong on the issues, not because its message is religious." One may oppose the use of religion to foster division rather than healing, or oppose the attempt of faith in some cases to co-opt the state for its own purposes. Nevertheless, he said, "The error, as a matter of secular politics, is to suppose that it is the Christian Coalition's *religiosity* rather than its *platform* that is the enemy" (Carter 1993, 266). That is, when religious believers advocate policies that may be questionable or even dangerous, the problem stems not from their religious motivations per se, but from what their religious motivations impel them to advocate (277). It is not linking God to political ends that has sometimes caused matters to go awry, but rather "the choice of secular ends to which the name of God was linked" (229).

For example, traditionalists who opposed the decriminalization of same-sex expressions of sexuality and who currently oppose same-sex marriage may employ religious arguments about God's intentions for reproduction and family life. Opponents also couch their views in terms of what arrangements are most conducive to stable families and child rearing. Although authoritative determinations of what God intends are hard to find, compared with conclusions rooted in rational argument and empirical data, the key issue is a different one. Absent cogent and compelling reasons to the contrary, a liberal democratic polity should avoid exclusions based on either religion or sexual orientation that create two classes of citizens: those who are favored and those who are disfavored. As Amy Gutmann explains, "Discriminatory exclusion is harmful when it *publicly expresses* the civic inequality of the excluded even in the absence of any other showing that it *causes* the civic inequality in question" (Gutmann 2003, 97).

Arguments made in favor of either civic equality or inequality for some classifications of citizens may be either religiously based or secular. Carter pointed out in 1993 that the Reverend Martin Luther King Jr. certainly used religious arguments in leading the civil rights movement (Carter 1993, 38, 48, 228). What rendered King's arguments convincing, however, was not specifically that they were religious. If his arguments had been purely secular, this also would not have lent them greater credibility. To paraphrase Carter, if King's message was right for America, it was because his message was right on the issues, not because his message was in part religious. In the case of sexual orientation in general and same-sex marriage in particular, it is not traditionalists' religiosity but their platform that is the problem. King argued that skin color is not a legitimate reason for civic inequality. In the United States we have long held that religious belief is not a legitimate ground for civic inequality, although for unpopular religions this leitmotif has sometimes been honored in the breach rather than the observance. In this book I argue that sexual orientation and attraction is also an illegitimate basis for civic inequality.

The Claims of Marriage

The anticipated effects of the recognition of same-sex marriage have garnered much discussion over the last several years. Even before a few states legalized same-sex marriage, traditionalist opponent James Dobson, founder of Focus on the Family, said in 2003, "The institution of marriage is on the ropes," as a result of the Supreme Court's decision in *Lawrence v. Texas* (539 U.S. 558 [2003]) overturning the Texas antisodomy law, as well as Canada's acceptance of same-sex marriage (Dobson 2003). "Barring a miracle . . . the family as it has been known more than five millennia will crumble, presaging the fall of Western civilization itself" (Dobson 2004, quoted in Coontz 2005, 273).

Marriage is the most intimate of private commitments, yet it also possesses a public character. In its civil aspect marriage comprises both rights and obligations that span both the marriage itself and also its possible dissolution. Ideally marriage benefits both the couple as individuals and as a unit and also society at large. Although it is rooted in mutual consent, its public character means that one consents to a status, a model of marriage reinforced by laws that may both privilege and punish. In the United States the model has historically involved "lifelong, faithful monogamy, formed by the mutual consent of a man and a woman, bearing the impress of the Christian religion and the English common law in its expectations for the husband to be the family head and economic provider, his wife the dependent partner" (Cott 2000, 3, see also 133, 178; Reid 2008, 158–59). As Stephanie Coontz notes, social changes have greatly expanded ways in which young people can now deploy their resources and opportunities and fill available social roles. Marriage therefore exerts less influence on people than formerly. However, Coontz observes, "for most Americans, marriage is the highest expression of commitment they can imagine," and individuals work on their marriages to a degree unimaginable in many past generations. To put this differently, Coontz quotes Mae West, saying, "'Marriage is a great institution. But I ain't ready for an institution,' . . . Now people want to live in a relationship, not an institution" (Coontz 2005, 278).

Even as an institution, however, marriage is not monolithic. What we call "marriage," Claire Snyder suggests, may comprise not only a civil contract but also a personal bond, a community-recognized relationship, and a religious rite. Because same-sex couples who wish to marry already share a personal bond, are often recognized as couples by their communities, and increasingly participate in religious rites, Snyder holds "that many lesbian and gay couples are already married, despite the fact that the government refuses to legally recognize those marriages" (Snyder 2006, 16; see also Pinello 2006, 8). Many traditionalists, especially those who oppose same-sex marriage, emphasize the religious aspects of marriage above the others. Some same-sex couples bear witness to their personal bonds by engaging in public ceremonies that may or may not be religious; others eschew public ceremonies when, as in most states, they do not carry legal meaning (Hull 2006, 26–115). Queer theorists not only reject such ceremonies as meaningless without the conferral of legal partnership status, but they also reject marriage itself because it empowers the state to regulate personal relationships (Snyder 2006, 16–17). What many fail to recognize, Snyder asserts, is the extent to which local community recognition of personal bonds has historically been constitutive of marriage (19).

This point is well demonstrated by Nancy Cott in her account of the gradual extension of governmental control over personal relationships in the early history of the United States. "The dispersed patterns of settlement and the insufficiency of officials who could solemnize vows meant that couples with community approval simply married themselves. Acceptance of this practice testified to the widespread belief that the parties' consent to marry each other, not the words said by a minister or magistrate, mattered most" (Cott 2000, 31; see also Snyder 2006, 17–19; Cherlin 2009, 45–46). Although in time state legislatures regulated access to legal marriage, states' desire to promote monogamous relationships and the building of stable households led courts to presume in doubtful cases that a couple was married, often on the basis of circumstantial evidence, just as accused persons were presumed innocent unless proven guilty. Marriage was considered a common right. Otherwise, the offspring of too many parents would be held illegitimate. Overall, Cott explains, "A couple's known consent to marry and general repute as married was sufficient, so long as there was 'public recognition' of the marriage—meaning acknowledgement by the informal public" (Cott 2000, 40, see also 30, 39). That is, "The institution requires public affirmation. It requires public knowledge—at least some publicity beyond the couple themselves" (1–2; see also 101). Simultaneously, however, the practice of recognizing informal relationships as marriages co-opted couples into acquiescing to a particular conception of matrimonial relationships, or the sort of status relationship described above. "In accepting self-marriage, state authority did not retreat, but widened the ambit of its enforcement of marital duties. By crediting couples' private consent, the law drew them into a set of obligations set by state law" (40). Similarly, states developed divorce laws that allowed the termination of marital relationships by means other than "self-divorce" or desertion. But by defining what constituted proper marital behavior, "the states in allowing divorce were perfecting the script for marriage, instructing spouses to enact the script more exactly" (52; see also 48–49).

This brief sketch from Cott should indicate, first, that the social institution of marriage presents varying facets that carry implications for the current controversy over same-sex marriage. Those who wish to marry civilly already possess a personal bond, are often regarded as married by their communities, and may have participated in a public ceremony, religious or otherwise, that solemnizes both that bond and that public regard. Second, however, marriage as a social institution reflects a tension between personal choice and public regulation. Although personal choice is primary, it may be co-opted by the state either to regularize relationships or to prevent the recognition of some kinds of relationships as constituting marriage. To use Cott's terminology, some relationships may be excluded altogether from the "script" that is being perfected. If personal bonds and some degree of community recognition historically have grounded the confirmation of relationships as civil contracts of marriage, same-sex couples and their allies have a precedent for making their own case in this regard.

Analogies between consent to the marriage contract that initiates family relationships and consent to the social contract that legitimates political authority are a standard feature of liberal theory. Once again, however, what one consents to is a status. Nonconforming groups can be made to conform, such as the Mormons in Utah, who abrogated polygamy in 1890 (Cott 2000, 120). Alternatively, some groups might be excluded from marriage altogether, as illustrated by nineteenth-century antimiscegenation laws as well as by today's laws and state constitutional amendments defining marriage as between one man and one woman. In the nineteenth century the terms of marriage were not to be left to individual discretion. Moreover, couples understood that they had to comply with state requirements if they wanted to marry and that they could not marry on their own terms—an understanding that elevated the status of legally defined marriage (101, 110). Overall, the private, contractual side of marriage diminished in importance in the nineteenth century as the public definition of the institution increased. The implication was that "the institution of marriage had to be insulated or salvaged from misuse by irresponsible, unsuited, or defiant couples," which in turn "created an atmosphere of moral belligerence about Christian monogamous marriage as the national standard" (128; see also Metz 2010, 3–15).

Although this description of nineteenth-century beliefs resonates with some of the opposition to same-sex marriage today, Cott suggests that in other respects marriage has been disestablished. That is, just as the special status given to one religion faded in many Western nations when a variety of religious institutions proliferated, "by analogy one could argue that the particular model of marriage which was for so long the officially supported one has been disestablished" as "plural acceptable sexual behaviors and marriage types have bloomed." As in the early years of United States history, many are now willing to accept "marriage-like relationships *as* marriage" (Cott 2000, 212). Couples in these relationships seek endorsement from their own communities but benign neglect from others, as the private, contractual aspect of marriage is once again asserted. Governments have in part colluded in this shift, because they have been able to enforce family support obligations outside of formal marriage relationships (213; see 212–15; Coontz 2005, 256–57, 278–80).

Cott correctly suggests that the disestablishment parallel fails with respect to same-sex marriage, because public authorities do not recognize every marriage-like relationship as marriage. In most jurisdictions in the United States only like-minded communities, such as informal networks of friends and relatives or sympathetic religious entities, not public authorities, will recognize these unions. The 1996 Defense of Marriage Act not only defined marriage for federal purposes as comprising one man and one woman, but also provided that states would not be required to accord full faith and credit to the actions of other states that marry same-sex couples (Cott 2000, 218–19). Like a number of countries, however, some states have formally provided various alternative arrangements, such as civil unions and domestic partnerships in which same-sex couples may participate and which are often accompanied by all the material benefits that these states provide to couples who are civilly married. As of 2005 unmarried partners living

together could access benefits at almost half of the five hundred largest corporations in the United States. In France an individual can enter a legal
resource-pooling relationship by designating virtually any other person to
receive material benefits and legal privileges. "Two sexual partners can take
advantage of this arrangement. So can two sisters, two army buddies, or a
celibate priest and his housekeeper" (Coontz 2005, 279). The crucial difference for same-sex couples is that although their relationships may comprise
personal bonds, community recognition, and perhaps religious rites, many
same-sex couples also desire the public recognition that only a civil contract
by the state provides.

For some commentators this is asking too much. The deconstitutionalization of antisodomy laws means that same-sex couples may live as they
choose without public interference. Moreover, the free exercise clause of the
United States Constitution protects the rights of religious communities to
celebrate same-sex unions through religious rites. Nevertheless, citizens do
care what the state thinks. As Daniel Brudney explains, "It is worth reflecting that people who otherwise seem hostile to state institutions, who deem
them corrupt, wicked, or at best a necessary evil, nevertheless deeply want
the state to endorse their point of view" as representative of "the people."
He suggests specifically that this desire underlies the arguments of both opponents and proponents of same-sex marriage. "That dispute is increasingly
not about the provision of concrete legal rights and benefits . . . but about
whether the term 'marriage' is to be applied to a relationship—and applied
not by a minister, priest, rabbi, or imam but by an agent of the state" (Brudney 2005, 832). In other words, lack of interference with private beliefs and
practices is insufficient. What justice requires is positive public action or
approval, the provision of a public context or framework within which all
committed couples may, if they desire, bear witness to these commitments.
Many same-sex couples do in fact create public commitment celebrations
that mirror marriage ceremonies and that often appropriate the language of
marriage, using "public ritual to communicate the reality of their relationship . . . as well as to assert the fundamental sameness or equality of their relationship with heterosexual marriages" (Hull 2006, 42). Some couples even
discover, often after the fact, that this public commitment strengthens their
relationship and increases their sense of its durability (50–52; see 26–77).

Interracial couples whose marriages were at one time prohibited or
unrecognized present the closest parallel to the current desire of same-sex
couples to marry. Before the passage of antimiscegenation laws, antebellum
abolitionists emphasized the "moral horror" of American slavery's failure to

recognize the marriage or family rights of slaves. As Richards suggests, "Slavery, understood as an attack on intimate personal resources, stripped persons of essential attributes of their humanity." Some have argued, in fact, "that it was the racist attack on the intimate life of slaves that was at the very heart of the atrocity of American slavery" (Richards 2005, 67–68; see also Cott 2000, 57–59). Antimiscegenation laws later continued this abridgment of "the basic human right of intimate life in a way that sustained the sectarian sexual mythology of the subhuman image of African Americans" (Richards 2005, 131). During the era of slavery, not only did white masters freely use the bodies of female slaves for their own sexual gratification, but they also refused to treat the marriages of their slaves as binding—making it easier to break up slave families to sell some members. Even during the colonial period, English colonies had used race and color as the basis for criminalizing interracial marriages. The aim of these laws as well as those passed after the Civil War was to maintain the purity of the white race in particular (Cott 2000, 41). Antimiscegenation laws were not viewed as a hardship imposed upon individuals of either race, because blacks and whites were equally prohibited from marrying those of the other race (100–102).

Despite some effort to pass a national constitutional amendment prohibiting interracial marriage, however, in 1948 in *Perez v. Sharp* (32 Cal. 2d 711, 198 P.2d 17 [1948]) the California Supreme Court struck down the state law banning the marriage of a white to "a Negro, mulatto, Mongolian, or member of the Malay race" on the grounds that the ban violated the equal protection guarantee of the Fourteenth Amendment to the United States Constitution (Cott 2000, 184–85). In 1967 in *Loving v. Virginia* (388 U.S. 1 [1967]), the United States Supreme Court similarly struck down the Virginia law making interracial marriage between a black and a white person a felony. Invalidating antimiscegenation laws nationwide, *Loving* rejected the argument that such laws disadvantaged both races equally, contending that they were instead intended to maintain white supremacy (Cott 2000, 198; see also Coontz 2005, 256).

Just as antimiscegenation laws were designed to prevent the degradation of white persons, Richards argues that the traditional condemnation of same-sex relationships has in part been rooted in their perceived "degradation of a man to the passive status of woman," a stigma that itself is premised on ancient assumptions about the degraded nature of women (Richards 1999, 98; see also Richards 2005, 111–12, 137–38). As Andrew Koppelman observes, "Just as miscegenation was threatening because it called into question the distinctive and superior status of being white, homosexuality is threatening because it calls into question the distinctive and superior status of being male" (Koppelman 1988, 145; see also Richards 1999, 83, 163; Richards 2005, 137–38, 141). Koppelman and others also argue that prohibiting same-sex marriage constitutes sex discrimination by specifying that individuals who marry must marry opposite-sex partners. That is, the availability of a marriage license depends upon one's own sex and the sex of the individual one proposes to marry (Koppelman 1994). All who wish to marry are similarly situated; and in this reading, conditioning a license on the gender of the aspiring spouses constitutes a denial of equal protection of the law.

Commentators differ, however, as to the appropriateness of the antimiscegenation analogy. For example, although he supports same-sex marriage as a fundamental right, Evan Gerstmann notes that men and women are actually treated alike by most states because neither may marry partners of their own sex, the position traditionally argued by those against interracial marriage and by the dissent in *Loving* (Gerstmann 2008, 51–53; see also Sunstein 1997, 209–10). Using *Loving* to argue that same-sex couples, like interracial ones, should be allowed to marry is problematic for Gerstmann, because the Virginia antimiscegenation law existed within a context designed to maintain white supremacy by segregating the races, particularly whites from everyone else. The impermissibility of same-sex marriage neither targets one gender as inferior nor seeks to segregate men and women—quite the opposite (Gerstmann 2008, 53–57). States were legalizing same-sex sodomy even before *Lawrence*, but they continued to firmly oppose same-sex marriage. The argument "that the same-sex marriage ban is best understood as a policy that discriminates against women . . . would be difficult to say . . . to gay men with a straight face" (Gerstmann 2008, 58; see 51–61).

In contrast, David Blankenhorn, a zealous defender of traditional marriage, ironically argues that proponents of antimiscegenation legislation in the past and of same-sex marriage now actually share a great deal in common. For Blankenhorn, marriage carries the public purpose of forming families that unite children to their biological parents and unite the parents to each other. Enforcing racial separation through antimiscegenation laws corrupted marriage by preventing the formation of such families. Recognizing same-sex couples, in his opinion, similarly corrupts marriage by sanctioning a form of the institution that is not first and foremost mindful of the welfare of children. Opponents of interracial marriage then and proponents of same-sex marriage today both seek "to restructure marriage and use it for a special purpose." Then, the intention was to preserve white supremacy;

now, "that purpose is to gain social recognition of the dignity of homosexual love" (Blankenhorn 2007, 177–78; see 171–79).

Nonetheless I agree with Richards and Koppelman that the analogy between antimiscegenation laws and the same-sex marriage ban is appropriate. Where *Loving* overturned the preservation of a hierarchy or caste system that enshrined white supremacy, the same-sex marriage ban maintains a caste system that privileges heterosexuality over nonheterosexuality. In other words, Gerstmann correctly asserts that sexism per se is not the problem. He fails to see, however, that the problem is heterosexism. The ban on same-sex marriage does not target one gender as inferior to another. It does target one type of sexual orientation as inferior to others, rendering the liberty interests and citizenship status of gays and lesbians as unworthy of the same treatment accorded those of straight persons. Contrary to Blankenhorn's argument, both antimiscegenation laws and same-sex marriage bans interfere with family formation and also family preservation, especially in circumstances where same-sex couples are rearing children from former marriages. If same-sex marriage proponents desire the recognition of "the dignity of homosexual love" (Blankenhorn 2007, 177–78), surely one function of this recognition is the stable grounding of families headed by same-sex couples as well as those headed by opposite-sex couples. It is the opponents of same-sex marriage, not its proponents, who assign a special purpose to marriage: valorizing heterosexual relationships over same-sex relationships.

Antimiscegenation laws and the same-sex marriage ban also both attempt to force individuals into the procrustean bed of rigid categories. Cass Sunstein, for example, argues that *Loving* is decisive in the context of same-sex marriage. Both opponents of interracial marriage and opponents of same-sex marriage have insisted on the rigidity of superficially factual categories whose meanings are socially constructed. Sunstein says, "I believe that the prohibition on same-sex marriages, as part of the social and legal insistence on 'two kinds' [of people], is as deeply connected with male supremacy as the prohibition on interracial marriage is connected with white supremacy. Same-sex marriages are banned because of what they do to—because of how they unsettle—gender categories" (Sunstein 1997, 211; see 208–11). That is, there is a factual element to the distinctions that societies make regarding race and gender, but these distinctions are constructed, often subconsciously, in ways that go far beyond genetic differences and secondary sexual characteristics. Sunstein also agrees with proponents like Richards that the immutability of a characteristic "is neither a necessary nor a sufficient basis for treatment as a 'suspect class'" by the courts. Racial discrimination, for example, "would not become acceptable if scientists developed a serum through which blacks could become whites" (215). On the other hand, bans on driving may be applied to the blind even when an individual's blindness is immutable. Overall, however, people generally resist the unsettling of categories with which they feel comfortable. Jack Turner explains, "The will to white supremacy is the will to Manichaeism—the will, that is, to divide the world into neat categories of pure and impure, innocent and guilty, good and evil, black and white, and to plant one's identity on the right side" (Turner 2008, 667). The categorical divide at issue in this case is of course the divide between same-sex couples and opposite-sex couples.

The "don't ask, don't tell" policy in the United States armed forces, repealed in 2010, exemplified both a caste system that privileged heterosexuality over nonheterosexuality and also an attempt to fit individuals into rigid categories. Moreover, this policy penalized individuals not only for what they did but also for who they were. Nathanial Frank describes the policy as it was originally passed by Congress in 1993: "The ultimate policy defined 'homosexual conduct' as any physical activity that 'a reasonable person would understand to demonstrate a propensity or intent to engage in homosexual acts'" (Frank 2009, 83; see also 110; Gerstmann 1999, 73–74, 78). Although President Bill Clinton argued, in Frank's words, "that people should be disqualified from serving in the military based on something they do, not based on who they are," the implementation was such that any acknowledgment or suspicion of homosexual status created a "presumption that the service member is engaging in homosexual acts or has the propensity or intent to do so" (84, 110). An additional memo in 1995 stipulated that a service member could only rebut this presumption—as one was permitted to do in a military hearing—by actually proving that he or she did not have this propensity, later reinterpreted as a likelihood of engaging in homosexual acts (174–76).

Therefore, as Frank asserts, "While lawyers can argue that 'don't ask, don't tell' targets only conduct, it clearly targets status as well. In fact, with the help of the rebuttable presumption and the propensity clause, the policy defines conduct so broadly that it makes a mockery of the distinction between conduct and status. And this was the point." As Frank exhaustively demonstrates, it was the possible presence of same-sex desire itself, not actual conduct, that alarmed many heterosexuals (Frank 2009, 177). Moreover the attempt to draw a rigid line between heterosexuals and nonheterosexuals was grounded not on an unquestioned military necessity but on an unwillingness to acknowledge publicly that gays already served in the military. This unwillingness in turn required blurring the line between conduct and status.

"The notion that gays and lesbians must conceal their true selves to preserve the comfort of other troops is based on resistance not to the *presence* of gays in the barracks but to *knowledge* of that presence" (292). As William N. Eskridge Jr. puts it, the "don't ask" portion of "don't ask, don't tell" "concedes that morale and unit cohesion are not unduly threatened by the presence of *closeted* gay personnel. Thus, the problem has less to do with identity or conduct itself than with the expression of that identity or conduct to others" (Eskridge 1999, 185; see 183–95; Warnke 2007, 216). Overall, the policy was grounded on heteronormativity, the idea that heterosexuality was the norm and therefore superior to nonheterosexuality. Maintaining this hierarchy in turn required a broad definition of homosexuality that blended status and conduct. This prevented an "unsettling" of rigid categories, in Sunstein's terms, and preserved the supremacy of heterosexual norms. Now that gay and lesbian troops may serve openly in the armed forces, this hierarchy should disappear over time. Moreover, once openly nonheterosexual individuals take on the responsibility of fighting and dying for their country, public opinion should shift further in the direction of acknowledging that these individuals should also have the right to participate in civil marriage.

The social construction of distinctions to magnify or exaggerate their factual elements also becomes apparent in the way public authority has oscillated between (1) legitimizing and protecting marriage as an institution ostensibly rooted in nature and (2) defining marriage to suit its own purposes. The recognition of "self-marriage" and "self-divorce" in early American history described above—that is, the formation and dissolution of unions without legal sanction—suggests that marriage is a social institution run in large part by its participants. State recognition of marriages and divorces bestow a stamp of civil approval on what is already recognized informally by couples and their communities. Yet the increasing formalization of rights and obligations, as well as the exclusion of parties whose relationships do not follow the prescribed script, increasingly suggests human construction. Yet "legislators . . . hardly wanted to admit that marriage was 'state-conferred'—that they themselves, rather than nature or God, defined its outlines. They tried to have it both ways with marriage in political discourse—picturing it as a rock of needed stability amidst eddies of change, while also acting to define and redefine marital obligations" (Cott 2000, 219).

Currently, where marriage has been disestablished by the legal recognition of parallel relationships, this development represents a reversion to the older, more minimalist model. Same-sex couples and often opposite-sex couples who are unmarried in the civil sense have personal commitments, are recognized by others as stable couples, and may participate in alternative arrangements offered by the corporations where they work or the political subdivisions where they live. In Cott's analogy, the hegemony of one model of relationship, like the special status of one religion, has given way to pluralism. Where marriage has not been disestablished, however, parties such as same-sex couples in most jurisdictions cannot marry and in many jurisdictions do not have access to alternative relationships that are legally or publicly recognized. Where there is but one model of civilly recognized relationship whose entrance requirements do not fit the realities of some couples' existences, these couples are left in the same position as those who cannot subscribe to an established religion and for whom there are no alternatives for corporate belief and practice. The existence of alternative arrangements for some, but of little or nothing for others, exacerbates the public expression of civic inequality, in Gutmann's terms (2003, 97)—inequality that is harmful even when the exclusion in question does not cause this inequality. I argue that the absence of a civil marriage option for same-sex couples both causes inequality and also bears witness to the existence of that inequality.

In fact, withholding civil marriage from same-sex couples violates a fundamental right: the right to marry the partner of one's choice. In overturning Virginia's antimiscegenation law, the Supreme Court declared, "The freedom to marry has long been recognized as one of the vital personal rights essential to the orderly pursuit of happiness by free men" (Loving v. Virginia, 388 U.S. 1 [1967], at 12). Gerstmann agrees, saying, "It is difficult to conceive of ourselves as morally autonomous beings without the freedom to marry the person we love; thus, it is not surprising that marriage has long been considered one of our fundamental rights" (Gerstmann 2008, 115). For Richards, the fundamental right to an intimate life, like the right to conscience, "centrally frames enduring moral interests in loving and being loved, caring and being cared for, intimately giving value to the lives of others and having value given to one's own life" (Richards 2005, 132). In turn the ability to marry frames and accords public recognition and respect to the right to an intimate life. As chapter 3 explains, the Supreme Court has suggested the existence of a fundamental right to marry, for example by ruling that a state may neither require judicial permission to marry for individuals under court orders to support minor children, nor limit marriage by prison inmates only to situations in which compelling reasons to marry exist. Finally the court ruled in 1923 in *Meyer v. Nebraska* (262 U.S. 390 [1923]) that substantive liberty rights exist that cannot be invaded without due process of law. These comprise not only freedom from bodily restraint or interference, but also the individual right to contract, to engage in common occupations, to pursue knowledge, "to marry, establish a home and bring up children, to worship God according to the dictates of his own conscience, and generally to enjoy those privileges long recognized at common law as essential to the orderly pursuit of happiness" (399).

Although Gerstmann does not appear to recognize the symmetry between white supremacy as the historical grounding for denying marriage to interracial couples and heteronormativity as the current basis for denying it to same-sex couples, he does posit four criteria for identifying fundamental rights under the equal protection clause, all of which in his view push same-sex marriage into this category (Gerstmann 2008, 145–60; see also Gerstmann 1999, 151–81). First, precedent supports a fundamental right to marry that he believes should apply to all. Second, the vindication of established rights can require the protection of other rights. For example, the right to form relationships, to establish a home, and to fulfill one's moral interests in love and care, in Richards's terms (Richards, 2005, 132), may be best promoted through the framework and stability of civil marriage. Third, Gerstmann notes, the government exercises monopoly power over the dispensation of marriage licenses, just as it does for driver's licenses. With exclusive power over civil marriage and divorce, the state can permanently deny the exercise of some rights and therefore needs to surmount higher hurdles if it wants to curtail these. Finally, access to marriage is not a political question, as the Supreme Court has defined it. Unlike the distribution of income and wealth, marriage more closely resembles speech or religious exercise, where greater access for some does not mean lesser access for others. If access to civil marriage is a fundamental right, the objections by opponents of same-sex marriage that the people or their elected legislators—not courts or "activist judges"—should decide whether same-sex couples may marry lose their force. Access to a fundamental right is not subject to a popular vote. If curtailing access by same-sex couples to the benefits of an institution that is freely available to traditional couples represents a public expression of civic inequality, the denial is even more inequitable if access to the institution is a fundamental right.

The Claims of Citizenship

When a single model of relationship is augmented by a plurality of options, some wonder whether the current desirability of civil marriage warrants the expenditure of energy that animates same-sex marriage advocates and their allies. Because a great many material benefits that accompany civil marriage are also tied in varying degrees to civil unions and domestic partnerships, some may feel it makes more sense to expand the current smorgasbord to include more and better options, a view definitively espoused by skeptics about marriage (discussed further in chapter 3).

An interesting comparison, however, may be made between the current status of marriage and that of national citizenship. Citizenship, like marriage, is less essential than it was before as a source of rights and benefits. In the view of Peter Spiro, birthright citizenship has been grounded on the expectation that individuals will develop their affective ties and community attachments in the land of their birth. This expectation is belied today, however, both by increasing global mobility and also by the ability to maintain ties with communities outside those in which one resides. From this perspective, birthright citizenship is overinclusive. In another sense, however, the practice is underinclusive. Individuals living in border communities are often equally fluent in both cultures, although knowledge about American government, history, and culture is common worldwide. "Happenstance Americans," then, may include individuals born in the United States who experience few affective ties here, whereas this group does not include those who might claim ties and knowledge of the culture but remain outside the circle of birthright citizenship. With the possibility of naturalization in other than one's birthright nation after birth and the growing acceptance of multiple nationality, Spiro observes a self-reinforcing departure from strong definitions of national community. "The larger the group of happenstance citizens, the less likely the status will be consequential, which renders existing citizens more accepting of expansive admission criteria and the addition of nominal members, which in turn entrenches the lack of consequence" (Spiro 2008, 31; see also 19–25). More simply, "*Once everyone is an American, no one is an American. . . .* Once the difference disappears, the identity disappears with it" (52).

As with marriage, however, many believe that citizenship as a formal status still matters. But is citizenship a matter of will or of fact? For some, formal citizenship should be contingent on the consent of the political community in question. Too much emphasis on de facto ties "represents an ascriptive infringement of the community's democratic authority to shape its own destiny" (Schuck and Smith 1985, 40). For others citizenship is grounded on a moral claim deriving from facts about individuals' relationships with a society. Ascription "implies that people are *entitled* to citizenship in any state in which they have sufficiently powerful social ties. They cannot legitimately be deprived of such citizenship against their will" (Carens 1987, 426; see 423–36). The first view argues that it is the community's decision to bestow the status of citizenship that renders individuals members. The second view believes that de facto membership in the community through social ties is what should eventually earn individuals the de jure status of citizenship. The liberal principle of consent, which is typically associated with choice and empowerment, can become a tool of exclusion (Jacobson 2006, 645–54), whereas ascription may increase the possibility of inclusion.

Like citizenship, marriage might be defined as a status bestowed on those desirous and capable of taking on the responsibilities associated with full membership in a community. Historically, marriage signaled full citizenship, as men assumed the rights and responsibilities attendant to heading a household (Cott 2000, 133; see also 178). The self-marriage practices of our early history suggest an ascriptive interpretation of marriage. That is, committed couples whom the community recognized as such had already formed relationships that entitled them to be regarded as married. Their de facto ties earned them the right to the de jure status of marriage. As states widened the scope of their authority, however, marriage became a more exactly defined formal status. Successful aspiration to marriage was in a greater degree contingent on the consent of the political community, as represented by the matrimonial law of the several states. In this consensual model, marriage rested not only on the consent of the individual parties who were to be married but also on the civil consent of the state in whose eyes the couple wished to be seen as married. Because the possibility of consent also implied the possibility of nonconsent, this development put governments in a stronger position to withhold consent to marriages of which they disapproved, such as those involving polygamy, miscegenation, and now same-sex relationships. The current availability of state-sanctioned alternative institutions such as domestic partnerships and civil unions represents a kind of halfway house: Couples have more choices in the level of commitment they wish to make, but same-sex couples most often have fewer choices than other couples. In the ascriptive model their commitments should entitle them to the recognition attendant to civil marriage; but in the consensual model most states do not afford them the opportunity to attain this status.

Spiro argues that because legally resident aliens increasingly have rights virtually equivalent to those held by citizens, the status of citizenship adds little value to the mix. Despite strenuous attempts in the 1990s to tighten the social safety net in ways that excluded noncitizens, these efforts have been considerably softened. Although aliens are generally barred from voting, they may engage in political participation directly through campaign contributions and membership in interest groups, as well as indirectly through advocacy on their behalf by their homeland governments (Spiro 2008, 81, 83, 91–95; see also Citrin et al. 2007, 33). Moreover the international influence of universal human rights claims has devalued the importance of traditional diplomatic protections against the mistreatment of citizens by foreign governments. In other words, access to national citizenship plays a lesser role than formerly in protecting the rights and interests of both noncitizens in the United States and citizens abroad. Finally, nonstate associations, both subnational and international, increasingly represent the interests of both individuals and groups beyond national borders (e.g., the Mormon church or the International Olympic Committee), and for some these loyalties may represent a higher priority than that of national citizenship (Spiro 2008, 140–48). Not all eligible individuals desire citizenship in the nation-state (117). "Membership in the state is no longer the only game in town" (110).

Somewhat similarly, the institution of civil marriage has decreased in value. Alternative institutions such as civil unions and domestic partnerships confer many of the benefits of civil marriage, although not all. States have been able to enforce many of the obligations of marriage, such as child support, on individuals who are unmarried. Many couples eligible to marry choose not to do so, either because they are uninterested in the rights and interests that marriage protects or because the rights and interests that they do prioritize are not protected by civil marriage. If institutions such as national citizenship and civil marriage carry diminished importance, perhaps we should move beyond these institutions and place our hopes elsewhere.

Some, however, care deeply about the status of civil marriage or the status of formal citizenship. Whether national citizenship is the gold standard of community membership is beyond the scope of this book. Rogers Smith points out, however, that historically legal distinctions between white and nonwhite citizens, men and women, and citizens of European descent and Native Americans represent types of differentiated citizenship that belie the notion that United States citizenship is a matter of legal uniformity. Differentiations need not be invidious; the Canadian province of Quebec and its francophone citizens exemplify a status that has been sought after and welcomed by Quebecois. Nevertheless, "It is enormously difficult to decide whether differently situated persons with different bundles of rights and duties are nonetheless meaningfully equal in their civic standing" (Smith 2009,

914). The problem is deciding when a difference in the classification of individuals and groups "represents a way of promoting rough civic equality in the face of actually differing resources, opportunities, and aspirations, and when doing so instead imposes on some inappropriately subordinated or marginalized civic statuses" (915).

Legal alternatives to marriage may be regarded as instances of differentiated citizenship. That is, couples who undertake civil unions or domestic partnerships may stand in a different relationship to the states in which these are concluded than do couples who undertake civil marriage in those states. Even though some states confer on these couples all the material benefits of marriage without the title, they do not have access to the federal benefits of marriage regarding Social Security, inheritance, and so on. Even same-sex couples who may marry in a few states do not have access to these federal benefits. The purposes of the Defense of Marriage Act were not only to relieve states of having to recognize same-sex marriages concluded in other states but also to deprive same-sex couples of the federal benefits that typically accompany marriage by restricting these benefits to marriages comprising one man and one woman. The question, then, is whether these differentiated statuses provide a "rough civic equality," or whether they in fact constitute an inappropriate subordination and marginalization (Smith 2009, 915).

Spiro concludes that "American citizenship no longer reflects or defines a distinctive identity" (Spiro 2008, 161). In Smith's view, however, Spiro does not attend to the social or psychological aspects of citizenship or "how much people feel that their national citizenship is crucial to their identity" (Smith 2009, 930). Smith argues that most people not only want community memberships that provide physical and economic security but also "want to believe those community memberships have ethical worth" (932). They have been socialized to believe that the nation-state embodies this type of community. Although not all value and seek national citizenship, many do.

The same may be said of marriage. The institution of civil marriage provides material benefits often inaccessible to the unmarried—but those who wish to marry, whether same-sex or opposite-sex couples, want something more. They desire to make a public and formal statement and recognition of their commitment by participating in the institution that they consider the gold standard for committed relationships. For them marriage provides emotional security, and their participation in this institution has ethical worth. Although Tamara Metz persuasively argues that the liberal state is unsuited to provide the transformative ethical authority afforded by a community of shared worldviews (Metz 2010, 114–19), this point does not matter to those seeking to marry. Whatever the available alternatives, the fact that they themselves desire inclusion renders their exclusion a matter of subordination and marginalization. In the ascriptive model of citizenship, they may be "married" in their own eyes and in those of their immediate communities, and they may have undertaken a religious ceremony of commitment. So they can remove those quotation marks, however, they desire the civil recognition that only civil marriage can provide. But in the consensual model of citizenship, recognition depends upon the grace and favor of the state.

In regard to citizenship, Smith notes that because people are socialized to identify their own well-being with that of "particular preexisting societies, many are likely to respond to leaders who tell them that any extensive embrace of new arrangements is dangerous and immoral" (R. Smith 2009, 933). This point also may be applied to marriage. Skeptics about marriage itself may attribute the desire of many to marry civilly to a form of false consciousness resulting from socialization. That is, they argue that people falsely identify their own well-being with the status of being married. However, those who are skeptical of any changes in the institution of marriage are vulnerable to leaders who argue that the inclusion of same-sex couples is dangerous to the well-being of the family and is ethically or religiously immoral as well. Same-sex couples who wish to marry do not want to alter the substance of marriage; they simply wish to be included in the institution as it already exists. Unlike the Quebecois, and unlike opposite-sex couples who can marry if they choose, same-sex couples do not want to maintain a special status compared with that of other couples. This distinction is crucial in deciding whether a differentiated status results in civic equality or marginalization.

Those who for whatever reason are skeptical of the institution of civil marriage resent its elevated status and resist the pressure toward inclusion. Alternative institutions are somewhat analogous to subnational institutions and the arrangements sometimes provided to minority nations to aid efforts to maintain their cultures and identities (Kymlicka 1995, 60–69, 78, 95–101, 177–78). Same-sex couples who do want to marry, in contrast, may be compared to ethnic groups or immigrants who do wish to assimilate but who are not allowed to do so, because of either the strangeness or the perceived threats posed by their beliefs and practices. They may be offered civil unions or domestic partnerships, but many desire more. In fact same-sex couples are more disadvantaged than ethnic groups that are the result of immigration. Same-sex couples are generally birthright citizens who did not choose their citizenship, yet their equal citizenship and their entitlement to its benefits are not recognized. Their inability to "assimilate," to participate in the institution of civil marriage, cannot help but promote a subordination and marginalization that is inappropriate. These circumstances fulfill Gutmann's criterion for the harm created by discriminatory exclusion, a public expression of civic inequality even though this exclusion does not *cause* this civic inequality.

In subsequent chapters I argue that as long as civil marriage exists as a public institution, civic equality requires the inclusion of same-sex couples. This requirement can be defended, moreover, through the religion clauses of the First Amendment. In a liberal democracy, public policy is properly subject to discussion and contestation. Individuals disagree and will continue to disagree about the merits of same-sex marriage. If liberal democracy is to be neutral among rival conceptions of the good, one solution is to determine what policy or combination of policies best embodies this type of neutrality. As I argue in chapter 2, however, the meaning of neutrality is itself subject to dispute. What may appear neutral given certain presuppositions and assumptions appears anything but neutral when scrutinized in a different context. Chapter 3 lays out four major positions that generally characterize people's divergent views about same-sex marriage and addresses the strengths and weaknesses of each. Chapter 4 addresses establishment issues, and chapter 5 takes up free exercise positions. Finally, chapter 6 considers same-sex marriage in the context of the culture wars.

Although I have firm views about the merits of same-sex marriage in this controversy, I also agree with Alasdair MacIntyre that conflict plays a major role in the moral development of both individuals and of communities. "It is through conflict and sometimes only through conflict that we learn what our ends and purposes are" (MacIntyre 1981, 153). More specifically, "When an institution—a university, say, or a farm, or a hospital—is the bearer of a tradition of practice or practices, its common life will be partly, but in a centrally important way, constituted by a continuous argument as to what a university is and ought to be or what good farming is or what good medicine is. Traditions, when vital, embody continuities of conflict" (206). Although MacIntyre might not approve of my analogy, the institution of civil marriage certainly bears a tradition of practices, and it is in MacIntyre's spirit that I proceed.

CHAPTER 2

The Impossibility of Neutrality

What unites conflicting viewpoints on same-sex marriage is the implied conviction that the definition of civil marriage makes a statement about who is—and who is not—an equal citizen of the liberal democratic polity. As Jyl Josephson puts it, marriage is viewed as "the holy grail of gay politics by opponents and proponents alike" (Josephson 2005, 269). Participation in this institution offers certain rights and material benefits, to be sure, but this is not all it does. "Marriage posits a specific desirable form for intimacy and family life—despite contemporary reality—and reinforces that form through legal, economic, political, and social privileges" (271). In other words, the contours of the institution of marriage represent an endorsement of a particular preferred view of how citizens should conduct their lives. Not all individuals or couples aspire to marriage, even when their ascriptive ties entitle them to that status if they seek it. Others do aspire to marriage, but the government withholds consent because it deems some couples unsuited to this status as it is currently understood. Whether sought or unsought, however, marriage as a civil institution looms as a constant presence in the lives of all citizens as they negotiate their relationships, both with each other and also with the public authority that defines and controls access to this preferred model of life.

If marriage is to model, at least implicitly, a preferred ideal of life, conflicting views about who is allowed to do the modeling should not be surprising. The increasing public regulation of marriage has historically been accompanied by the implication that the institution "had to be insulated or salvaged from misuse by irresponsible, unsuited, or defiant couples" (Cott 2000, 128). In the debate over the inclusiveness of civil marriage, this understanding explains both scrutiny of the ethical worth of individuals desiring to formalize same-sex relationships and also disagreement about what message might be sent by inclusiveness. For example, according to Evan

Gerstmann, some scholars suggest that in terms of the state's monopoly on the legal benefits accompanying marriage, same-sex marriage simply respects these couples' freedom of association; but others believe that because society endorses the marital relationship, allowing same-sex couples to participate in it would signal that same-sex relationships deserve respect. For scholars in the first group, "given the state monopoly on licensing, it is no more an endorsement of homosexuality to grants gays and lesbians marriage licenses than it is to grant them driver's licenses." For the second group of scholars, in the context of interracial marriage, "Who would dispute that one reason most people oppose a ban on the latter is to show that the love and commitment of interracial couples is as worthy of respect as those of same-race couples?" (Gerstmann 2008, 43). Gerstmann points to the endorsement test often used in religious jurisprudence: If a reasonable person can view a government practice as an endorsement of religion, the practice violates the separation of church and state or, more specifically, the establishment clause of the First Amendment. Therefore because some reasonable persons "*could* view government recognition of same-sex marriage as an endorsement of same-sex relationships, . . . it is not irrational to reject a policy because it *might* have the effect of endorsing an undesired practice" (44; see also Gerstmann 1999, 136). Although Gerstmann himself endorses the idea that marriage to the person of one's choice is a fundamental right that therefore bypasses this jurisprudence, the example illustrates why in many contexts no policy can appear neutral.

The government properly regulates many human activities on moral grounds, and in these areas it cannot be neutral. It does not, however, generally use religious beliefs as a justification for doing so, even when civil laws against murder, for example, coincide with religious injunctions against it. Janet Jakobsen and Ann Pellegrini wonder, "Why does religion seem like the natural and appropriate basis for public policy concerning sex, but not for other ethically charged questions" such as poverty or the death penalty (Jakobsen and Pellegrini 2004, 5)? Freedom to marry the person of one's choice should be the right of every citizen, they maintain, but instead it is held out as a reward to those who form "the right kind of family. What kind of freedom is this when enjoyment of it requires subjection to narrow, exclusionary, and even sectarian understandings of who and what constitute family?" (9; see 9–13). As chapter 1 describes, moral questions always inform debate, but morality is not limited to religion, especially not to particular interpretations of what religion dictates. By continuing to endorse an ideal of marriage and family for which religious argument is seen as dispositive, the government endorses some religious arguments over others and also endorses religious arguments over nonreligious or unconventionally religious arguments. Even when public authority conscientiously pursues a neutral stance, however, no policy can appear neutral among conflicting claims on divisive issues. Why this is so is the subject of this chapter.

Neutrality as Metatheory

Many modern liberal theorists hold that a hallmark of liberalism is the state's neutrality among rival conceptions of the good. This claim has rested sometimes upon moral skepticism, the idea that no rational basis exists for making the best choice among different ways of life, and sometimes upon moral autonomy, the idea that each individual must define the good to be pursued in his or her own manner. Other contemporary liberals argue, however, that even a liberal polity cannot espouse neutrality among rival conceptions of the good. William Galston maintains, for example, that "liberalism is the theory, not of the neutral state, but of the minimally committed state" (Galston 1991, 93). The liberal state, like any other, must make binding determinations of public policy that are implicitly grounded in specific assumptions about human nature, proper conduct, well-ordered institutions, and just practices. "In such cases, neutrality is never violated, because it is never possible. Every polity, then, . . . establishes at least a partial rank-order among individual ways of life and competing principles of right conduct" (96–97). Unlike nonliberal states, however, "the liberal state rests solely on those beliefs about the good shared by all its citizens, whereas every other state must coercively espouse some controversial assumptions about the good life" (93).

I argue that unless a state proceeds on libertarian premises and comprises only libertarians, even a liberal state is premised on beliefs about the good that not all citizens share. Galston is correct, however, that neutrality is never possible, if he means neutrality across the board. Different kinds of neutrality may exist in different contexts, because neutrality has meaning only when it can be measured or judged in terms of some independent standard. If a state were to require every citizen to belong to one of a range of organized religious groups, for example, it would be neutral among these religions, but it would not be neutral in the eyes of citizens whose commitments were to unlisted religious groups or to no religion at all. This point illustrates the difficulty with nonpreferentialism in religious jurisprudence: the claim that a government that evenhandedly accords benefits to religious groups is not establishing religion. First, true evenhandedness not only is difficult to effect but is also politically unrealistic when unpopular or minority religious groups are involved. Second, even if evenhandedness exists, nonpreferentialism is not evenhanded between religion and nonreligion.

Likewise, if a state recognizes only one form of civil connection for committed couples but limits this connection to opposite-sex couples, it is neutral in the eyes of opposite-sex couples because any opposite-sex couple may avail themselves of it. But it is not neutral in the eyes either of same-sex couples who desire a civil connection or of those who support the rights of same-sex couples. Moreover, if a state makes a civil connection available to all couples, same-sex and opposite-sex alike, including legal and material benefits that are not extended to couples who do not desire this formalized commitment, the latter couples would still not find it neutral. In the first case, when it limits civil connection to opposite-sex couples, the state is neutral in offering benefits to civilly connected opposite-sex couples, but it is not neutral with regard to who may seek this connection. In the second case, the state is neutral regarding inclusiveness, but it is nonneutral in terms of how it bestows the benefits of civil connection, because they go only to those undertaking this formal commitment. The first case is analogous to an establishment of a single religion, which disadvantages both those who follow other religions and also those who follow no religion. The second case is analagous to nonpreferentialism, which ostensibly advantages all religions equally but disadvantages the nonreligious.

Putting this differently, Patrick Neal notes, "Although liberalism is neutral with regard to *conceptions* of the good, it has a very distinct *conceptualization* of what it means to have a conception of the good" (Neal 1997, 37–38; see 34–47). Neal's example of the limits of neutrality is an individual who believes that one can properly develop the moral virtues one values only in the context of the small, homogeneous Athenian polis. Although the liberal state respects diversity, in that you may become a lawyer and I a professor, this individual may not become part of a society constituted like the Athenian polis. This individual cannot pursue his or her conception of the good privately, because it can be pursued "only insofar as this pursuit is collectively undertaken on the basis of essentially shared ends which are understood by the participants to be definitive of themselves as selves" (40–41). Although the liberal may object that this hypothetical individual is trying to satisfy his or her own ends by imposing his or her own conception of the good on others, each is actually arguing for a different *conceptualization* of conceptions of the good, or metatheory of the good, which each claims is universally applicable. When the affirmation of a conception of the good is viewed as a private choice, in the language of metatheory, "it is not without public consequence; for if the good is a matter for private individual choice, then it is not a matter for public political determination" (45). In other words, although a liberal society or state allows choice within a range of preferences, it cannot allow choice among all preferences that might conceivably exist, because its very espousal of core commitments produces one range of preferences that excludes others.

This is why, Neal says, "The positive defense of liberalism cannot be that it is neutral amongst preferences; it must be a defense of the *kind* of preferences liberalism produces" (Neal 1997, 28). Commitment to the complete range of possibilities for diversity is unachievable, as is the realization of a thoroughgoing neutrality. The metatheoretical perspective advanced by Neal reveals that liberalism and the neutrality of broad value pluralism can be incompatible. Although the liberal state is often viewed as a response to the existing diversity of incommensurable goods, Pratap Bhanu Mehta explains, "Liberalism, if it is to give itself any identity and content at all, has to argue for precisely such values that, in the case of conflict, trump others" (Mehta 1997, 723).

A defense of liberalism therefore cannot rest upon its hospitality to diversity across the board; it must instead be grounded in the particular range of values or preferences that its given interpretation of liberalism puts forward. This range may include hospitality to diverse conceptions of the good, but within that range it cannot include conceptualizations whose effectiveness relies upon an essential identification with only one conception of the good. This metatheoretical perspective also supports the point chapter 1 makes about Rosenblum's foundationalist integralists, who seek to apply religious law and authority to every aspect of life. If, in Galston's terms, the practice of religious belief—or for that matter, any belief system—requires control over the whole of life, including the sociopolitical environment, this demand may work in voluntary communities that sequester themselves from the larger society. It is not, however, compatible with a liberal society and state, in which individuals expect the freedom within broad limits to live their lives as they see fit.

Purported neutrality toward conceptions of the good itself then constitutes a metatheory of the good, as it eliminates conceptions that can only be realized, in Neal's view, in communities that are not themselves neutral toward conflicting interpretations of the good. Moreover, even communities that strive for neutrality on some definition must espouse public policies that do not appear neutral to all. Creppell notes that despite John Locke's advocacy of religious toleration, for example, Locke wrote that civil authority, not individuals, must define its limits. Although Locke believed that the correct test for public interference with religious rituals and practices is that of actual bodily injury to the individual or the body politic, not offense to others' sensibilities or beliefs (Creppell 1996, 224), the definition of injury is itself problematic and depends on one's beliefs and perspectives. Therefore the civil authority must establish a worldly criterion of injury to life, liberty, and property that then determines the appropriate scope of religious belief and practice. The line between the civil and the religious is an object of civil determination, rather than one of conscientious belief, and it may change along with the demands of the public interest, which is itself civilly determined (McClure 1990, 373–81; Locke 1689, 48–50). The criterion of "worldly injury" is an attempt to make civil law neutral with respect to religion, but it does so by rendering irrelevant any consideration of or reference to the validity or appropriateness of religious practices on their own terms. Because the norms of religious believers often differ from those of unbelievers, just as sacred norms do from secular ones, no stance appears neutral to all.

For Locke, then, civil enforcement to prevent a purely religious harm to some is illegitimate when this causes civil harm to others, as Creppell explains. Because civil authority determines the boundary of religious practice, civil law that is neutral with regard to the religious truth of particular practices is indeed not neutral or politically indifferent toward the practical embodiments of some religious visions of the good society. As Kirstie McClure suggests, the difficulty is that "the civil discourse of facticity itself has become a site riddled with conflicting interpretations of which particular sets of social 'facts' are to be considered indicative of the sort of 'harm' appropriately subject to political jurisdiction" (McClure 1990, 383; see 382–84). Although McClure's focus is Locke's concern with religious practices that may be questionable because they constitute worldly injury to the life, liberty, or property of others, this interpretation also applies to civilly benign practices that partisans of particular religious and ethical beliefs may view as injurious.

For example, people who believe that abortion is wrong because the fetus is a human being from the moment of conception hold different worldviews and accept different sets of social facts about the nature of social morality and the proper role of women and children than do those who believe that abortion is rightly a matter of personal choice (Luker 1984, 158–91). Opponents of abortion rights want to use their own set of social facts to reconstitute as civilly injurious the legality of abortion that pro-choice advocates and civil law classify as benign. Similarly, those who believe that abortion is a matter of personal choice argue that the severe limitation on reproductive choice represented by the criminalization of abortion constitutes worldly injury to the civil interests of women, to their agency, and to their moral and personal autonomy. Because each side begins with a different set of social facts, they hold different views regarding what is injurious and what is civilly benign. Neither camp wants to have its viewpoint denied empirical validity and relegated "to the category of speculative truths without worldly effect" (McClure 1990, 384; see 384–86). Moreover, the two sides conflict not only in their conceptions of the good but also, in Neal's terms, in their metatheory, or conceptualization of these conceptions. For those who are pro-life, controversial matters such as abortion should be subject to public political determination. Individual self-determination negates their desire to live in a polity that is united in pursuit of the essentially shared end of respect for human life at all stages of existence. For those who are pro-choice, intimate and personal matters concerning reproduction and sexuality are at the core of individual identity and self-definition. The idea that these choices should be subject to the will of others whose values they do not share embodies the tyranny of the majority.

The role of metatheory is evident in other contemporary disputes. With regard to religion, a strict separationist interpretation of the First Amendment that banishes most religious symbols from the public square does not appear neutral to those who support a public acknowledgment of their religious heritage as well as their secular heritage. To separationists, however, these religious symbols and ceremonies represent a nonneutral public endorsement either of some religions at the expense of others or of religiosity in general at the expense of nonbelief. Alternatively, accommodationists believe that denying public funds to social service agencies that retain their religious character or discriminate in hiring penalizes religious belief and imposes a burden on the free exercise of religion. In contrast, separationists believe that when public monies are at stake, all recipients, whether secular or religious, must be expected to adhere to the same rules (Gill 2004; Kmiec 2008, 111, 118). Policies that appear neutral to one group thus appear nonneutral to the other. Each side possesses a different conceptualization of what it conceives to be the proper relationship between religion and the state and therefore holds a different vision of neutrality.

Similarly, differing sets of social facts indicate conflicting interpretations of who is harmed and how they are harmed when same-sex couples are included or not included in the institution of marriage. Traditionalist opponents of same-sex marriage view marriage as a long-standing institution that binds sexual intimacy to parenting. The inclusion of same-sex couples dethrones this social fact and by extension endorses other versions as equally worthy. Those whom I call traditionalist proponents of same-sex marriage focus not on the gender of the participants but rather on the social fact that long-term commitments can enhance stable relationships, which should be encouraged and rewarded. Skeptics about marriage point to the rigidity of an institution that publicly defines its relevant benefits and burdens, rather than leaving them to choice. Finally, liberal, rights-based advocates of same-sex marriage focus on the social fact of the denial of basic human rights involving association, conscience, and individual moral and personal autonomy; they view marriage as instrumental to the expression of the moral and ethical agency of its voluntary participants.

These conflicting sets of social facts also influence diverse views on the proper forum for decisions about who may marry. If society recognizes marriage as a private choice available to all committed couples, this move has the public consequence of removing the definition of marriage from the public square as a matter for public political determination. If, however, the public through representative government is allowed to determine what sorts of couples may marry, this not only limits the private choices available to same-sex couples but also has the public consequence of defining the public square as one that distinguishes between insiders, who are viewed as full members of the community, and outsiders, who are not. Moreover, proponents and opponents of same-sex marriage hold not only different conceptions of the good but also different conceptualizations (or metatheories) of conceptions of the good. Liberal proponents and skeptics alike recognize that although individuals may hold divergent conceptions of what is good for them, it is individuals who hold them and who should decide how to act on them. Their conceptualization of these conceptions, then, is based on the individual. Traditionalist proponents as well as opponents of same-sex marriage, in contrast, differ in their conceptions of whom marriage should include, but their conceptualizations are rooted in what they see as promoting social stability. Like Neal's individual who longs for the Athenian polis, they believe that couples can pursue the good of commitment in a truly effective manner only within the contours of a society that upholds and reinforces it as a bedrock institution.

Neutrality and Moral Assessment

Despite the parallels between religious belief and sexual orientation and the resulting implications for the free exercise of both, many people to whom religion is important see an irresolvable conflict between nondiscrimination concerning sexual orientation and the religious belief that leads some to see same-sex intimacy as sinful. In the opinion of Marc Stern, "The legalization of same-sex marriage would represent the triumph of an egalitarian-based ethic over a faith-based one, and not just legally. The remaining question is whether champions of tolerance are prepared to tolerate proponents of a different ethical vision. I think the answer will be no" (Stern 2008, 57). He does not believe that clergy will be penalized for refusing to perform marriages that contravene their religious beliefs (1). He does fear, however, that widespread acceptance of same-sex marriage plus civil rights laws that prohibit discrimination on the basis of sexual orientation will compel religious institutions and individuals to treat same-sex couples as married even if this violates their beliefs (25), based on both actual and hypothetical examples. In the view of some commentators, Jonathan Turley says, already "the government has abandoned a neutral position in its dealings with political or religious groups in favor of enforcing nondiscrimination policies. In doing so, the government has taken sides on religious or cultural controversies through the denial of tax exemption or access to state-run charity programs" (Turley 2008, 60). Although Turley does not oppose same-sex marriage and prefers that the term "civil union" be applied to the government-sanctioned connection known as civil marriage, he argues that organizations with fundamental commitments based on faith and morals should not suffer discrimination because they insist on living by these views (61).

This conflict once again implicates McClure's civil discourse of facticity. As Thomas Caramagno observes, rights advocates assert that nondiscrimination laws simply allow gays and lesbians openly to enjoy the same rights as heterosexuals, such as finding housing and employment and participating politically in the lives of their communities. "And since invisibility is not required of other minority groups, does it not constitute an inequality for LGBTs [lesbian, gay, bisexual, and transgendered]?" Some Christians reply, however, "that protecting LGBTs' freedom to live openly by their own beliefs infringes upon Christians from living openly by theirs" (Caramagno 2002, 193). That is, lesbians, gays, bisexuals, and transgender individuals believe that these Christians are acting antisocially and immorally by resisting antidiscrimination protections based on sexual orientation, whereas religious activists believe that gay rights advocates are acting antisocially and immorally by trying to stigmatize the religious for living out their faithful, conscientious religious beliefs. Caramagno explains, "Anti-discrimination laws and sodomy laws both impose values. States are put in the paradoxical position of protecting each group's core beliefs while simultaneously outlawing acting out those beliefs," or at least openly doing so (Caramagno 2002, 193). The government could be neutral by refusing to protect any group, regardless of religion or sexual orientation, from discrimination, but it would do so at the expense of unleashing private discriminatory practices that "can be just as effective at marginalizing a despised group as institutionalized disenfranchisement" (195; see 190–97), a point with historical resonance for unpopular minorities of all kinds.

If the state cannot be neutral among rival conceptions of the good, in a metatheoretical sense, how then might one define neutrality within the range of preferences that the liberal state offers that is sufficient to support both pluralism and the protection of individual rights that are among its core features? Chai Feldblum provides a provocative account of neutrality that specifically addresses sexual orientation. She begins by identifying three possible views of same-sex sexual activity. First, one might believe that such activity morally harms both individuals and their communities and is therefore to be strongly discouraged. Second, one might hold that same-sex sexual activity is neither good nor harmful but is more like an abnormal health condition that people typically eschew, implicitly because of the difficulties posed by living with it. Third, one might believe "that gay sexual activity has the same moral valence as heterosexual activity and that gay people are basically similar to straight people" (Feldblum 2008, 128). Statistics show that a great many people adhere to the second view. Although many do not see all sexual orientations as equal and do not support marriage for same-sex couples, neither do they want their relatives to suffer discrimination on the basis of their sexual orientations (129).

Although she herself subscribes to the third viewpoint, as do I, Feldblum believes that the second, middle position points the way to a definition of moral neutrality that could be described as agnostic about the good. For her, "When the government decides, through the enactment of its laws, that a certain way of life does not harm those living that life and does not harm others who are exposed to such individuals, the government has basically staked out a position of moral neutrality with regard to that way of living," one that stands "in stark contrast to those who believe that the particular way of living at issue is morally laden and problematic." In other words, the government is not saying that same-sex relationships are either bad or good. Feldblum suggests, however, that if the government enacts civil rights laws that prohibit discrimination on the basis of sexual orientation, "it is disingenuous to say that voting for a law of this kind conveys no message about morality at all." When the government prohibits discrimination in housing, employment, and places of public accommodation, the state has "made the prior moral assessment that acting on one's homosexual orientation is not so morally problematic as to justify private parties discriminating against such individuals in the public domain" (Feldblum 2008, 131). Although same-sex sexual activity is neither bad nor good then, at least it is deemed not harmful, unlike domestic violence or rape, and therefore those who engage in it warrant protection from discrimination.

Feldblum's definition of neutrality toward sexual orientation is one that we already use toward religion. When the government protects against religious discrimination, it is not stating that religion is either bad or good. Such protection does imply, however, a prior moral assessment that practicing one's religion does not harm the individual, does not harm others exposed to this practice, and is not morally problematic enough to justify religious discrimination. This protection also means, moreover, that discrimination on the basis of religion is wrong. Therefore within a broad range individuals who engage in the practice of religious belief warrant protection. From a metatheoretical perspective, then, Feldblum's definition of neutrality is not in fact neutral, because it cannot simultaneously encompass both the view that one sexual or religious orientation is superior and the view that all share an equal plane and must therefore be protected from discrimination. However, from the perspective of first-order liberal theory, Feldblum's definition of neutrality may be regarded as neutral because it does not prefer one sexual orientation to another or to total celibacy, just as laws against religious discrimination do not prefer one religion to another or to nonreligious practice. Therefore, laws prohibiting discrimination on the basis of sexual orientation or religion do support sexual or religious pluralism and neutrality within the range that a liberal state can offer. Nonetheless, from a second-order or metatheoretical perspective, sexual and religious pluralism is itself grounded in the defense of moral and personal autonomy that I view as instrumental to the expression of moral and ethical agency (Gill 2001, 13–42). In this sense then, Feldblum's conception of neutrality is not neutral.

This point may be illustrated by Feldblum's argument that the absence of antidiscrimination laws also sends a message about morality. "When the government *fails* to pass a law" prohibiting discrimination "on the basis of sexual orientation, . . . or *fails* to allow same-sex couples access to marriage . . . , the government has similarly taken a position on a moral question. The state has decided that a homosexual or bisexual orientation is not morally neutral, but rather may legitimately be viewed by some as morally problematic" (Feldblum 2008, 132; see 131–33). The same argument applies to religion. That is, if the record demonstrates that some religions are traditionally despised, and the government allows majority sentiment to prevail by doing nothing, it has taken a moral position. Although some people will always view certain sexual orientations or religions as morally problematic—and they are entitled to do so—the government's failure to act means that public authority is itself signaling that these orientations or religions are problematic. Because the liberal state purports to be hospitable to diversity within a particular range of activities not deemed harmful to others, it must step up to protect ways of life within that range that are not morally problematic according to its own prior moral assessment.

Romer v. Evans (517 U.S. 620 [1996]) may exemplify this point. The political subdivisions in Colorado that passed antidiscrimination laws forbidding discrimination in housing and employment based on sexual orientation engaged in a prior moral assessment. That is, they judged that revealing one's sexual orientation, in Feldblum's terms, "was not so morally problematic as to justify private parties discriminating against such individuals in the public domain" (Feldblum 2008, 131). The *Romer* court evidently agreed. Correspondingly, however, if Colorado had failed to pass such laws, or the *Romer* court had failed to overturn Amendment 2, this would also have constituted a moral assessment, implying that revealing a minority sexual orientation was indeed morally problematic and should therefore be discouraged. One cannot, of course, be denied a housing situation or a job if one simply conceals a nonheterosexual orientation. However, one should not have to conceal a matter that is central to identity, like sexual orientation, any more than one should feel compelled to conceal one's religious convictions. The outcome of *Romer* indicates governmental neutrality about the moral worth of sexual orientation. Nevertheless whenever a public authority draws the line between what is sufficiently morally problematic that it should be forbidden and what is sufficiently unproblematic that the activity or practice should be allowed and perhaps protected through civil rights laws, the public authority does so on the basis of a moral assessment about the range of preferences that a liberal state should encompass. In my view, the range includes a wide latitude of activity and practice that moral pluralism and personal autonomy alike require, thereby instantiating neutrality within that range. From a metatheoretical perspective, however, this range will never appear neutral to all, because it is nonneutral between the idea that some sexual orientations are preferable to others and the conviction that discrimination on the basis of sexual orientation is wrong.

Ranges of Diversity

If the liberal state necessarily encompasses preferences within a particular range, rather than all preferences that might conceivably exist, we cannot avoid the question of what that range should be. This question requires engaging in politics to persuade others that one particular range is more compatible than another with one's particular interpretation of liberalism. We must take care not to assume too quickly that any given consensus is the correct one, to be maintained without question against those who might challenge it. Neal suggests that when we agree to take certain matters off the political agenda, we assume an identity of political interests as a given. "But what if this assumption is wrong?" he asks. "What if political actors and interests are thought of not as entities pre-existing the process of political activity, but as properties which emerge and constitute themselves within and through that process?" (Neal 1997, 124). Neal's example is in fact the rights of individuals experiencing same-sex attraction, which until recently was neither discussed nor included on the political agenda. "Commentators and activists, however, have *made* themselves and their interests *recognizable* by engaging in various forms of political activity" (125; see also Warren 1996, 263; Gill 2001, 38–42). Another example is the insistence by some that unborn persons possess rights as potential persons. What we want to avoid is "closing the channels through which 'free and equal persons' manifest themselves in ways recognizable by others" (Neal 1997, 124). Avoiding a rush to judgment "turns on a commitment to live life without the assurance that ours is the right, good, holy, or rational way to live," in the words of Bonnie Honig (1993, 194). If traditions embody continuities of conflict, as MacIntyre suggests, this commitment requires openness to interpretations of the liberal tradition that may appear alien at the outset.

In chapter 1 I state that although sexual orientation, like religious belief, is a central facet or constituent of personal identity, some individuals tolerant of diverse religious beliefs are often less tolerant of diverse sexual orientations. However, others who champion secularly based nondiscrimination laws fear that granting seemingly justifiable religious exemptions will undermine civic equality. "They see any exemption or weakening of resolve as likely to erode hard-earned gains," or as "a back door effort to undermine equality rights generally" (Stern 2008, 28; see 27–28). From another perspective, however, both gay advocates and religious advocates benefit from a neutral government that does not seek to withdraw tax exemptions, for example, from private organizations using their rights of free speech and association in ways with which the government disagrees (Turley 2008, 75–76), any more than it seeks to suppress rights claims by those who have historically been objects of discrimination simply because many religious individuals disapprove of these claims. If sexual orientation and religious belief both constitute central facets of personal identity, can these claims be balanced?

In a discussion of antidiscrimination legislation based on sexual orientation that may pose burdens on religious belief for some religious people, Feldblum posits the hypothetical example of a couple running a Christian bed-and-breakfast establishment. The owners state clearly in all advertising that they run a Christian business and will not accommodate cohabiting unmarried couples, whether they are same-sex or opposite-sex, or same-sex married couples unless these couples agree to rent separate rooms and not engage in sexual activity while in residence. To allow otherwise, for these owners, would condone activity that they consider sinful. If they are sued because (again hypothetically) the state has an antidiscrimination law based on sexual orientation and marital status, they are likely to lose even if they claim that their free exercise of religion is burdened, because their religion does not require that they operate a bed and breakfast. If the state does not have such an antidiscrimination law, a same-sex married couple, perhaps previously unaware of the owners' policy and desiring accommodations, will be turned away and will therefore receive treatment unequal to that accorded an opposite-sex married couple (Feldblum 2008, 123–24). Feldblum's point is that these sorts of conflicts tend to be framed as zero-sum games in which liberties such as religious freedom and equal treatment are unalterably opposed. She does not claim that there is a neutral solution under which no one loses. She does suggest that commonalities exist.

Society readily accepts the idea that although individuals and religious communities have complete freedom of belief, they are not necessarily free to engage in every practice that flows from these beliefs. Civil authority necessarily defines the limits of religious practice, and some manifestations of belief may be forbidden because they are deemed harmful to one's fellow citizens or to the larger community. We tend to conclude that curtailing religious practice, though regrettable, does minimal damage because, after all, we are not pressuring people to change their beliefs. As Feldblum points out, however, if religious people tell the same-sex married couple in her example that they should not object to abstaining from sexual activity while staying at the Christian bed and breakfast because, after all, they are not prohibited from having or acknowledging a gay identity, civil rights advocates will quite properly object. To Feldblum it appears "the height of disingenuousness, absurdity, and indeed, disrespect to tell someone it is permissible to 'be' gay, but not permissible to engage in gay sex. What do they think being gay means?" (Feldblum 2008, 143; see 142–43, 123–24).

Feldblum reacts similarly "to those who blithely assume a religious person can disengage her religious belief and self-identity from her religious practice and religious behavior. What do they think being religious means?" Although religion is grounded in belief, certain practices flow from these beliefs, and "the day-to-day *practice* of one's religion is an essential way of bringing meaning to such beliefs" (Feldblum 2008, 143). In her view, "Gay people—of all individuals—should recognize the injustice of forcing a person to disaggregate belief or identity from practice" (142; see also 124). She classifies both sexual orientation and religious belief into two broader categories, representing different types of liberty interests, the invasion of which requires greater justification than do other kinds of state action. "Identity liberty" encompasses intimate and personal choices central to one's autonomy and constitutive of one's identity, such as sexuality, marriage, procreation, and family relationships. "Belief liberty" refers to "the liberty to possess deeply held personal beliefs without coercion or penalty by the state" (140) and appears similar to freedom of conscience. Although these two liberty interests are closely linked, Feldblum describes belief as a separate liberty interest subject to due process protections, because beliefs that "constitute an important core aspect of the individual" may derive from either religious sources, secular sources, or spiritual sources that are not traditionally religious, all of which she argues should be accorded the same weight. "What should be relevant for a liberty analysis is whether such beliefs form *a core aspect of the individual's sense of self and purpose in the world.* An individual may be able to meet this standard whether his or her beliefs are religiously or secularly based" (130; see also 125, 140). Liberty interests may still "be *justifiably* burdened by the government because of the needs of society" (135). But Feldblum supports a wide scope for the exercise of both kinds of liberty, because both are central to individual identity. For this reason she defends such conduct under the due process clauses of the Fifth and Fourteenth Amendments, rather than under the free exercise clause of the First Amendment (125, 140–49).

In her final disposition of this conflict, however, Feldblum implicitly admits that no solution is truly neutral. Nondiscrimination laws that include sexual orientation are in her view neutral, not only because they suggest that this status is neither bad nor good but also because in her opinion sexual orientation is as morally neutral as hair color (Feldblum 2008, 141), and therefore discrimination on the basis of either is wrong. However, when identity liberty concerning sexual orientation conflicts with belief liberty concerning religion, Feldblum says, "I find it difficult to envision any circumstance in which a court could legitimately conclude that a legislature that has passed an LGBT equality law, with no exceptions for individuals based on belief liberty, has acted arbitrarily or pointlessly" (152). Establishing a baseline allowing people with a morally neutral characteristic to live openly, safely, and with dignity reflects the public good, in her view. Feldblum suggests that we should still acknowledge that this stance poses an obstacle to belief liberty by limiting the ability to engage in some of the practices that flow from one's beliefs. Admitting this obstacle, moreover, may properly impel legislative bodies to enact certain exemptions to these nondiscrimination laws when they are passed (150–53). Open acknowledgment of this conflict is healthy. Nevertheless, Feldblum says, "Protecting one group's identity liberty may, at times, require that we burden others' belief liberties" (156).

I argue that the liberal state can encompass only a particular range of preferences rather than all preferences that could possibly exist. If belief in liberty or liberty of conscience is as broadly defined as Feldblum advocates, the problem is that the same breadth that helps to ground equality claims for LGBT persons can simultaneously justify discrimination against them on religious grounds. Locke suggested one way to negotiate this conflict. In his 1689 *Letter Concerning Toleration*, Locke argued with respect to corporate belief "that no Church is bound by the Duty of Toleration to retain any such Person in her Bosom as, after Admonition, continues obstinately to offend against the Laws of the Society" (30). Without the freedom to expel recalcitrant members, faith communities as well as other close-knit groups could not retain a forum within which they may express and practice their shared values (Spinner-Halev 2000, 171). Locke cautioned, however, that this separation may not be accompanied by any action that would constitute civil injury, as "Civil Goods . . . are under the Magistrate's Protection." With respect to individual belief, "No private Person has any Right, in any manner, to prejudice another Person in his Civil Enjoyments, because he is of another Church or Religion. All the Rights and Franchises that belong to him as a Man, or as a Denizen, are inviolably preserved to him. These are not the Business of Religion" (Locke 1689, 31; see also Spinner-Halev 2000, 174). Although like-minded individuals must be free to associate without threat from those who might alter their values through their membership, a liberal state must also guard against the danger that establishment of an orthodoxy can pose for the exercise of alternatives.

The protection of diversity within a context of equal citizenship, then, requires the recognition both of the value of acceptable difference and also of the necessary conditions for its flourishing. Amy Gutmann suggests, "Discriminatory exclusion is harmful when it *publicly expresses* the civic inequality of the excluded even in the absence of any other showing that it *causes* the civic inequality in question" (Gutmann 2003, 97). Gutmann here argues that the entrance to discriminatory voluntary associations should sometimes be opened up even when blocked entry does not directly harm individuals, "because the standing of citizens as civic equals should be *expressed* as well as supported by associations that distribute public goods and services" (98). Although the status of private, voluntary associations is beyond the scope of this chapter, the public conditions for the flourishing of religious and sexual difference are not. Civic equality, in my view, not only may require a qualified noninterference with belief or identity and practice, but also may require public action that may prevent the creation of two classes of citizens. If, as Locke suggested, private persons and organizations have no right to "prejudice another Person in his Civil Enjoyments" because of religion—or by extension, sexual orientation—neither should public authority (Locke 1689, 31). When a great many individuals or organizations parallel one another in religious, ethical, or moral stances that disadvantage some other individuals and groups, moreover, public authority cannot simply stand by, as it did for decades on the issue of racial discrimination by both private and public entities. Otherwise it effectively sanctions the public expression of civic inequality. How it provides the necessary conditions for the flourishing of diversity is of course the hard question, one that requires closer examination of the conflicting meanings of neutrality.

Ranges of Neutrality

In a widely recognized contrast, Nancy Fraser distinguishes between economic injustice—one rooted in the structure of society and exemplified by exploitation, marginalization, and deprivation—and cultural or symbolic injustice—exemplified by cultural domination, nonrecognition or invisibility, and disrespect. These types of injustice are intertwined, and they both disadvantage some groups of people more than others. Nevertheless, suggests Fraser, the remedies for these types of conditions differ. Economic injustice requires transforming political and economic structures, or a focus on redistribution. Cultural injustice requires cultural or symbolic change that raises the value of disrespected identities and cultures, or else it requires a focus on recognition— that is, the redistribution of economic resources cannot engender respect for the disrespected. Gays and lesbians, Fraser asserts, suffer from both heterosexism, or "the authoritative construction of norms that privilege heterosexuality," and homophobia, or "the cultural devaluation of homosexuality." Although gays and lesbians suffer from economic injustice when they are not hired or are fired on the basis of sexual orientation or when they are denied economic benefits that derive from conventional family status, the harassment, discrimination, and violence they may suffer derive from "an unjust cultural-valuational structure," the remedy for which is recognition (Fraser 1997, 18; see also 13–16). Although Fraser does not say so, the economic injustices experienced by gay, lesbian, bisexual, and transgender persons arguably flow from the devaluation of their sexual identities by much of the larger culture, or the sorts of cultural injustices that describe a failure of recognition. The remedy, then, "is to revalue a despised sexuality, to accord positive recognition to gay and lesbian sexual specificity" (19).

The importance of cultural recognition is developed in detail by Anna Elisabetta Galeotti, who expands upon the idea that although we typically think of inequality as stemming from an unequal distribution of resources and opportunities, "public consideration as members of the political and social community" may also be lacking (Galeotti 2002, 8; see also 9–14, 61). Recognition of full membership in the community may require not only toleration of personal liberty in the private sphere but also its extension to the public sphere. Although some object that public recognition involves endorsement of the content or intrinsic value of particular differences, thereby conflicting with the liberal ideals of impartiality and neutrality, Galeotti suggests that "differences can be recognized not for their intrinsic value, which is not up to the political authorities to determine, but instrumentally, for the value they have for their bearers." Public recognition then means that a different identity or practice is accepted or included "in the range of the legitimate, viable, 'normal' options and alternatives of an open society" (15; see 14–15, 73, 100–101, 103–5). This point is reminiscent of Feldblum's contention that when the government concludes a particular way of life harms neither those living that life nor those exposed to it, its position is one of moral neutrality toward that way of life, viewing it as neither good nor bad.

In the realm of religion Galeotti distinguishes between toleration, or noninterference with individuals' religious and moral views by public authority, and neutrality, or not favoring some views and their adherents over others in the public sphere. "With reference to citizens, then, while toleration grants them freedom of conscience, neutrality grants them the right not to be discriminated against because of their conscience" (Galeotti 2002, 26). This distinction parallels that between the religion clauses of the First Amendment. That is, the free exercise clause respects the dictates of the individual conscience, but the establishment clause prevents favoritism toward some manifestations of conscience over others, or in Gutmann's terms, the public expression of civic inequality (Gutmann 2003, 97). As a solution to religious warfare, Galeotti explains, toleration of private manifestations of conscience during the Protestant Reformation was not incompatible with the establishment or endorsement of a state religion. With the development of the secular state, however, the accompanying ideal of neutrality renders religious differences politically irrelevant. The focus on individual rights means that differences are tolerated in the private sphere but ignored in the public sphere. Although citizens do not necessarily have to hide differences in a public sphere that is blind to them, "an influential interpretation—embodied in the continental ideal of *laicité*—has equated neutrality with a public sphere to which everyone belongs qua citizen, and where no particular loyalty, identity, or group that might threaten the general will is allowed" (Galeotti 2002, 27; see 23–27).

Galeotti's view of neutrality is congruent with Neal's, mine, and by implication Feldblum's: That is, neutrality can never be absolute but instead is a matter of context and interpretation (Galeotti 2002, 53–58). Neutrality, as I argue above, only has meaning when measured or judged in terms of some standard independent of neutrality itself. If this standard depends on the civil discourse of facticity, in McClure's terms (McClure 1990, 383), that determines which sets of social facts are relevant for determining fairness or neutrality, neutrality cannot in and of itself be the desired goal without some further qualification of its meaning. Galeotti makes a distinction between neutralist liberalism, in which toleration is the precondition or "principle on which the legitimacy of liberal institutions is grounded" (Galeotti 2002, 48), and perfectionist liberalism, for which "full political toleration should in principle be limited to those differences which can be accommodated within the fairly open boundaries of the liberal conception of the good," excluding those that may threaten the ethical integrity of the liberal order (41–45; see also Gill 2001, 13–42). Perfectionist liberals believe that toleration is properly grounded in respect for ethically substantive liberal values, and they therefore believe that neutralist liberals strip liberalism of meaningful content (Galeotti 2002, 37). Neutralist liberals, in turn, believe that perfectionist liberals betray the promise of toleration, inclusiveness, and universalism, making liberalism just another particularistic political ideal in which the state implicitly takes sides among rival conceptions of the good (44, 55). Although those whom Galeotti calls the "new autonomists" have extended their framework to endorse cultural rights and multicultural policies that support minority cultures, they retain the perfectionist liberal attitude of pragmatic toleration that may exclude full recognition (45–47).

Galeotti seeks to rescue the concept of neutrality from charges of emptiness or meaninglessness. She argues that neutralist liberalism has a constitutive ethical core of nondiscrimination that can be interpreted to grant public relevance and sensitivity to social differences (Galeotti 2002, 57). Public blindness or indifference may protect the private pursuit of minority conceptions of the good or ways of life, but it ignores embedded privileges and costs in the public realm, stemming from a history of discrimination—privileges and costs that are reinforced by attitudes shaped by this history (59; see also Jakobsen and Pellegrini 2004, 45–50). Today, because toleration and noninterference with religion are assumed, society emphasizes neutrality as equal freedom of expression and association. "Thus the present-day conflict does not concern (not primarily, at least) incompatible differences of value and culture . . . , but the unequal public standing of those professing minority views, who, therefore, demand toleration as a means of getting fair access to the public sphere" (Galeotti 2002, 66; see also 62–65).

In the United States contemporary religious jurisprudence has focused on religious groups' equal access to public educational facilities and on public funding for faith-based social services and religiously affiliated schools. This religious jurisprudence highlights these groups' perceptions that they possess unequal public standing. They seek to fulfill the promise of toleration by redeeming its worth in the public square. One interesting point about Galeotti's account is that by attributing this type of ethical content to neutralist liberalism, she moves it closer to perfectionist liberalism. Whereas perfectionist liberals believe we should accord public toleration and recognition only to social differences in accordance with liberal ideals, as a neutralist liberal Galeotti believes we should accord public toleration and recognition to acceptable but marginalized conceptions of the good if their adherents are to enjoy public standing comparable to that of adherents to majority conceptions. That is, perfectionist liberals focus on preserving the integrity of liberal values and the liberal order by according full recognition only to those who measure up to a particular standard. Neutralist liberals, in contrast, assume a rough compatibility between conceptions of the good held by citizens of the liberal order and that order itself. They then focus on the conditions necessary for these citizens' equal public standing or, in Gutmann's terms, civic equality (Gutmann 2003, 97). Where perfectionist liberals see the proverbial glass as half empty and seek to move individuals and groups whose liberal credentials are lacking closer to liberal values, neutralist liberals view the glass as half full, seeking outcomes that equalize the positions of individuals and groups whose liberal credentials are already assumed. As Galeotti (2002) explains the matter, if some individuals are marginalized and excluded on the basis of their group membership, "then the normative response cannot be toleration as non-interference, but toleration as the symbolic recognition of differences as legitimate options in pluralist democracy" (67).

A common interpretation of neutralist liberalism, Galeotti explains, is that differences that are unfamiliar may be displayed publicly, but only if it is clear these are expressions of private beliefs or identities. A private choice, that is, may be displayed as such, but not as a public statement that might appear to "constitute a demand for special consideration of the difference in question, thus representing a breach of the notion of institutional blindness and an illegitimate invasion of the public sphere by what is legitimate only as an object of private choice" (Galeotti 2002, 70; see also 100–101). Majority views, however, may enjoy both private and public visibility, although society often fails to notice this fact. Controversy over the French national policy of complete secularism in public education, for example, was sparked in 1989 by Muslim schoolgirls who appeared wearing headscarves in public schools, an action interpreted as a challenge to the principle that religious belief and affiliation are matters of private conscience and should not invade the public domain. Galeotti (1993) notes that the liberal public sphere, however, has always recognized the particularistic collective identity of the white Christian male (600–601; see also Galeotti 2002, 121–36). Because white Christian males wear no markers, in contrast to the yarmulkes that Jewish males wear, for example, it may appear that no sign of identity exists. But this conclusion is mistaken. In France, as Norma Moruzzi describes, both secular republicans and Roman Catholics agreed "that wearing a headscarf in class was militantly anti-French and should not be tolerated" (Moruzzi 1994, 656; see also 659–60). Moruzzi's point is that the left's defense of French national culture as being secular coincides with the right's defense of it as being Christian. Public bareheadedness is interpreted as a secular practice, but it is a religious marker to those whose religious traditions do carry specific markers, like yarmulkes or headscarves. The same is true of the fact that Sunday is the only full holiday in the French school week. A seemingly secular practice has a religious definition and identity to those whose holy days are other than Sunday. Secularists and Christians, Moruzzi explains, "can both energetically defend the cultural practices of that school system because those practices are amenable to both traditions" (664). In other words the nonneutrality represented by secularism is compounded by a second sort of nonneutrality: favoring the religious practices of the dominant group in French culture. Even public policy that is designed to exclude particularistic identities, then, unwittingly "disguises particularism and partiality under the pretense of universality and impartiality" (Galeotti 1993, 601; see also Babst 2002, 72–79).

Individuals with a minority sexual orientation are ideal candidates for Galeotti's framework. Because sexuality is practiced in private, it does not require a public forum in civil society comparable to facilities for religious worship. Because gays, lesbians, and bisexuals *can* closet their sexual identities, unlike most racial minorities and many ethnic minorities, it is a short step for those uncomfortable with their presence to conclude that they *should* closet their identities. If gays, lesbians, and bisexuals are open about who they are and experience difficulty, for example, in seeking employment or housing without antidiscrimination provisions or in seeking election or appointment to public positions, some may believe that they in fact ought to have disguised their sexual identities and may be unsympathetic. Under the classic interpretation of liberal toleration, Galeotti (2002) observes, "Homosexuals have rights, not as full-blown individuals, but only as desexualized persons. Their sexual life is tolerated at the price of being kept under cover, which in turn means that their different identities are excluded from the viable alternatives that make up the norm" (173; see also 11). Their complete identities possess no public standing, and this lacuna constitutes, in Gutmann's terms, a public expression of their civic inequality (Gutmann 2003, 97).

In Galeotti's discussion of the history of religious conflict, classic toleration may be sufficient when everyone assumes that there is a single truth and that differences stem from conflicting interpretations of this truth (Galeotti 2002, 62–66). This assumption resembles nonpreferentialism, which accords equal treatment to all or most religions but assumes that nonreligion is beyond the pale. With disestablishment, however, public authority is expected to be neutral among rival conceptions of the good. This neutrality requires public recognition or positive consideration of difference, because there exists no publicly established or officially accepted norm, of which differences are merely competing interpretations. The positive consideration of difference that characterizes public recognition supersedes a merely neutral stance of public blindness, but it does not necessarily mean a positive evaluation of the differences in question. Rather, this positive consideration legitimates the public presence of difference, signifying citizens' "inclusion in the public sphere on the same footing as those whose practices and behavior are 'normal.' This inclusion implies the acceptance of the corresponding identity and, hence, the acceptance of those who are marked by such identities" (101; see also 103–5, 175–77, 194–95). If this positive attitude is expanded to all acceptable differences, in Galeotti's view it is impartial (73; see 73–75) and is therefore consistent with neutralist liberalism.

Galeotti argues that her conception of public recognition is a neutral middle way between toleration of an unpopular way of life as a necessary evil and the recognition of its positive moral value. This neutral middle way merely includes varied sexual orientations and identities as part of the broad range of normal options offered by and visible within a liberal society. "Thus it is not toleration as recognition that implies a positive moral evaluation and promotion of homosexuality, but, rather, it is the usual view of toleration which works to discourage homosexuality" (Galeotti 2002, 176; see 175–77). That is, whereas conservatives hold that classic toleration means acceptance but that public recognition constitutes moral approval, Galeotti suggests that today classic toleration as public blindness means that sexual minorities are accepted only in that they are not subject to negative attention or persecution by public authority. They may appear in public as members of sexual minorities, but they do so with the understanding that their orientations are public manifestations of their private identities and are not to be interpreted as constituting any sort of demand on public authority. Public recognition, in contrast, connotes the judgment that sexual minorities represent one of many viable options; but in Galeotti's view it does not represent promotion, endorsement, or an evaluative judgment of moral value. Although neutrality can never be absolute and must be defined within a context, for Galeotti justice and inclusiveness require public recognition of social differences that are not already part of the dominant consensus.

The difference between toleration and recognition resonates in the context of the "don't ask, don't tell" policy of the United States armed forces, repealed in 2010, which was ostensibly blind to differences in sexual orientation. The context of heteronormativity within which this policy existed, however, meant that heterosexuals might both ask and tell, and they did not need to refrain from discussing their personal lives or else disguise them by changing the names or pronouns they used to refer to those with whom they shared their private lives. From Galeotti's conception of recognition, it also follows that she supports including same-sex couples in the institution of civil marriage. Substantive arguments for and against this inclusion are discussed in detail in chapter 3, but here I allude to these arguments insofar as they support same-sex marriage as an example of public recognition.

Like some traditional couples, some same-sex couples may not wish to marry, and people of varying sexual orientations regard the institution of marriage as confining rather than liberating. Moreover, because many material benefits that accompany civil marriage can be accessed through various forms of recognized partnership, some believe that seeking inclusion in civil marriage as such wastes resources and political capital on a goal of benefit that is symbolic at best (Galeotti 2002, 180–83). For Galeotti, however, the symbolism is crucial. The legitimation of same-sex marriage means public recognition of the relationships of committed couples who choose to participate in this institution. "Marriage should be accessible to homosexuals if their sexual orientation is to be regarded as a viable option on the same footing as that of heterosexuals. The point is not to define an ideal lifestyle for homosexuals, whether or not this involves marriage, but to provide them with the same opportunity as heterosexuals to pursue their ideal of the good life, within or outside the gay community, in a marriage or in a partnership" (187; see also 179, 182).

By denying same-sex couples the symbolic legitimacy that marriage offers to opposite-sex couples, the government measures same-sex unions by a standard that it does not and cannot apply to traditional unions. Although conservative opponents of same-sex marriage assert that the traditional two-parent family is the ideal setting for rearing children, "this argument assumes what must actually be demonstrated," Galeotti says. Rather "it is the cultural dominance of the traditional model of the family that makes it 'ideal' in the eyes of the majority" (Galeotti 2002, 188). Moreover, the fact that families headed by same-sex couples have not been considered a legitimate or viable option contributes to the feelings of alienation or abnormality that children of same-sex couples may experience, comparable to the reaction previously experienced by children of divorced parents. It is not difference in itself that gives rise to discomfort, Galeotti implies; it is the cultural hegemony of the traditional family that renders difference "different" and marginalizes those who exhibit difference. In general "the state has consistently given up any perfectionist ideal of marriage and family, limiting its paternalist intervention in favor of children to cases on unquestionable harm: abuse, violence, or physical deprivation" (189). It is inconsistent, she suggests, for the state now to revert to this ideal regarding same-sex marriage.

Overall, for Galeotti formal citizenship rights that are protected by toleration are not enough to convey the full membership in society that equal public standing and civic equality require. Public recognition, on the other hand, "is not a resource to be distributed, but, rather, designates the capability to make use of citizenship rights and social opportunities" (Galeotti 2002, 193). It protects the value or worth of these rights and opportunities, as well as the existence of a range of meaningful options with which individuals may identify (205–9). Some kinds of social difference are more disadvantaged than others within the framework of the dominant consensus. Galeotti's conception of public recognition does not, however, accord special rights as such. Rather her conception empowers individuals by allowing them to participate in the public sphere as whole persons. Because both the armed forces and the institution of civil marriage are public institutions, the inclusion of individuals and couples experiencing same-sex attraction simply allows them to access these institutions on the same terms as heterosexuals. Service in the armed forces and marriage appear to most to be neutral practices in which individuals commonly participate. Gays, lesbians, and bisexuals, however, could for many years serve in the military only by hiding their sexual identities, and today they can actually marry only in a few jurisdictions. Accordingly, just as public bareheadedness in France is interpreted as a neutral, secular practice, full disclosure of one's personal life in the military or a decision to marry seem matter-of-fact, but they are in fact markers of heterosexuality because of their unavailability to those who cannot share in them. The heteronormativity of the dominant culture obscures this fact and promotes the invisibility of sexual difference.

Implications

If we apply Galeotti's contrast between toleration and social recognition to the controversy over same-sex marriage in the United States in particular, we find that the dominant culture does not exemplify even neutralist liberalism, let alone the perfectionist liberalism of personal autonomy. Despite the lack of a formal establishment of religion and the constitutional guarantee of the free exercise of religion, Jakobsen and Pellegrini observe, "Christianity, and often conservative Christianity, functions as the yardstick and measure of what counts as 'religion' and 'morality' in America" (Jakobsen and Pellegrini 2004, 13; see also 21–22, 47, 104, 109–10). Ethical views that do not fit within or at least overlap this consensus often go unrecognized as moral values. Concerning sexual orientation, the role of Christianity is occupied by heteronormativity, which "describes the moral and conceptual centrality of homosexuality in contemporary American life" (28). That is, as Jakobsen and Pellegrini explain, heterosexuality represents the norm, and the idea that alternative sexual practices possess ethical significance is unconsciously overlooked or ignored. In regulating the expression of sexuality, whether formerly through sodomy laws or presently through resistance to same-sex marriage, "the secular state understands itself to be doing so not in the name of religion per se, but in the cause of a universal morality. And yet, time and again particular religious interpretations provide the state's last best defense for its policies concerning sex" (22; see also Babst 2002). Just as secular republicans and Christians in France united in opposing headscarves for Muslim schoolgirls as being anti-French, some secularists and religious people with traditional moral values can and do unite in the United States to oppose same-sex marriage as being contrary to American tradition. In both cases particularism and partiality are portrayed as universality and impartiality.

Jakobsen and Pellegrini view the history of tolerance for social differences as intertwined with the history of religion in the United States. Americans see their nation both as one that offers religious freedom and equality and also as a Christian nation (Jakobsen and Pellegrini 2004, 45, 47). "There are still those in America who are central and those who are marginal, but tolerated" (49). Even under a more protective standard than is now in force, the Supreme Court "could not see its way clear to ruling in favor of a free-exercise exemption that would support a non-Christian religious practice" (110; see 109–10). According to Wendy Brown, below the surface tolerance ultimately lies a discourse of power. Although it carves a middle road between suppression and assimilation, it manages threats represented by difference by maintaining that difference. "What is tolerated remains distinct even as it is incorporated" (Brown 2006, 28). Historically, where liberal equality is premised on sameness, tolerance is grounded on difference. Hence tolerance functions as a supplement to liberal equality, as a tool for managing that which cannot or should not be made the same, even as the discourse of tolerance itself "produces the differences it seeks to protect" (47; see also 7). Although toleration is certainly preferable to hatred, we can infer from these critics that toleration also cannot help but maintain relations of dominance and subordination between a magnanimous majority and a minority that is the recipient of its grace.

My exposition demonstrates that understandings of both tolerance and neutrality can be manipulated. Jakobsen and Pellegrini, for example, cite the October 26, 1998, issue of *Time*, which followed the murder of Matthew Shepherd in Wyoming. The cover story was titled "The War over Gays." The wording of this title outlines two extremes: (1) those intolerant of gays, who want to deny them rights and perhaps commit violence against them; and (2) gays and those perceived as activists for gay rights. Those who hate and those who fight against hate are morally equal combatants in the war, this headline implies. On the sidelines stands the general public, by implication both tolerant and innocent of involvement. Jakobsen and Pellegrini explain, "Because the tolerant middle must be distinguished from both sides of any political conflict, the 'violence' of our social life can be projected onto either side of a political debate regardless of the specifics of the situation" (Jakobsen and Pellegrini 2004, 58; see 53–61). The general public in turn is not expected to make judgments and perhaps to take a stand against injustice; instead, it is simply expected to tolerate the extremes while perhaps inwardly condemning both sides. "If each side is as bad as the other, it is impossible to distinguish between them" (59).

This example casts the public as neutral, but no neutral position really exists here. Both Feldblum and Galeotti view the protection or recognition of a way of life as morally neutral because it signifies that this way of life is unproblematic. As we have seen, however, this protection or recognition also implies a moral assessment that the way of life is legitimate and that discrimination or nonrecognition is wrong, whereas failure to protect or recognize it signifies its questionability. This imprimatur of legitimacy cannot simultaneously signify neutrality. In Jakobsen's and Pellegrini's example from *Time*, the "War over Gays" article title not only portrays the general public as a tolerant middle. It also suggests that neutrality is possible and that there is a safe place to hide to remain uninvolved in the controversy. Although public recognition is neutral on a first-order level when compared with classic toleration, it is not neutral on a second-order, metatheoretical level. Other portrayals—this time in Britain in the 1980s, in connection with debates over gay rights—distinguished between the "dangerous queer" and the "good homosexual" worthy of inclusion; as Anna Marie Smith explains, the latter is "self-limiting, closeted, desexualized, and invisible" (Smith 1997, 121; see also 121–25; Burack 2008, 10, 114). Finally thinkers on the religious right have claimed tolerance for themselves by embracing "traditional tolerance," which holds the conviction that some practices are wrong or sinful in tension with the imperative that those who practice them should still be respected. "New tolerance," however, is condemned as an ethical relativism that blurs value distinctions between right and wrong (Burack 2008, 12; see also Jakobsen and Pellegrini 2004, 1–4). These examples highlight Galeotti's distinction between classic toleration, which has too often been predicated on invisibility, and social recognition, which expands the kinds of social differences that are publicly accepted as viable options.

As we have seen, not only is neutrality a matter of context, but in a given context individuals of different viewpoints define neutrality differently. However, if civic equality means that differences acceptable in a liberal polity need not be invisible but rather can be publicly expressed, a logical conclusion might be that those who oppose civil rights for sexual minorities or same-sex marriage have the same entitlements enjoyed by those who advocate for these rights. Of course those on all sides of any controversy have the right to express their viewpoints, to support candidates for public office that espouse these viewpoints, and so forth. Feldblum argues that just as same-sex sexual activity flows from a gay or lesbian sexual identity, certain kinds of religious practices and activities similarly flow from adherence to particular religious beliefs. However, some religious individuals who are dedicated to returning American society to godliness claim that their free exercise of religion—not simply in private but also in the public square—is infringed by antidiscrimination laws or by the legal inclusion of same-sex couples in the institution of civil marriage. Although subsequent chapters address this issue more thoroughly, I address it briefly here.

As suggested by Jakobsen and Pellegrini, more religious freedom does not need to mean more government support for religion in the public square. As members of society, they say, "We [all] want the freedom to be religious and the freedom to be religious differently. And we want both these positions to count as the possible basis for moral claims and public policy" (Jakobsen and Pellegrini 2004, 12–13; see also 111–13). Secularists tend to emphasize the separation of church and state but not religious freedom, whereas religionists tend to emphasize religious freedom but not separation. That is, emphasizing the disestablishment of religion is often equated with minimizing and even denigrating the importance of religious practice; but emphasizing the free exercise of religion is associated with supporting religious dominance, especially as understood by those who believe religion and morality require a Christian interpretation. For Jakobsen and Pellegrini, however, disestablishment is a precondition of free exercise. It allows people to be traditionally religious, differently or nontraditionally religious, or nonreligious. In the area of sexual orientation and practice, the disestablishment

of heteronormativity, or of the assumption that heterosexuality is the norm
and measure of sexuality, does not mean that asexuality is the norm. Rather
disestablishment opens space for people to be heterosexual, gay, lesbian, bisexual, or asexual if that is their orientation, without being disadvantaged
in the context of the dominant consensus. The state is neutral with regard
to the comparative merits of being heterosexual or gay, just as it is neutral
about Roman Catholicism and Judaism (120–21). It is not neutral in the
metatheoretical sense, however, because it views being heterosexual, gay, Roman Catholic, or Jewish all as viable options that are compatible with the
civic equality of all citizens.

This metatheoretical nonneutrality is the sticking point for social conservatives and the religious right. They do not see nonheterosexual orientations as viable options, which explains why Galeotti's conception of social
recognition would not be convincing to them. Accordingly, in my view,
advocates for minority sexual orientations must further draw out the comparison between religion and sexuality. If we accept religious variations as
viable options, we must do the same with variations in sexual orientation.
Jakobsen and Pellegrini argue that we do not need to agree about the moral
status of homosexuality. "If we were to move outside the framework of tolerance to a framework of freedom, . . . it would be possible for those of us
who believed that homosexuality is a sin to embrace the religious freedom of
those who thought otherwise. This stance is not the tolerance of loving the
sinner and hating the sin. It is the democracy of religious freedom in which
one group's idea of sin does not limit the freedom of those who believe and
practice differently" (61). In chapter 3 I address specific grounds that have
been adduced to support or oppose the inclusion of same-sex couples in the
institution of civil marriage.

CHAPTER 3

Same-Sex Marriage

Social Facts and Conflicting Views

The impossibility of defining neutrality and of instantiating policies that embody this quality reveals itself in conflicting views engendered by the topic of same-sex marriage. Although one might expect that traditionalists oppose same-sex marriage and that liberals support it, the landscape is more complex. Traditionalist opponents link their opposition to the maintenance of a long-established morality among citizens, as one might predict. However, there are also traditionalist advocates of same-sex marriage, who believe that including same-sex couples in the institution of marriage will smooth the apparent rough edges of same-sex relationships, promoting stability and the welfare of both individual participants and the larger community. In contrast, queer and feminist skeptics as well as some libertarians fear that widening the institution's reach will force some to enter into contracts that are ostensibly freely chosen but that in reality amount to a preordained status, while others who do not marry would be even more marginalized than now. Finally, liberal advocates see the ability to marry the individual of one's choice as a right of equal citizenship, whether or not particular couples choose to avail themselves of it.

For some observers the inclusion of same-sex couples in the institution of marriage promotes neutrality, or at least impartiality toward all couples who otherwise meet given requirements, because this potentially includes all committed couples in an institution important to full citizenship. After 1967, when the Supreme Court in *Loving v. Virginia* (388 U.S. 1 [1967]) struck down the Virginia statute that criminalized and invalidated interracial marriages, states that opposed them could no longer prohibit them and were forced to recognize them as legitimate. As Mark Strasser notes, however, this recognition did not mean that these states endorsed them.

"In *Loving*, the Court recognized that Virginia's anti-miscegenation law was a manifestation of the state's preference for some of its citizens over others," in itself a sufficient reason to strike down the law (Strasser 2002, 104; see 99–113). Chief Justice Earl Warren wrote in *Loving*, "There is patently no legitimate overriding purpose independent of invidious racial discrimination which justifies this classification" (Loving v. Virginia, 388 U.S. 1 [1967], at 11). This reasoning was echoed twenty-nine years later by Justice Anthony Kennedy in *Romer v. Evans* (517 U.S. 629 [1996]), which struck down Colorado's Amendment 2 prohibiting antidiscrimination laws that protected sexual orientation and which disputed its supporters' views that such laws amount to a governmental seal of approval on homosexuality. In Kennedy's opinion the rights to seek passage of laws protecting minorities are not special rights but "are protections taken for granted by most people either because they already have them or do not need them; these are protections against exclusion from an almost limitless number of transactions and endeavors that constitute ordinary civic life in a free society" (631; see 630–31). Overall, he wrote, "Amendment 2 classifies homosexuals not to further a proper legislative end but to make them unequal to everyone else. . . . A State cannot so deem a class of persons a stranger to its laws" (634–35).

Strasser argues that although commentators correctly distinguish between permitting and endorsing particular practices, some incorrectly infer that accommodation constitutes endorsement rather than permission. When the state accommodates different religions, it does not endorse one or some over others. Strasser explains, "Just as the endorsement test in Establishment Clause jurisprudence precludes the state from treating nonadherents of a particular faith as outsiders who are not full members of the community, an endorsement test should preclude the state from denying individuals the right to marry merely because it wants to tell those individuals that they are outsiders who are not full members of the community" (Strasser 2002, 105; see 104–5, 133–45). In other words if the nonrecognition of interracial marriage had the effect of maintaining white supremacy, the nonrecognition of same-sex marriage has the effect of maintaining the moral supremacy of heteronormative ideals. Or to apply *Romer* to the marriage issue, those who participate in the institution of marriage receive many benefits such as family leave, health insurance, disability insurance, pension and Social Security benefits, inheritance, and favorable treatment in income and estate tax matters, not to mention civic recognition and respect. To extend these civil protections and respect to same-sex couples does not grant them special rights but rather simply grants them an equal footing, rendering them the beneficiaries of advantages already enjoyed or taken for granted by opposite-sex couples. Any endorsement so conferred is bestowed on marriage as a status that committed couples traditionally seek, not on the sexual orientation or genders of individuals in any given couple who seek this status.

For other observers the public recognition of same-sex marriage is not a neutral event, because it extends to same-sex couples not only toleration but also endorsement of same-sex relationships. Evan Gerstmann, himself a proponent of same-sex marriage, suggests that allowing same-sex couples to marry signals that these relationships deserve respect and therefore constitutes an endorsement (Gerstmann 2008, 42–46; see also Gerstmann 1999, 127, 136). Because of this ambiguity Gerstmann prefers the argument that marriage to the partner of one's choice is a fundamental right, given the government monopoly on certain privileges (Gerstmann 2008, 154; see also 73–116). Applying the strict scrutiny standard, the government could ban same-sex marriage, like libelous speech, if the government deems it a true threat to society and considers the maintenance of traditional marriage to be a compelling state interest. However, it would then have to justify the ban "by reference to social interests other than pure majoritarian social preference" (74). This justification implicitly puts the burden of proof on those who want to disallow same-sex marriage, rather than on those who want to allow it. Nevertheless Gerstmann's view that accommodation implies endorsement resonates with the point that Anna Elisabetta Galeotti makes about public recognition. That is, because recognizing same-sex relationships accommodates them as viable options among others in a liberal society and state, it therefore conveys legitimacy on such relationships. Although to some, same-sex marriage as public recognition is a neutral middle way between grudging toleration and positive moral approval, not everyone views the inclusion of same-sex couples in this manner. The question of what message would be sent by recognizing same-sex marriage animates these differing opinions, at least implicitly. In this chapter I explore four viewpoints on same-sex marriage.

Traditionalist Opponents of Same-Sex Marriage

For traditionalist opponents of same-sex marriage, such as Maggie Gallagher, marriage as a universal human institution "is everywhere the word we use to describe a public sexual union between a man and a woman that creates rights and obligations between the couple and any children the union may produce" (Gallagher 2003, 18). The social institution of marriage communicates a shared ideal of exemplary relationship, but this institution is in crisis because we have forgotten "its great universal anthropological imperative: family making in a way that encourages ties between fathers, mothers, and their children—and the successful reproduction of society" (19). For Gallagher marriage is an institution beyond individual choice and will. Although couples may choose to marry, once they do so, the institution takes on a life of its own apart from the participants' individual desires, creating rights and obligations between husband and wife as well as between them and any resulting offspring (18). Referring to the high degree of unintended pregnancy, Gallagher asks, "If it is choice and contract that create parental obligation, why do these mothers have any obligations for the creatures of their bodies? . . . On a less theoretical plane, why are we hounding poor men for child support, for babies for which they never contracted?" Reliable fathers in particular are "cultural creations," she says, products of the expectation that sex and parenting go together. The idea that parental obligations result only from free choice puts the well-being of children at risk (17).

Similarly, according to David Blankenhorn of the Institute for American Values, "Marriage's main purpose is to make sure that any child born has two responsible parents, a mother and a father who are committed to the child and committed to each other" (Blankenhorn 2007, 153; see also 15, 35, 49, 59–61, 83, 102, 155, 248–54). If marriage comes to be regarded simply as a particular kind of close personal relationship, its private aspect will subsume and swallow its public function: the social priority of children's well-being. Marriage is a public social institution that exists prior to and then defines any couple who participates in it. Couples cannot privately define marriage to fit their particular circumstances, Blankenhorn asserts. "On their wedding day, couples become accountable to an ideal of marriage that is outside of them and bigger than they are" (18; see 18–19). Although he is sympathetic to the exclusions faced by same-sex couples, "the central argument for gay marriage is not an argument about marriage, but an argument about basic rights" and human dignity (171; see also 141–44). The more open to choice that family forms are, the more likely it is that vulnerable children will be shuffled around among adults who, however much they may care for these children, are there because of voluntary ties that they might at some point choose not to maintain. "Do we want, in pursuit of a good cause, to transform marriage once and for all from a pro-child social institution into a post-institutional private relationship?" (201; see also 175, 183–212). For Blankenhorn the goals of both antimiscegenists and same-sex marriage advocates corrupt the institution for their own purposes: to preserve white supremacy, for antimiscegenists; and "to gain social recognition of the dignity of homosexual love," for same-sex marriage advocates (177–78; see 171–79), a goal that marriage is not designed to achieve.

Although caring families may form through adoption, where one or both parents are biologically unrelated to their children, to Blankenhorn adoptive families and stepfamilies all betoken a failure or unhappy ending—through widowhood, divorce, remarriage, the mistreatment or abandonment of children—of traditional, biological family formation and maintenance. "For this reason, despite all the good it does, adoption is ultimately a derivative and compensatory institution. It is not a stand-alone good, primarily because its existence depends upon prior human loss" (Blankenhorn 2007, 191; see 189–94). The use of reproductive technologies as a personal prerogative is less benign than adoption, he argues, because rather than providing for already existing children, they seek in many cases "to bring into this world children who by definition can never be cared for by their two natural parents" (192). Some may wonder whether traditional opposite-sex marriage—all too often characterized by infidelity, domestic violence, desertion, divorce, remarriage, and such—instantiates the ideal that Blankenhorn seeks. He might respond that although families are populated by flawed human beings, there is a difference between coping with these deviations from the ideal and deliberately creating family forms that can never hope to approximate the ideal.

Although some traditionalists focus on stable families' prerequisites for rearing children, others take a more abstract approach to the defense of traditional, opposite-sex marriage. Advocates of what is called the new natural law believe that secular, biologically based arguments can ground traditional marriage. In the view of Robert George, a proponent of this new natural law, the idea that allowing same-sex couples to marry renders matrimonial law morally neutral is logically incoherent. Although this idea appears neutral with regard to the sex of the participants, it is decidedly nonneutral between the view that the institution of marriage should include same-sex couples and the view that traditionally defined marriage is so valuable, both individually and collectively, that society should uphold it as the only legitimate form of marriage. For George, "Marriage is a two-in-one-flesh communion of persons that is consummated and actualized by acts that are procreative in type, whether or not they are procreative in effect" (George 2003, 120). In nonmarital acts, which include not only masturbation and sexual activity between persons not married to each other but also sexual activity by a married couple that does not lead to vaginal intercourse, sexual satisfaction and the sexual use of the body are instrumental to pleasure, the release of tension, or the expression of affection. "In marital acts, by contrast, . . . the end, goal, and intelligible point of sexual union is the good of marriage itself" (120–21). Because the law is a moral teacher, George argues, it should eschew any attempt at neutrality between the idea of marriage as "an intrinsic human good" and the notion that marriage is a malleable convention, the contours of which may be made and remade to suit individual desire and will. Marriage is an ideal of human relationships in which couples may fully participate only if they understand its nature, "yet people's ability properly to understand it and thus to choose it depends upon institutions and cultural understandings that transcend individual choice" (128; see also Kohm 2003).

For Lynn Wardle the availability of same-sex partnerships and civil unions devalues and weakens the institution of marriage, in which "the union of two persons of different genders creates something of unique potential strength and inimitable potential value to society. It is the integration of the universe of gender differences (profound and subtle, biological and cultural, psychological and genetic) associated with sexual identity that constitutes the core and essence of marriage" (Wardle 2003, 196). Any claimed right to intimate association cannot ground new constitutional rights to institutions—whether marriage-like arrangements or same-sex marriage— that protect close or intimate relationships outside of traditional marriage (197–99). Richard Wilkins argues that although individuals are the ones who marry and procreate, the state correlatively holds a substantial, surpassing, even compelling "interest in channeling and promoting responsible procreative behavior" (Wilkins 2003, 231). The value of privacy lies not in shielding individually defined intimate relationships but rather in protecting relationships with potential procreative power, in which society has already claimed a surpassing interest (232–33). For George, Wardle, and Wilkins then, recognition of same-sex marriage constitutes an endorsement of a second type of family making that ostensibly puts it on par with traditional marriage. Because all three believe that the latter model is vastly superior to any other, they reject any move that might give reasonable persons the impression that same-sex marriage is a worthy alternative.

The new natural law theorists ground their arguments on the moral claims that particular goods, such as marriage, exert on individuals as they strive to realize the kind of life best suited to human nature. Nicholas Bamforth and David A. J. Richards explain the work of John Finnis, who posits a set of basic human goods necessary to human flourishing; these include life, knowledge, play, aesthetic experience, friendship, practical reasonableness, and religion, defined as "speculation about the order of things" (Bamforth and Richards 2008, 63). Bamforth and Richards explain that for major natural law theorists Germain Grisez and Joseph Boyle, along with Finnis, the first principle of morality is that human beings are to do and pursue the human good, which means choosing and willing only that which is conducive to integral human fulfillment, the realization of good in all persons integrated harmoniously into an ideal community (66, 73). The satisfaction of individualistic or emotional desires and preferences is acceptable only "as part of the pursuit or attainment of an intelligible good other than satisfaction of the desire itself" (70). Although natural law theorists assert that individuals possess the capability of discovering natural law without religious premises and independently of particular religious beliefs, Bamforth and Richards argue in their detailed study that despite these thinkers' sincerity, the principles of the new natural law do in fact possess religious underpinnings. These principles have attracted attention from the hierarchy of the Roman Catholic church, and the new natural lawyers themselves have deployed their arguments to support the church hierarchy in the face of post–Second Vatican Council theological dissent (74–83).

Bamforth and Richards explain that the influence of the new natural law would not be a matter of concern, except that new natural law theorists such as Finnis, George, and Gerard Bradley have advanced their moral arguments through constitutional litigation, the press, and advice to President George W. Bush on a range of issues such as same-sex relationships, stem cell research, faith-based initiatives, and the proposed Federal Marriage Amendment barring same-sex marriage (Bamforth and Richards 2008, 83–88). Concerning marriage, these thinkers believe that only the one-flesh communion of husband and wife through the uniting of their reproductive organs, whether or not this results in procreation, allows them to experience and actualize the common good of their marriage. No other relationship can actualize this unity. Same-sex couples only hope in vain to experience it, and any other type of sexual relationship either inside or outside marriage constitutes only individual gratification (96–98). For the new natural lawyers, pleasure cannot properly ground sexual activity, because it is merely an instrument to achieve a good—it is not an intrinsic value (101). In sum any sexual activity apart from vaginal intercourse by a married couple, no matter how devoted a same-sex couple or an unmarried heterosexual couple might be, cannot express a true human good such as marriage. It is only a simulacrum, a futile attempt to reproduce (so to speak) a good that is incapable of reproduction outside the norm.

In Bamforth and Richards's view, the new natural lawyers depend upon the authority and teachings of the Roman Catholic church to lend content, justification, purpose, and reasoning to their assessments of heterosexual marriage, contraception, and abortion. Bamforth and Richards do not argue that individuals should not advance religiously grounded views in litigation or in the public square in general. They explain, "Our concern is instead to argue that, given the law's coercive potential and its role in regulating human behavior, it is crucial in a democratic society for *any* participant engaged in debate about the law to be clear about the nature and foundations of their argument. It does not matter whether that argument is religious, secular, or rooted in some further analytical category. Clarity, in a democracy, is crucial" (Bamforth and Richards 2008, 115; see also 93–115).

Having examined the writings of the new natural lawyers in detail, Bamforth and Richards conclude that for these theorists, "love of God, . . . as an uncaused cause which favors—for no other reason than its own goodness—the well-being of all, provides us with a new and much more powerful reason for pursuing the common good than would otherwise be available" (Bamforth and Richards 2008, 126). Moreover Bamforth and Richards explain that despite Finnis's recognition that people display diverse responses to a particular good, these theorists assert that "the only diversity that is permitted is in relation to the basic goods *as already defined*" (132). A long and rewarding relationship enjoyed by an unmarried couple, same-sex or opposite sex, cannot count as a good, because their "decision to engage in sexual acts as an expression of their love automatically violates the good of marriage" as it has already been defined (133; see also 139–46). Finnis even suggests that because the exclusivity and indissolubility of the true good of marriage do not define civil marriage, couples who marry civilly can only consent to imperfect marriages when these requirements are absent. In other words "the basic good of heterosexual marriage can never be perfect in a legal system which does not enforce the teachings of the Catholic Church" (148). Overall, despite its universalist claims the new natural law "is, at bottom, a faith-based theology," Bamforth and Richards explain. Although "the new natural lawyers deny that God's will is morally ultimate, . . . their conception of basic goods assumes a highly sectarian conception of God's will—namely that taught and defended by the Papacy" (187).

In fact the new natural lawyers share some similarities with Nancy Rosenblum's foundationalist integralists, discussed in chapter 1. New natural lawyers, unlike foundationalist integralists, do not seek political or social power as advocates of religion per se. However, new natural lawyers are similar to foundationalist integralists, in that they imply what Rosenblum calls "an exclusive connection between *particular* religious beliefs and . . . virtue," personal if not civic. Moreover new natural lawyers suggest that the goods and virtues they advocate are unavailable if their interpretation of religion, like that of foundationalist integralists, does not possess "a controlling place in public arenas and public law" (Rosenblum 2000a, 20).

The new natural lawyers' insistence on a procreational model of sexuality is sectarian not only because it is rooted in a particular religious tradition but also because it is an extremely narrow one. Some might think homosexuality is a misfortune, suggests Stephen Macedo, if they deem the ability to procreate to be part of a complete human life. If true, however, this fact does not need to lead to the conclusion that same-sex relationships are shameful or immoral or that their participants should be subject to legal discrimination, any more than marriages in which one or both partners are unable to have biological children. Although Macedo agrees with traditionalists that society should encourage people to settle down in monogamous relationships, "condemning all gays and lesbians on the basis of opposition to the promiscuous behavior of some gays (and, in truth, many heterosexuals also) is no better than condemning all men because some men rape women" (Macedo 1995, 264; see 263–64, 269–70, 285–87). For Macedo "The new natural law seems to exaggerate greatly the subjective, self-centered character of all nonprocreative sexuality" (281), whether committed same-sex relationships, contracepted marital sex, bathhouse sex, sex with prostitutes, or masturbation. It is simplistic "to portray the essential nature of *every form* of nonprocreative sex as no better than the *least valuable* form" (282; see also Macedo 1997, 90–93; Bamforth and Richards 2008, 245–61).

Macedo's overall criticism of the new natural lawyers is that their view is overly narrow as a basis for deciding what should ground the exercise of state power. Although moral arguments may be included in the political arena, he explains, "it is not fair to shape coercive political power based on any reasons whose force depends upon adopting a particular sectarian view, whether that sectarian view is a religious doctrine or a philosophical vision" (Macedo 2000, 34; see 34–35). Along similar lines, although the approach of Finnis and other new natural lawyers is not purely physicalist and instead focuses on the common good they impute to voluntary and uncontracepted marital sex, Paul Weithman suggests that Finnis defines the required complementarity of sexual partners too rigidly. If complementarity of diverse attributes and capacities is desirable in a couple, this complementarity may be present along many other axes than that of their complementary sexual organs (Weithman 1997, 238–40; see also Babst 2009, 190–93), whether they are a same-sex or an opposite-sex couple.

Although Weithman does not mention it, the scope of the complementarity he discusses is reminiscent of Charles Taylor's distinction between various kinds of common goods. Some goods are *convergent* common goods that we share collectively, as with the public goods of clean air or national defense. Others are *mediately* common goods that may be experienced individually but that take on added value when they are shared, such as when two Mozart lovers listen to Mozart together. Still other common goods, however, "are things that we value even more, like friendship itself, where what centrally matters to us is just that there are common actions and meanings. The good is that we share." He calls these *immediately* common goods (Taylor 1999, 168; see 166–70). That is, some goods are valued as instrumental to an enterprise; some are more enjoyable when shared; but still others represent "the bond of solidarity . . . based on a sense of shared fate, where the sharing itself is of value" (170; see also Bamforth and Richards 2008, 253–54).

These categories may be applied to sexual relationships in a way that broadens the scope of sexual complementarity beyond that required by the new natural lawyers. Institutions that encourage and reward the formation of committed long-term relationships may be compared to convergent goods—not because they are necessarily enjoyed by all, but because their existence facilitates the formation of bonds enjoyed separately, couple by couple. Sexual practices that a couple enjoys together are mediately common goods, more meaningful because they are shared than they are when practiced by either individual alone, as with masturbation, even if each thinks of the other. Finally, the shared bond of solidarity that is the context for the very existence of common meanings and actions, whatever these might be, is for the couple an immediately common good in an ontological sense. All of these types of common goods can apply to the intimate relationships not only of a traditional married couple practicing uncontracepted vaginal intercourse, but also of any other couple, whatever their sexual practices, whose emotional bond carries meaning for them. A broader conception of human good renders discussions of sexual practice less sectarian from both religious and philosophical perspectives.

Both the new natural lawyers and those who view marriage between biological parents as the optimum setting for rearing children value heterosexual marriage as a public good, one that grounds a possibly compelling state interest in confining marriage to heterosexuals. Only heterosexual marriages can produce children who are the biological offspring of both parents. However, as the *New York Times* reported in 2002, the respected American Academy of Pediatrics announced its support of second-parent adoption by the partners of gay and lesbian parents. Adoption protects children's best interests "because it guarantees the same rights and protections to homosexual families that are routinely accorded to heterosexual parents and their children," such as health insurance benefits from both partners, Social Security survivor benefits, and a legal relationship that governs custody, visiting rights, and financial support even if the couple separates. The chairman of the drafting committee, Dr. Joseph Hagan, explained, "This is really about the needs of children" (quoted in Goode 2002). The media have reported on some small studies published since 1980, several of which followed children for years. In these studies researchers found that on measures such as social adjustment, school performance, mental health, and emotional resilience, virtually no developmental differences emerged between children reared in same-sex households and those reared in traditional families. Wardle, however, suggested that the studies failed to probe aggressively, because they focused on issues relating to self-esteem and friendships rather than sexual behavior and drug use. All the studies agreed, however, that children of same-sex parents tend to face more teasing and bullying, making all the more remarkable their equality with children in traditional families, in terms of mental health and emotional resilience. A larger study published in 2004, based on a random survey rather than self-selection, likewise indicated comparable equality between children from the two types of families (Carey 2005).

However, in a 2001 review of twenty-one studies of children of same-sex parents, sociologists Judith Stacey and Timothy Biblarz found several differences within those studies that their authors ignored, most likely due to political anxiety about how such findings might be used. Reporting on Stacey and Biblarz's findings for the *New York Times*, Erica Goode explained that children reared in same-sex households "were less likely to have stereotyped notions of masculine and feminine behavior and more likely to aspire to occupations that crossed traditional gender lines," as well as being more tolerant and secure in their own identities. Young adult children of lesbian mothers were found more likely to be open to same-sex relationships than the children of traditional mothers, although they were no more likely to identify themselves as gay or lesbian (Goode 2001; see also Stacey and Biblarz 2005). As Stacey and Biblarz noted, most differences "cannot be considered deficits from any legitimate public policy perspective. . . . Because lesbigay parents do not enjoy the same rights, respect, and recognition as heterosexual parents, their children contend with the burdens of vicarious social stigma." Correspondingly, however, some of the strengths these children display, "such as a greater capacity to express feelings or more empathy for social diversity, are probably artifacts of marginality" that may disappear in a more overtly sexually pluralist society (Stacey and Biblarz 2005, 52).

Traditionalists such as Wardle, already on record as arguing that child custody should presumptively go to heterosexual parents, praised the publicity accompanying Stacey and Biblarz's findings (Goode 2001). His reaction in turn prompted a letter to the *New York Times*: "Does he prefer that children be close-minded, intolerant, psychologically weak, rigid and socially insecure?" (Mellinkoff 2001). Taking issue with Wardle's preference for heterosexual families, columnist Cindy Richards said she can understand him if studies showed that children reared in "Harriet and Harriet" families are more subject to abuse, neglect, or other mistreatment. "But this study," she observes, "says merely that kids raised by Harriet and Harriet, or Ozzie and Ozzie, are less likely to condemn other Ozzies and Harriets who find true love with someone of the same sex. How can that be an argument against allowing those couples to love, care for, and rear children?" (Richards 2001; see also Belkin 2009).

Galeotti suggests that what society should question is not the suitability of same-sex couples as parents, but rather the assumption that the dominant family model is the ideal environment for children. Although the link between reproduction and child rearing by biological parents is treated as the norm, from a historical standpoint this model is not always typical; it has also been accompanied by documented instances of abuse, violence, and neglect. "It is rather the cultural dominance of the traditional model of the family that makes it 'ideal' in the eyes of the majority, but it is also for this very reason that homosexual families may turn out to be a problem for children" (Galeotti 2002, 188; see 183–91). If children in these families feel abnormal or excluded, this is only because nontraditional families are considered deviations from the norm or the natural model. In Galeotti's view a political community should abandon "any perfectionist ideal of marriage." It should instead limit its intervention to protecting children from unquestionable harms such as abuse, violence, and physical or educational deprivation, "because any attempt to impose a particular model of family life as the natural and ideal environment in which to bring up children is unjustified, and implies an interference with personal liberty that is not in line with liberal institutions" (189).

Controversy over whether children are harmed by growing up in families headed by same-sex couples, or for that matter by single gay or lesbian parents, has proceeded through the courts. Although some states have even prevented gay or lesbian parents from rearing children who are their biological offspring from previous heterosexual relationships (Eskridge 1999, 275–77), more typical attempts to prevent gay and lesbian adoptions have been overbroad and have also revealed an antigay agenda. Florida directly prohibited adoptions by gays and lesbians in 1977, when Anita Bryant was successfully crusading for the repeal of a Dade County gay rights ordinance, whereas Mississippi and Utah banned such adoptions by prohibiting adoptions by unmarried couples. In 2008, however, a Florida judge ruled that a gay man could, with his partner, adopt two foster children he had been rearing since 2004. Judge Cindy S. Lederman said, "The best interests of children are not preserved by prohibiting homosexual adoption. . . . It is clear that sexual orientation is not a predictor of a person's ability to parent" (quoted in Almanzar 2008). Changing the law, remarked columnist Jacob Sullum, "does not require moral approval of homosexuality; it merely requires the recognition that being gay does not automatically make someone an unfit parent." Not doing so "elevates anti-gay ideology above children's welfare" (Sullum 2008; see also Eskridge 1999, 281–82). These sentiments were endorsed in 2010 by a unanimous Florida appeals court, which ruled that allowing gay men and lesbians to foster children while preventing them from adopting had no rational basis (*New York Times* 2010b).

For similar reasons in 2006 the Arkansas Supreme Court unanimously overturned a 1999 state welfare board ban on foster parenting by gays and lesbians. In addition the impetus behind the board's regulation was not child welfare "but rather [was] based upon the board's views of morality and its bias against homosexuals" (*New York Times* 2006). Arkansas voters responded in 2008, however, by approving a popular initiative prohibiting unmarried couples from fostering or adopting children, despite the fact that three times as many Arkansas children then needed adoptive or foster homes as the state had people willing to foster them (Brown 2008). Columnist Dan Savage noted that although the measure applied both to same-sex and opposite-sex cohabiting couples, a stated purpose of the law was thwarting "the gay agenda." Under this law a grandmother cohabiting with her opposite-sex partner, avoiding marriage for fear of losing pension benefits, could not foster or adopt her own grandchild; a gay man living with a male partner could not adopt the children of deceased blood relatives (Savage 2008). The *New York Times* pointed out, "Under Arkansas law, people convicted of major crimes, including contributing to the delinquency of a minor, remain eligible to adopt children or become foster parents. Single people who have no partner—or who have a large number of casual sexual partners—are also eligible. Anyone who is in a committed relationship, gay or straight, but is not married is automatically barred" (*New York Times* 2009a; see also Gerstmann 2008, 39). In 2010 a court overturned the ban as a violation of both due process and equal protection because despite the breadth of the act's potential application, a politically unpopular group was "specifically targeted for exclusion by the act" (*New York Times* 2010a).

These examples show not only that children exist who need homes, but also that children are already being reared by cohabiting gay and straight couples who may or may not have biological ties to these children, as well as by single parents, gay and straight. Although some fear that same-sex marriage promotes parenting that deviates from the ideal, family diversity is already a fact. Therefore, it seems that any compelling interest here centers on the welfare of children, however they may be reared. Because in the United States so many benefits for families accompany marriage alone, attending to the welfare of children ineluctably points toward allowing their parents to marry. Although skeptics about marriage such as Nancy Polikoff prefer arrangements where marriage matters less because material benefits accrue to individuals or dependents as such, rather than stemming from legal relationships between romantically involved adults, the current situation dictates that concern for the welfare of children means allowing their parents to marry. It is ironic that some marriage advocates, discussed below, encourage marriage between poor women and the fathers of their children, while simultaneously opposing marriage between adults who truly want to marry, many of whom are already rearing children. If marriage is the preferred setting for child rearing, it seems better for more children rather than fewer to live in a setting with married parents, even if the children are not the biological offspring of both legal parents.

Moreover, because no compelling evidence exists to demonstrate that liberalized policies toward same-sex couples affect the marriage and divorce rates of traditional couples, there is also no rational relationship, Gerstmann suggests, between the exclusion of same-sex couples from marriage and the goal of increasing the number of children reared by their biological parents. Although some think that the legalization of same-sex marriage or of registered partnerships for same-sex couples has correlated with a decrease in marriage and increase in cohabitation by opposite-sex couples (Kurtz 2004), other studies find this correlation illusory. Divorce rates have not increased; rather marriage rates have remained stable or have increased. Nonmarital birthrates have risen no faster in European countries with widespread nonmarital parenting and partnership laws than they have already risen. Finally, summarizing a paper by M. V. Lee Badgett, Gerstmann observes, "The average Scandinavian child spends more of his or her youth living with both parents than does the average American child" (Gerstmann 2008, 36; see 29–37; Badgett 2004). As the Supreme Judicial Court of Massachusetts explained in the 2003 decision instantiating same-sex marriage in that state, "Excluding same-sex couples from civil marriage will not make children of opposite-sex couples more secure, but it does prevent children of same-sex couples from enjoying the immeasurable advantages that flow from the assurance of a stable family structure in which children will be reared, educated, and socialized" (Goodridge v. Department of Public Health, 440 Mass. 309 [2003], at 335, citing Cordy dissent at 381; see also Struening 2009).

Gerstmann notes that it is possible that some unmarried same-sex couples decide not to use sperm donation or other reproductive technologies to have children together but might decide otherwise if they could marry. This point provides further ammunition to traditionalists such as Blankenhorn, who disapprove of reproductive technology when it increases the number of children not reared by both biological parents. Gerstmann counters, "But then the question is not whether these children would be better off with opposite-sex parents; the question is whether they would have been better off if they had not been born at all" (Gerstmann 2008, 38). One can argue, moreover, that parents who make such efforts to obtain children will be better parents than those who may not have intended to conceive.

Ironically, appellate courts in Indiana and New York have ruled that because traditional couples can produce children quickly and unexpectedly, it is *they* who need the protections of marriage, whereas same-sex couples, who must incur deliberate effort and expense to reproduce, are already so stable that their children do not need the additional stability that civil marriage provides (39–42). If this legalistic argument were the true reason for banning same-sex marriage, no one needs to worry about the unsuitability of same-sex couples for rearing children. The overwhelming impact of the same-sex marriage ban, Gerstmann concludes, "is to prevent children *already being raised in same-sex households* from having the protection afforded by the benefits of marriage, a policy that has the irrational consequence of punishing children for the 'sins' of their parents" (39). This reasoning is analogous to the legal requirement that the alien children of undocumented immigrants be admitted to public schools: Whatever reasons brought such children here, they will likely remain in the United States, and both they and society as a whole will benefit from their access to free public education. The fact that educating alien children can be viewed as a compensatory policy, like Blankenhorn's view of adoption, as a result of the failure to exclude their undocumented parents from national territory, does not detract from the value of this education.

Traditionalist opponents of same-sex marriage adhere to what Jyl Josephson calls an ascriptive understanding of citizenship. Ascriptive characteristics are those innate traits in individuals, like race or ethnicity, that are not typically a matter of choice. Same-sex couples may not marry because they do not meet the predefined requirement of heterosexuality, and opposite-sex couples must marry if they are not to forgo certain public benefits, as well as the civic respect that typically accompanies marriage. "This ascriptive status is not based on race or national origin, but on heterosexual identity and willingness to participate in and benefit from the state-sanctioned institution of marriage" (Josephson 2005, 272).

Many same-sex marriage proponents, however, are also traditionalists, but of a different sort. Their understanding of citizenship is also "one that ensconces a particular form of intimate relationship as the state-recognized norm" (Josephson 2005, 272), but it is inclusive toward same-sex couples as well as traditional couples.

Traditionalist Proponents of Same-Sex Marriage

Although traditionalist proponents of same-sex marriage differ from their opponents with regard to whom the institution should include, they share the conviction that the institution of marriage contributes to social stability. According to Nathaniel Frank, for example, "The main reason marriage is considered good for society is that committed relationships help settle individuals into stable homes and families. Marriage does this by establishing rules of conduct that strengthen obligations to a spouse and often to children." As a private relationship that is publicly contracted, marriage carries symbolic authority, Frank suggests—authority that can reinforce monogamy and stability in the face of temptation. Although he thinks some traditionalist opponents fear that the ostensibly weaker commitments of married same-sex couples will lower expectations of opposite-sex marriage, Frank himself believes that same-sex marriage serves the same function that traditional marriage serves: promotion of monogamy and stability. "The traditionalists may well be right that a monogamous relationship between two, unrelated, consenting adults makes a strong foundation for a stable family, and thus for a vigorous social order. They're just wrong that these two people have to be of different genders" (Frank 2004). From this perspective, whatever their sexual orientation, married couples have more in common with each other than either type of couple has with those who are unmarried.

Andrew Sullivan argues in fact that the very absence of social incentives, institutions, and guidelines with respect to same-sex relationships renders traditionalist opponents' expectations a self-fulfilling prophecy. To these opponents the public affirmation of same-sex relationships is not "a neutral event," he says, but instead "creates a social norm that says that sex is about personal gratification and not about marital procreation"—a scenario squarely opposed to the ideals of the new natural lawyers. Because "it devalues the social meaning of sex" (Sullivan 1996, 100), public affirmation of same-sex relationships "*in itself is an assault on heterosexual union*" (Sullivan 1996, 99). Traditionalist opponents want to preserve social and familial stability by refusing to acquiesce to—or endorse—the idea that homosexual and heterosexual lives are morally equivalent. Sullivan explains, "They mean by 'a homosexual life' one in which emotional commitments are fleeting, promiscuous sex is common, disease is rampant, social ostracism is common, and standards of public decency, propriety, and self-restraint are flouted" (106). For Sullivan, however, the simultaneous celebration of both the traditional family and the stable homosexual relationship actually valorizes heterosexual marriage as a model for commitment. To disapprove of homosexuality because of behaviors that might accompany this orientation is to ignore not only the nonmonogamous behaviors of straight couples, but also the fact that these consequences flow from the very disapproval that traditionalist opponents recommend (107–16).

In other words, although traditionalist opponents believe that same-sex marriage devalues traditional marriage by admitting participants who are unsuited to it, proponents believe that including same-sex couples adds value to same-sex relationships by making them more like opposite-sex ones. The recognition of same-sex marriage, then, constitutes an endorsement not of same-sex relationships in themselves, but rather of the ideal of long-term commitment that marriage represents. Because same-sex marriage "would integrate a long-isolated group of people into the world of love and family, . . . gay marriage would . . . help strengthen it, as the culture of marriage finally embraces all citizens" (Sullivan 2001, 7).

The hypothesis that marriage will transform same-sex relationships for the better is in part the converse of the nineteenth-century suffragists' hope that the enfranchisement of women would introduce the pure and virtuous morality of the private sphere into the public sphere, transforming and ennobling politics in the process. "Women would use the vote to change society, but the vote would not change women," Jean Bethke Elshtain summarizes (Elshtain 1982, 62; see 58–65). Sullivan conversely implies that society can use the public institution of marriage to change private same-sex relationships, but that the participation of same-sex couples will not change marriage as an institution.

Along related lines, Jonathan Rauch suggests that the growing prevalence of domestic partnerships and civil unions, accompanied by various material benefits, poses competition for the institution of marriage, thereby devaluing it as the unique option for committed couples, straight or gay. If the institution is undermined, he warns, "the culprit . . . is not the presence of same-sex couples; it is the absence of same-sex marriage" (Rauch 2005, 91). As more same-sex couples marry and are regarded as stable couples by their communities, "the marriage ban turns gays into walking billboards for the irrelevance of marriage" (92). Similarly, Rauch says, "Opponents of same-sex marriage who worry that gays would set a bad example by marrying ought to be more worried about the example gays are already setting by *not* marrying" (93). Marriage should not be regarded simply as a lifestyle option. Rather it should be expected of committed couples and should be privileged as "better than other ways of living. Not mandatory, not good where everything else is bad, but a general norm, rather than a personal taste" (81–82; see also 89). Where Sullivan argues that marriage strengthens same-sex relationships, Rauch suggests that civil recognition of committed same-sex relationships strengthens the institution of marriage. "Marriage is for everyone—no exclusions, no exceptions," he says (6; see also 42–43, 89, 94). Rauch argues that all couples should marry if they want the benefits of marriage, thereby reinforcing "marriage's status as the gold standard of committed relationships, at a time when marriage's competitors are gaining ground. And in so doing, it also preserves and strengthens marriage's legitimacy and sustainability as a social and legal institution. It stabilizes marriage for the long haul" (94). In Josephson's terms, Sullivan's and Rauch's understanding of marriage is, like that of their opponents, an ascriptive one. Although it includes both traditional and same-sex couples, it describes a preferred way of life that is mandatory for those who wish to partake of its accompanying public benefits.

Although Rauch supports marriage as an institution as strongly as Blankenhorn does, the two are deeply divided regarding same-sex marriage. Rauch, like Blankenhorn, views the well-being of children as a central focus of marriage, stating that "marriage is uniquely good for raising children" (Rauch 2005, 106; see 75, 107–19). He disagrees, however, with the emphasis that traditionalist opponents of same-sex marriage place on procreation. For him it is "the caregiving commitment [that is] at the heart, rather than the periphery, of marriage" (24; see 21–28, 65). The commitment to be there, to provide care and comfort "in sickness and in health," is the heart of the pair bond and not only precedes but also is necessary for rearing children. For the couple this commitment means that "because neither of us has anyone else, we are there for each other" in a way that no one else is (22). Rauch disagrees both with libertarians, who want to withdraw the state altogether from the business of marriage, and the "substituters," who advocate only do-mestic partnerships and civil unions for same-sex couples—"the ABM pact, for Anything But Marriage," an institution he calls "marriage-lite" (31, 43). Transcending both private contracts and benefits packages, marriage "is a contract between two people *and their community*" (32), a contract that both creates a bond and fosters mutual responsibility in ways that no other status can. Therefore, Rauch asserts, "Gay marriage is not so much a civil rights issue as a civil responsibility issue" (67; see also 58–59, 67–68; Eskridge 1999, 289). That is, same-sex couples want the legal underpinning necessary to fulfill their responsibilities both to their families, such as time off to care for their partners, and to their communities, such as rearing children and engaging in military service. Traditionalists, Rauch maintains, cannot logi-cally argue both for the importance of marriage for committed couples and also for confining it to opposite-sex couples. "They can defend marriage's normality or its exclusivity, but not both" (Rauch 2005, 93).

In the context of Kirstie McClure's civil discourse of facticity (McClure 1990, 383), both Blankenhorn and Rauch hold differing interpretations of social facts. Rauch sees same-sex marriage as civilly benign and even con-tributory to meeting important social needs, whereas Blankenhorn views it as civilly injurious to these purposes, saying, "If we could move toward this goal by embracing same-sex marriage, I would gladly embrace it" (Blanken-horn 2007, 20; see also 128, 130). Rauch asserts, "I have said and will always say that if same-sex marriage would destroy the institution of marriage, it is not worth having" (Rauch 2005, 69). Blankenhorn reserves marriage as the means of family formation for those who may procreate, whereas Rauch privileges it as the ideal status to which all committed couples should as-pire. Despite their differences, however, from the standpoint of the First Amendment religion clauses they resemble those who want to establish one religion. They want to allow other so-called religions, such as civil unions and domestic partnerships, but they argue that only marriage should carry the full public benefits befitting an institution that serves a definable public purpose. Blankenhorn does not object to civil unions for same-sex couples, because they do not impinge upon the integrity of traditional marriage as a child-centered institution (Blankenhorn 2007, 229–30). Rauch, however, wants to withdraw public support from alternative institutions. "What seems incontestable," he says, "is that empowering a bunch of competitors cannot do marriage any good, especially if the competitors offer most of the benefits with fewer of the burdens" (Rauch 2005, 53; see also 43, 48–49). He hopes that public support only for marriage, the gold standard of intimate relationships, will cause couples to lose interest in possible alternative "faiths." Although same-sex couples have been excluded from the established "religion," their inclusion will garner support for the establishment at the expense of other religions.

With regard to the free exercise of religion, for Blankenhorn the protection of children's rights to be reared optimally by their two natural parents is a compelling governmental interest that trumps both the otherwise worthy purpose of recognizing the value and dignity of same-sex relationships and the free exercise of religion by those same-sex couples who desire to marry. Rauch's view, in contrast, can be said to have an impact on free exercise for both same-sex and opposite-sex couples whose participation in alternatives to marriage will be burdened in comparison to participation in marriage. For Rauch, preserving the value of marriage as both an expression and a stabilizer of committed caregiving relationships is a compelling governmental interest that overrides couples' interests in the availability of other options.

In 2009 Blankenhorn and Rauch arrived at a kind of rapprochement in an article in the *New York Times*, in which they proposed a compromise position to which they were both willing to subscribe. Their proposal was a tripartite measure that they suggested Congress could enact in one unified bill. Congress would first recognize, as federal civil unions, both same-sex marriages and civil unions that have been granted by states, enabling same-sex couples to claim most of the federal benefits of marriage. Second, however, the federal government would recognize marriages and civil unions only in states with "robust religious-conscience exceptions" that would relieve religious organizations of any obligation to recognize same-sex unions and would protect them from the application of antidiscrimination laws, including obligations, for example, to grant benefits to an employee's same-sex spouse. Finally, the federal government would enact its own religious conscience exemptions. Blankenhorn and Rauch believe that because most state antidiscrimination laws that include sexual orientation also contain religious exemptions, same-sex couples could live with this proposal even if they would prefer not to. Similarly, Blankenhorn and Rauch believe that most Americans could live with the idea of federal civil unions even if they would prefer no legal recognition of same-sex relationships, "provided that no religious groups are forced to accept them as marriages" (Blankenhorn and Rauch 2009).

Although their proposal represents a sincere effort at acceptable compromise on a divisive topic, I do not believe it works. First, although granting material benefits at the federal level should not be underestimated, this book focuses on the same-sex marriage ban as a public expression of civic inequality. This expression may be exemplified not only by material inequality of treatment but also by symbolic inequality of status. When African Americans were treated in a separate-but-equal manner and were consigned to the backs of buses during the Jim Crow era, they arrived at the same destinations that those at the front did. This did not afford them equality of status, however, even though they rode buses rather than being forced to walk. Recent marriage cases in California and Connecticut were resolved in favor of marital status for same-sex couples, despite the fact that they already enjoyed most material benefits under the rubric of domestic partnerships or civil unions. In the words of one letter to the editor, "My partner and I fight for the same rights as heterosexual couples. So yes, we fight for equal tax privileges and spousal protections, but these are mere manifestations of what we truly fight for: equality. I am not willing to give up my status as a human being in the name of 'compromise.' I will continue to pursue the real goal of acceptance over tolerance" (Putnam 2009).

A second reason why I do not believe Blankenhorn and Rauch's proposal works is because it presages a confusing and impractical legal situation that would render federal civil union status a much lesser benefit than it appears at first glance. Depending upon the robustness of conscience protections in various states, couples in some states would enjoy federal civil unions and others would not. Moreover, state laws change over time. Couples whose state marriages or civil unions did not originally qualify for federal recognition might later be entitled to it. More problematically, couples whose state unions were initially federally recognized might be subject to future withdrawal if their state's protections were later watered down. For example, same-sex couples married in California before the passage of Proposition 8 retained their marital status even when new marriages could no longer be contracted. If this precedent obtained, couples could retain their status, but over time a direct correlation would no longer exist between state conscience protections and federal civil unions for same-sex couples. The spirit of Blankenhorn and Rauch's proposal implies that same-sex couples would have to relinquish federal status under these conditions. Couples' statuses would then be uncertain; their unions might be federally recognized at some times and unrecognized at others, perhaps changing several times over the duration if the laws of their states are in flux. These changes would depend not on these couples' own decisions but instead on the vagaries of state law. Because Rauch asserts that marriage is the gold standard for all committed couples, the creation of federal civil unions sets up yet another competitor, just as existing state programs do, thereby contributing to the "marriage-lite" institution that he deplores.

A third reason this proposal seems untenable is because it also appears questionable to some traditionalist opponents of same-sex marriage. According to Elizabeth Marquardt of the Institute for American Values, such a proposal does not address the central concern that children should be reared by their own married, biological parents. Instead it redefines parenthood by implying that "children need two parents but not necessarily their mother and father" (Marquardt 2009). To another commentator, John B. Donovan, both marriages and civil unions represent a contract with society, one that includes "respect for the needed feminine contribution to child-rearing as a complement to the needed masculine contribution. What the dual-gender couple gives society is further stability to its foundations, and society in turn gives honors and privileges" (Donovan 2009). As I have shown, however, any legal recognition of same-sex couples, whether by civil union or by marriage, does not indicate that fewer children than otherwise will be reared by their married biological parents. The lack of this recognition, however, affects the stability of the lives of children already being reared by same-sex couples. Moreover, because domestic partnerships are in some locales available both to same-sex and opposite-sex couples, Blankenhorn should worry that a federal imprimatur on something short of marriage might induce some opposite-sex couples to choose formalizations of their relationships that fall short of matrimony. Existing or subsequent offspring might then be reared by their biological but unmarried parents, an outcome he appears intent on avoiding.

Finally, Blankenhorn and Rauch's proposal does not work because the civil institution of marriage is after all a public institution. Couples who wish to enter this status should not have their ability to do so determined by the religious beliefs of others. Furthermore, their public status should not depend upon whether their state enacts and maintains laws that permit private persons and organizations to discriminate. There is a place for the protection of religious conscience. I argue in chapter 5 that the denial of marriage to same-sex couples violates their conscientious beliefs, and that the ban directly affects the way they live their own lives. Because marriage and civil unions, where they exist, are public institutions, entry should not depend upon satisfying the private biases of others. Allowing this sort of condition is, once again, a public expression of civic inequality. According to Marinelle Boyadzhiev, yet another commentator on the compromise proposal, "People may disapprove of the romantic relationships of others based on a number of reasons, religious or not, but preserving the rights of our citizens must outweigh minimizing the discomfort of those who, for any reason, dislike the details of the sex lives of committed, consenting adults" (Boyadzhiev 2009).

Traditionalist proponents of same-sex marriage do not necessarily base their positions on the need for civic equality. Although Macedo argues that coercive political power should not be grounded in sectarian religious or philosophical views of morality, he does believe that society has something to learn from the new natural lawyers, who "are fundamentally right in their insistence that we must make value judgments in the realm of sexual morality" (Macedo 2001, 27). Many people agree that heterosexual promiscuity, premarital sex, teenage pregnancy, and divorce threaten social stability. But "if promiscuity is a social evil," Macedo argues, "let society oppose promiscuity wherever it appears," rather than singling out gays as "peculiarly perverse" in their sexual practices (33, 34). Because Macedo, like Sullivan, suggests that male promiscuity can be harnessed by the stability of family life, we should "broaden the scope of legitimate sexuality to include committed gay couples" (Macedo 2001, 42). Like Rauch, Macedo wants to confer the benefits of marriage on those willing to undertake long-term commitments, thereby supporting the existence of social norms that in turn shape behavior (Macedo 1995, 289). The reason to make marriage more inclusive "should not simply be to distribute opportunities and options fairly to all. Rather, the point is to extend a moral norm that carries with it an expectation that one *will* get married, and a social judgment that people *should* get married." Like Rauch, Macedo believes that offering marriage as a "lifestyle option . . . will only further weaken an already weak institution and further demote the marital state from being an imperative expectation to a mere option" (297; see 294–300). Macedo defends liberal rights, but he calls his viewpoint "a judgmental liberalism," which "would defend a broad range of freedoms while insisting that people need not simply options but channels encouraging them to favor better over worse ways of life" (Macedo 1997, 93; see 93–100).

Despite proponents' enthusiasm for same-sex marriage as a means to channel wayward impulses, Macedo himself intimates that a wide range of dysfunctional behaviors characterizes heterosexuals, to whom the institution of marriage is wide open but who do not always value it. In 2002 President George W. Bush began an initiative to encourage marriage among low-income individuals. When the 1996 welfare law was reauthorized in 2006, it included $150 million to promote traditional marriage under the banner "Healthy Marriage Initiative." These funds can be used for high school curricula that emphasize the value of marriage, for public advertising campaigns, and for relationship skills classes for those who otherwise could not afford them. The ensuing controversy, sociologist Andrew Cherlin notes, was one over symbolism. "Should the government state symbolically that marriage is preferred over other family forms, or should it make the symbolic statement that all family forms are equally valued?" (Cherlin 2009, 127; see 121–30).

Although two-parent families are likely to earn more income than single-parent families, some commentators suggest that easing the economic distress experienced by two-parent families—and also, one infers, by single-parent households—sustains and promotes marriage and lessens poverty more effectively than classes on relationship skills do. Columnist Ellen Goodman, for example, noted in 2002 that 38 percent of poor children lived in two-parent homes and that only 1 percent of college-educated single mothers with full employment lived in poverty. She observed that it is far from clear whether single parents "are poor because they are unmarried, or unmarried because they are poor." Premarital counseling and couples' communication workshops might be fine, "but the only way the administration's proposal would actually reduce welfare rolls is if they hired poor women to lead the workshops" (Goodman 2002). According to Theodora Ooms of the Center for Law and Social Policy, moreover, we tend to view decisions regarding marriage, divorce, and procreation as private. Policy proposals to the contrary, Broder observes, "are viewed as counter to American values of individual autonomy and privacy" (Broder 2002; see also Lyall 2002; Cherlin 2009, 28–32). In the *New York Times* in 2002, Frank Furstenberg reviewed a study of teenage mothers in Baltimore, Maryland, that found that although more than half the mothers married their children's fathers, four out of five of these marriages eventually dissolved. Furthermore, those who married were no more likely to avoid welfare, continue their educations, or find stable employment than were those who did not marry. These mothers indicated a desire to marry in future, Furstenberg summarized, but not "until they find a man who offers them some prospect of economic support and won't 'act like another child,' as one woman explained" (Furstenberg 2002). As the *New York Times* later editorialized in 2004, poor women like many others dream of marriage—but not to men without jobs, skills, and hope. "To pour money into marriage and relationship counseling for people without economic hope is a very expensive version of spitting into the wind" (*New York Times* 2004; see also Smith 2007, 73–77; Polikoff 2008, 70–82). Cherlin finds that, in general, although marriage used to function as "the foundation of adult family life, now it is often the capstone" or "a symbol of successful self-development" (Cherlin 2009, 139, 140; see 136–43, 174–80).

As a final cautionary note to marriage enthusiasts, the participation of same-sex couples may reinforce marriage as the committed relationship of choice, according to H. N. Hirsch, but this participation may change and even radicalize some conceptions of what marriage requires. Regarding gay male sexuality, Hirsch finds that even among those who support same-sex marriage, some "believe people who want to have anonymous, promiscuous, or dangerous sex should be free to do so." To Hirsch these findings suggest "that gay citizens are able to separate sex and love." Although same-sex couples desire the emotional and financial commitments of marriage, "it is generally more widely accepted, at least among gay men, that sexual fidelity is a separate matter, and is not a required element of a strong and lasting emotional bond" (Hirsch 2005b, 292). If so, the spread of same-sex marriage could have a profound impact on the institution of marriage. "A great many heterosexual marriages falter over the issue of sexual exclusivity; a great many gay 'marriages' incorporate non-monogamy into their explicit self-understanding. It is hard to imagine that the legal and social recognition of the latter will not profoundly influence the former" (293; see also Jakobsen and Pellegrini 2004, 145). Although the suffragists believed that the enfranchisement of women could change politics without being changed by politics, eventually politics changed women more than women changed politics. Although both Sullivan and Rauch suggest that the participation of same-sex couples in marriage will change these relationships more than same-sex relationships will change marriage, Hirsch at least hints at some reason to anticipate the reverse.

This information points to one conclusion. Even if marriage is ideally supposed to be an institution beyond individual choice and will, the facts suggest that marriage, like other intimate relationships, has always been and currently is defined by couples to fit their particular circumstances. Individuals should enter or leave any intimate relationship with deliberation and forethought, especially where children are involved. However, just as individuals who are pro-choice may regret the number of abortions, especially those resulting from carelessness, but still hold that pregnant women should be able to make their own decisions in light of their personal circumstances, these individuals may also hold that people should be free to enter and leave intimate relationships without legal pressure to jump through myriad hoops before doing so. Although dependent children should be protected, neither pressure on adults to marry nor roadblocks that adults must surmount to divorce constitute sure means to this end. Some relationships grounded in marriage may last longer than some based only on cohabitation, but neither is the rock of stability that some imagine. On the one hand, if same-sex couples are deemed unsuitable to function as marriage partners or as parents, many traditional couples should also be barred, and many lone parents should not be rearing children at all. On the other hand, marriage by same-sex couples should not be regarded as a panacea for familial instability when it does not function as such for traditional couples.

Skeptics about Marriage

The fact that the traditional marriage contract has historically meant consent to a status, as Carole Pateman puts it, has made some feminists, libertarians, and skeptics in the queer community—which celebrates what is different or unique about gays and lesbians—wary of same-sex marriage or of marriage as a desirable goal for all citizens. For Pateman, although the social contract has operated as a paramount metaphor for conditions of autonomy, women traditionally have been subordinate to men according to the terms of a hypothetical or imaginary sexual contract, the scope and terms of which are not freely chosen but are authorized by the state (Pateman 1988, 135–42). Susan Moller Okin vividly portrays gender inequalities experienced by married women who have chosen lower-paying, subordinate careers in the expectation that their future husbands will be the primary breadwinners; their status before and during marriage—and after, if they divorce—is thereby determined by this initial trajectory (Okin 1989). She reports, moreover, on studies showing that both cohabiting heterosexual couples and cohabiting same-sex couples, particularly the latter, are much less likely to assume a traditional division of labor than married couples are (140; see also 149).

Whereas traditionalist advocates of same-sex marriage see institutionalized expectations as a benefit that militates in favor of extending marriage to same-sex couples, skeptics view such expectations as a weakness of marriage in general and therefore a burden on all couples. Because marriage is an arrangement whose terms are externally defined by the state, rather than internally defined by its participants, greater inclusiveness without reforms such as those Okin suggests simply means including more couples in an inherently restrictive institution. Again, will same-sex couples change marriage, as traditionalist opponents fear, or will same-sex marriage change same-sex couples, as traditionalist proponents hope and skeptics fear?

From both John Rawls's perspective and a libertarian perspective, one may argue that disestablishing the institution of marriage can end the tug of war among competing viewpoints about who should define it. Writing from a Rawlsian perspective, Edmund Abegg suggests that we should allow the state itself to perform only civil unions but also let it recognize marriages as civil unions, within limits, if the marriages are solemnized by religious communities. This suggestion harmonizes with political liberalism's characteristic eschewing of comprehensive ethical and moral views (Abegg 2006). From a libertarian perspective Richard Stith asserts, "The argument for legal recognition of same-sex unions does not seek liberty. It seeks state involvement in what would otherwise be free personal relationships" (Stith 2004, 263) and is, as many skeptics argue, not in the best interests of many who now seek such unions. Stith wants to grant legal recognition only if or when children are being parented, to protect family members and reward those whose burdens eventually benefit the entire community (266–69). Both Abegg's and Stith's proposals still tie the receipt of material benefits to a civil institution based on recognizing couples whom the state assumes are romantic partners.

Marriage skeptics such as Valerie Lehr criticize the rigidity of marriage on other grounds. Benefits that commonly accompany marriage might more justly be extended to any individual that a person chooses, regardless of the sort of relationship that obtains between them. An unmarried or unpartnered working woman, for example, should be able to choose the elderly mother she is supporting as the recipient of her family health insurance benefits when her mother lacks adequate health care. Extending marriage to those previously excluded will not help those who need benefits but who cannot or will not marry, such as those whose self-identified families comprise a network of close friends. "That is, the extension of marriage rights might well make it harder for us to form the 'families' that we choose by extending the reach of family as defined and regulated currently" (Lehr 1999, 33). Lehr promotes a libertarian approach to family formation that does not eschew according privileges and obligations to families once they are formed. She wants us to contest the norm of state regulation rather than extending it, a position "that encourages a cultural transformation" in the ways we think about adults, children, and the giving of care in general (34; see also Lehr 2003, 127–42; Lehr 2009, 164–69). As Shane Phelan suggests, "The central role of legally recognized marriage in mediating family and state confounds modern attempts to distinguish spheres of life. . . . One need not take a particular normative position on this interrelation in order to recognize its pervasiveness and its structuring role in modern Western societies" (Phelan 2001, 71).

Janet Jakobsen and Ann Pellegrini wonder, for example, why matters such as finances and health insurance need to be bundled into packages that accompany sexual relationships. In their view "we need to disaggregate, or unbundle, the set of social goods brought together under the rubric of sex and marriage (or even domestic partnership)" (Jakobsen and Pellegrini 2004, 141; see 140–47). As currently practiced, "marriage effectively creates a two-tier system that allows the state to regulate relationships. Why should anyone have to submit her or his consensual relationships to the state for either recognition or regulation? Why should some consensual ways of doing intimacy and family get the stamp of state approval and others not?" (142). Connecting this point to the interplay between the disestablishment and free exercise of religion, Jakobsen and Pellegrini argue that although the state should disestablish and refuse to endorse any particular form of sex or family as the official model, it should not privatize sex or family by withdrawing its supporting roles concerning heath care, child care, housing, and such. "We focus on free exercise, on public practices of freedom, rather than on the privatized freedom of choice offered by political liberalism and the market" (144; see 143–44). One may infer that just as the disestablishment of religion facilitates the free exercise of nonmajority beliefs and practices concerning religion and conscientious belief, the disestablishment of one particular family form promotes the free exercise of nonmajority beliefs and practices concerning the shape of one's intimate associations and close relationships. Moreover, just as the free exercise of religion may require protection through public policy, so also the freedom to form and sustain close relationships may require grounding in public policy, involving positive state action.

Skeptics about marriage then represent the other side of the coin shared by traditionalist proponents of this extension. Where traditionalist proponents endorse the institution of marriage as beneficial both to individuals and to society as a whole, arguing that this benefit is why it should be available to all committed couples, the skeptics withhold their endorsement from the institution of marriage altogether. Although some couples benefit by marrying, a great many couples and individuals—straight and gay—may not. Legal recognition of same-sex marriage extends a benefit to some, but it extends to others a forced choice between the rigidity of marriage and exclusion from a valuable status. As Josephson puts it, skeptics "share a serious concern that same-sex marriage will establish a new form of ascriptive citizenship that appears to include sexual minorities, but in fact excludes most LGBT persons" (Josephson 2005, 274; see also Polikoff 2008, 7–10). Recognizing same-sex marriage once again endorses a preferred way of life. By extending this option to more couples, however, this move ironically renders more problematic the status of those who cannot or do not, for philosophical or personal reasons, want to participate.

To remedy this problem, Nancy Polikoff argues that we need to extend the benefits that typically accompany marriage to individuals in any relationship of emotional and economic interdependence, gay or straight, married or not, and that these benefits should be offered in ways that empower individuals in a broad range of situations. "The most contested issue in contemporary family policy is whether married couple families should have 'special rights' not available to other family forms" (Polikoff 2008, 2). Although couples should be able to choose marriage for its religious or cultural meaning to them, Polikoff argues, "they should never have to marry to reap specific and unique legal benefits" (3; see 3–10, 84). Both the conservative marriage movement (those who, from either a secular or religious perspective, advocate for heterosexual marriage as the uniquely valuable setting for intimacy and child rearing) and the marriage equality movement (those who advocate for marriage for gay and lesbian couples) valorize marriage as a special legal status that is rightly accompanied by special rights and benefits. These movements differ only in regard to which couples should be admitted to this status. Although the courts have eliminated sex-based classifications that once grounded the gendered nature of marriage, as well as those that favored children born to married parents over those born out of wedlock (23–33), the law still privileges adults who marry over those who do not. Rather than fighting to include some of those excluded in the rarified status of marriage, Polikoff advocates redefining family in ways that recognize its diversity, thereby making marriage matter less as a basis for the legal benefits that all families need, whether or not a family is grounded by a marriage (47, 57–61, 84).

Polikoff suggests through numerous examples that the marriage equality movement "positions the gay rights movement on the wrong side of the culture war over acceptable family structures. More alarming, the logic of the arguments made to win converts to marriage equality risks reversing, rather than advancing, progress for diverse family forms, including those in which many LGBT people live" (Polikoff 2008, 98). The argument that including same-sex couples will strengthen marriage implies that this is "an unqualified accomplishment," and it always occurs "in a context that asserts the *superiority* of marriage. Marriage must be strengthened, its advocates declare, to protect society from the damage that a proliferation of diverse family structures causes" (99–100). Although same-sex couples that lack legal recognition do face problems, for Polikoff marriage is *not* a superior solution to the difficulties that both these and other types of families confront (103). Marriage equality supporters, for example, argue that children are better protected when reared by married parents. If, however, the same-sex or opposite-sex partner of a child's biological or legal parent participates in a second-parent adoption, then this second parent may rear the child without question, and any entitlements accruing to this parent benefit the child if something happens to the original parent, whether or not these parents are married. "A child does not need his parents to be married to get these rights; the child needs his parent to be legally recognized as his parent" (100; see 100–102, 52–54, 85–88; Tronto 2004; Fineman 2004).

Similarly, advocates of marriage equality note that because the federal Family and Medical Leave Act (FMLA) limits the type of persons needing care for whom a worker may take unpaid leave, same-sex couples need access to marriage to care for their spouses if such care becomes necessary. A hypothetical woman who is gravely ill, however, "doesn't need a spouse; she needs care"—which could be provided by a spouse but also by a domestic partner, relative, friend, or group of friends (Polikoff 2008, 103; see 103–7, 168–73). For Polikoff, a proposed federal Healthy Families Act would improve upon FMLA by allowing seven days annually of paid sick leave not only for the employee but also "for the purpose of caring for a child, a parent, a spouse, or any other individual related by blood or affinity whose close association with the employee is the equivalent of a family relationship" (172). This standard is already followed by employees of the federal government. Overall, however, the problems that supporters of marriage equality want to solve through same-sex marriage are broader than this proposed solution. Therefore, instead of making marriage matter more by broadening its reach, Polikoff argues, we should instead construct solutions "that make marriage . . . matter less" (107; see also 47, 84, 98; Cossman 2004).

Surveying the relationship between marriage and civil benefits in other nations that provide legal rights to unmarried couples, Polikoff concludes that "the problem in America is not that we deny marriage to gay men and lesbians but that we value married couples exclusively in providing access to laws that all families need" (Polikoff 2008, 111; see also 123–26). Unmarried couples who voluntarily support and take responsibility for one another, for example, have assumed the special obligations we typically associate with married couples, and therefore they should also receive the special rights we have historically reserved for married couples. "In fact, it is nonsensical to deny a benefit, such as health insurance coverage, to a couple who *are* supporting each other on the ground that they are not *required* to do so. Giving privileges to those who make an unenforceable promise of commitment over those who have carried out that commitment is the triumph of formalism over function. It's the life together, not the promise, that the law should recognize" (129; see 127–31). Like the view that individuals' ties within and relationships to a society, not their formal status, should entitle them to national citizenship (discussed in chapter 1), Polikoff's viewpoint is an ascriptive one. It differs, however, from the ascriptive view espoused by traditionalist opponents of same-sex marriage whom Josephson describes: an ascriptive view that emphasizes the unchosen, innate characteristics of opposite-sex couples that uniquely qualify them for marriage and disqualify same-sex couples. Polikoff's ascriptive approach centers on benefits, not on marriage; the ties and commitments that couples and nontraditional families alike demonstrate are what entitle them to the benefits that have historically accompanied marriage, whether or not they are married.

In accordance with the principle of valuing all families, Polikoff wants to revise laws to support the needs of children above those of able-bodied spouses or partners, support children's needs in all types of families, and recognize situations involving adult interdependency such as illness, disability, or financial need. She demonstrates how these changes can work in a variety of areas, including medical decision making, hospital visitation, family and medical leave, the dissolution of relationships, inheritance laws and pensions, wrongful death, workman's compensation, and Social Security. What matters to her in all these circumstances is not the legal relationship between individuals, but rather the function carried out by those upon whom others depend (Polikoff 2008, 198, 202, 206; see 137–207). She also supports the idea of designated family relationships, in which individuals designate specific persons as family who can make decisions regarding health care and the disposition of remains if the individuals should become incapacitated; this idea also allows designated persons to inherit property. This designation promotes autonomy, because these individuals would be designated on the basis of individual choice rather than by preexisting legal requirements (129–37). All of these reforms would aid same-sex couples who do not have the protections of marriage, but they would also aid heterosexual couples and nontraditional families whose needs are not met through conventional arrangements.

Polikoff suggests that although these reforms appear far-reaching, policymakers and public and private employers increasingly recognize and offer benefits to those in a broad range of personal relationships because they do not want to validate same-sex relationships specifically (Polikoff 2008, 144, 152). Therefore, "A victory for diverse family forms," she argues "protects more LGBT people because it includes a wider variety of LGBT relationships. When the law includes *unmarried* heterosexual couples . . . it's a total win" (144; see also 152–57).

In sum, Polikoff suggests that the movement for marriage equality is flawed because it plays into the hands of the conservative marriage movement, which valorizes traditional, heterosexual marriage above all other relationships. By retaining special rights for married couples, advocates of marriage equality think they are being inclusive. To Polikoff, however, these advocates seem not to recognize that despite these gains, many more individuals are still excluded from needed civil benefits. These advocates, she implies, suffer from a form of false consciousness. In Jason Pierceson's (2009) opinion of Polikoff's efforts, "The great contribution of her work is to demonstrate the ways in which the U.S. welfare state is tied to marriage and how those not married are left out of this policy framework" (130). Pierceson agrees that protection for diverse types of families requires more than the inclusion of same-sex couples in the institution of civil marriage. He argues nevertheless that one cannot realistically expect legislative bodies to emulate other Western democracies by rewriting hundreds of policies to de-emphasize the role of marriage in their operation, simply because policy advocates such as Polikoff can show that these reforms are rational. Advocates of marriage equality adopt a more pragmatic and incremental approach by tying their arguments to existing policies for the distribution of social benefits. Pierceson explains, "It makes sense politically, especially when advocating for four percent of the population, to gain access to already developed policy frameworks rather than calling for a radical, though noble, change in social policy." He also takes issue moreover with Polikoff's criticism of marriage's superior status in the liberal state. "She places the relationship with one's intimate life partner on par with the relationship to a second cousin who lacks health insurance" (Pierceson 2009, 132).

Straight and gay couples who are currently married are not likely to appreciate the equivalent of a legal declaration that although the state will protect their benefits, there is nothing special about their relationships. As William N. Eskridge Jr. argues, marriage is in part an agreement to limit one's future choices, like any other trajectory that crucially shapes one's life. Because of this, he says, "Partnership is important because it provides an intense focal point for one to transcend one's 'self' and to deepen one's identity through intimate interaction with another self." Moreover, whether one considers love between parent and child or love between partners, "the love is as much a consequence as a cause of the mutual expectation that the relationship will be a lasting one" and is "conducted within a mutual understanding of lasting commitment" (Eskridge 1997, 286; see also Eskridge 1999, 282–89; Hull 2006, 42–57, 125–26). Milton C. Regan Jr. explains that, independent of its legal consequences, "as a social institution, marriage plays a crucial role in serving as a sense of value that can give meaning to personal choice" (Regan 2004, 72; see also Ball 2003, 103–12). Eskridge therefore resists moves that seek entirely to replace status with contract, explaining that "a risk of conceiving our interhuman relationships as nothing more than families we choose—a marketplace of intimacies—is to neglect or even sacrifice the advantages of relational features that are constitutive of self" (Eskridge 1997, 278). Choice is a necessary but not a sufficient condition of fulfilling relationships. Eskridge explains, "Gay families must rest on something more profound than choice . . . gay families are good for gay people and good for America" by providing a context for the living out of personal commitments (Eskridge 1999, 278; see 278–84, 288–89).

According to Gordon Babst, Polikoff's argument in theory allows the state to strip all of marriage's current benefits from the institution and to award them along the lines she advocates—but simultaneously to retain its power to exclude same-sex couples from a relationship with unique status and prestige in American society (Babst, pers. comm.). As I emphasize throughout, same-sex couples who wish to marry want the material benefits that currently accompany it, but they and their advocates desire, at least as much or even more, the symbolic value of marriage, meaning the public expression of civic equality that they have traditionally been denied. For Polikoff, marriage might lose its desirability without the material benefits. For Tamara Metz, in contrast, marriage possesses not only a material but also a "meaning" side. Marriage is a preexisting social as well as a legal institution. It has a comprehensive purpose, accounting for both personal relationships and the relationships between couples and their communities; and it relies on formal, public recognition by an ethical authority that may function both to solidify and to alter or transform individuals' self-understandings. Because, unlike traffic laws, marriage laws command not only behavior but also belief, marriage is more like religion than it is like other legal statuses. Metz explains, "No matter how civil union is defined, no matter what concrete benefits it carries, it cannot draw on the same social, cultural, and emotional associations and histories upon which marriage draws" (Metz 2010, 98; see also 85–111; Metz 2004, 101).

Nevertheless, Metz argues for disestablishing marriage as a state institution and replacing its material side with the status of intimate caregiving unions through which the state can achieve its public welfare goals. More important for present purposes, the "meaning" side would be accounted for by voluntary religious and cultural entities that are more suited than the liberal state is to inculcating comprehensive values that shape and reinforce both behavior and belief (Metz 2010, 133–39). As the nonestablishment of religion guarantees that the right to vote does not depend on one's religion, "so too the disestablishment of marriage would guarantee that government-provided benefits for intimate caregiving would not hinge on an individual's public acceptance of a particular vision of marriage" (141; see also 136, 151, 159). If couples were to seek marriage only "when they wanted meaningful recognition from a community that held ethical sway in their lives," moreover, this would maximize the chances "that marital status would be acquired in the context of a community of shared understandings about marriage" and would increase the transformative potential of marriage (143; see 141–47, 114–19). Although I am sympathetic to Metz's analogy between religious and marital nonestablishment, couples wanting to marry do view the state as an ethical authority, whether they ought to or not. If marriage as a state-conferred status disappears, it may indeed cease to carry its current prestige. This consideration is a hypothetical one, however, and it should be addressed only if Polikoff's and Metz's suggested reforms are in large part enacted.

Meanwhile, although I agree with both Polikoff and Pierceson that greater civil protections are needed for individuals and all types of families, I concur with Pierceson that marriage as it is currently practiced is a special status, and that advocates of marriage equality are correct to seek the inclusion of same-sex couples. First, marriage constitutes a solid gain both in current material benefits and in civic equality for these couples. Second, and more important, same-sex couples who wish to marry should have the right to do so. They should not be told that this desire is an instance of false consciousness and that more rational reflection will reveal the hollowness of their goal. In reality, same-sex couples who desire to marry have arguably engaged in greater reflection about the advisability of marriage than have many traditional couples who take the institution for granted. Absent a compelling interest in excluding them, they should be welcomed.

Liberal Rights Advocates of Same-Sex Marriage

Finally, liberal rights advocates of same-sex marriage regard the ability to marry the partner of one's choice as a basic human right. As the Supreme Court stated in *Loving*, "The freedom to marry has long been recognized as one of the vital personal rights essential to the orderly pursuit of happiness by free men" (Loving v. Virginia, 388 U.S. 1 [1967], at 12). Like many rights, it need not be exercised by everyone, but it should be available to those who wish to pursue it. In the view of David Richards, what most properly triggers strict scrutiny of distinctions based upon particular traits is neither their immutability nor their salience nor the political powerlessness of groups characterized by such traits. Rather the true evil of discrimination grounded in race, sex, religion, or sexual orientation lies in the cultural dehumanization of individuals, which he terms moral slavery. "This structural injustice is marked by two features: first, abridgment of basic human rights in a group of persons, and second, the unjust rationalization of such abridgment on the inadequate grounds of dehumanizing stereotypes that reflect a history and culture of such abridgment" (Richards 1999, 53; see also 3–4, 17–18, 22, 50, 55, 84, 86; Richards 2005, 39–40, 105–6; Bamforth and Richards 2008, 164, 217–18, 222–24, 234). That is, the dominant culture devalues some human beings as bearers of rights and then justifies this devaluation on the basis of history and experience that themselves bear the marks of this original dehumanization.

Once devalued, these individuals lose the ability to define their own identities, because their identities are culturally constructed for them by the dominant culture—a form of intolerance that Richards describes as a violation of "the inalienable right to conscience, which I identify as the free exercise of the moral powers of rationality and reasonableness in terms of which persons define personal and ethical meaning in living" (Richards 1999, 18). The fundamental right to an intimate life, like the right to conscience, "protects intimately personal moral resources . . . and the way of life that expresses and sustains them in facing and meeting rationally and reasonably the challenge of a life worth living" (74; see Bamforth and Richards 2008, 197). This right "centrally frames enduring moral interests in loving and being loved, caring and being cared for, intimately giving value to the lives of others and having value given to one's own life; to be denied respect for such powers is, literally, to be deemed subhuman, incapable of the moral interests that give enduring value to living and sustain that value in others, often over generations" (Richards 2005, 132).

As with racism and sexism, Richards argues, the traditional status of those experiencing same-sex attraction has reflected a structural injustice that has abridged the basic rights of conscience, speech, intimate life, and work. Rather than being consigned to a servile social status, however, these individuals have been exiled from any conception of a moral community because of the unspeakable nature of the sexual expression by which society defines them, resulting in "a kind of cultural death, naturally thus understood and indeed condemned as a kind of ultimate heresy or treason against essential moral values" (Richards 1999, 90). For example, as Richards explains, the aim of Colorado's Amendment 2, overturned by the Supreme Court in *Romer v. Evans*, "was decisively that advocates of gay and lesbian identity should be compelled to abandon their claims of personal and ethical legitimacy and either convert to the true view or return to the silence of their traditional unspeakability" (Richards 1999, 92; see also 70, 90, 126–27; Richards 2005, 107–8)—similar to expectations about those who follow a traditionally despised religion like Judaism (Richards 1999, 93; see also Richards 2005, 108–9). As with conventional assertions of religious orthodoxy, this opposition is unrelated to the immutability or saliency of dissenting views and is itself a sectarian form of moral orthodoxy (Richards 1999, 91–93; Richards 2005, 118–19; Bamforth and Richards 2008, 226–27).

Although rights of conscience may admittedly be abridged under some circumstances, Richards suggests that such abridgment must be "justified on compelling secular grounds of protecting public goods reasonably acknowledged as such by all persons" (Richards 1999, 18) or else requires "a compelling public reason, not on grounds of reasons that are today sectarian (internal to a moral tradition not based on reasons available and accessible to all)" (78; see also 50, 86, 97; Richards 2005, 135–36). Richards does not believe that these grounds exist. First the procreational model of sexuality is "a sectarian ideal lacking adequate secular basis in the general goods that can alone reasonably justify state power" (Richards 1999, 98; see also Richards 2005, 69–70, 104, 135–37; Babst 2002, 51–59); the Supreme Court has supported this point in striking down laws against contraception and abortion. Maintaining a close link between sex and procreation is arguably a legitimate aim, but it does not command universal allegiance and should not be enforced at the expense of those who do not define their lives in this manner. Bamforth and Richards believe that sexual orientation merits suspect classification status similar to that accorded to race, gender, and religion, based on the culture of moral slavery—that is, subordination through the denial of equal constitutional rights and the prejudice of homophobia—and on "the aggressive sectarian religious expression of such prejudice against the conscientious claims of gay and lesbian persons to justice in public and private life" (Bamforth and Richards 2008, 223; see also 220; Frank 2009, 40–41, 45, 51–52).

The right of adults to have the intimate lives they choose has been variously based on respect for privacy, on equality, and on autonomy. Privacy arguments do not necessarily defend the moral value or worth of the activities they purport to protect. The defense of privacy is often a stand-in, moreover, for equal respect for persons as moral agents or choosers. Finally, the right to privacy is ill suited to prohibiting discrimination in the workplace, in the public square, and most especially in the seeking of legal recognition for one's partnership through marriage or some alternative public status (Bamforth and Richards 2008, 191–200). Patricia Boling similarly suggests that "our privacy is not always empowering or protective. Keeping something private—our preference for same-sex partners, for example—may keep others from finding out about something we do not want them to know. But it may also make it more difficult for us to claim that the ability to choose sexual partners freely is a matter of legitimate public and political concern. Privacy is protective, but it can also *deprive* issues of public significance" (Boling 1996, 146; see 146–48, 56–59; Gill 2001, 197–204). For Boling privacy can be a liberatory value, but it can also operate as a conservative value used by the dominant consensus to reinforce traditional relationships and forms of intimacy (Boling 1996, 103; see 85–90, 101–3). An emphasis on privacy moreover valorizes negative freedom from interference, as opposed to the positive freedom that can ground state action in recognizing same-sex relationships (Pierceson 2009, 120–21, 127–28; see also Pierceson 2005, 32–38, 45–46, 49–50, 125; Ball 2003, 103–12; Eskridge 1999, 302).

Equality arguments, however, do not indicate whether the parties under discussion merit the same or similar treatment, why those particular parties are in fact comparable, or why differences in the treatment of the two parties are wrong. As Bamforth and Richards explain, equality tells us "*that* two persons (or couples) deserve analogous treatment, rather than *why* such treatment is merited. . . . We need to find an argument prior to equality—involving some distinct scale of value—in order to explain why the differential treatment is unjust." Similarly, as I argue in chapter 2, neutrality exists not in the abstract but only in the context of some particular range of options. Therefore, it has meaning only when it is measured or judged in terms of some standard independent of neutrality itself. Bamforth and Richards similarly note that both privacy and equality arguments "ultimately depend for their force upon a deeper underlying value or values. This suggests that, in the interest of clarity, it is the underlying value(s) that we should invoke directly" (Bamforth and Richards 2008, 211; see 200–211). Carlos Ball argues that the "dispute over the legal status of same-sex relationships is not whether the State should remain morally neutral on the goodness and value of those relationships, but is instead the underlying (and value-driven) question of whether same-sex relationships are *worthy* of legal recognition and protection" (Ball 2009, 76; see also 84–86; Ball 2003, 91–99; Feldblum 2009, 205–14).

Therefore, for Bamforth and Richards as for me, the autonomy argument is the correct grounding for the rights of consenting adults to intimate lives of their own choosing, including the right to marry. "Sexual/emotional desires, feelings, aspirations, and behavior . . . are of central importance for human beings": both because any sexual encounter involves an "unparalleled degree of human interdependence," reciprocity, and exchange (Bamforth and Richards 2008, 212; see 211–27), and also because of the infinite variety of sexual tastes that human beings possess. Individuals' understandings of their sexual identities as well as their freely chosen sexual and emotional relationships deserve respect. Furthermore, sexual intimacy that satisfies basic human needs and capabilities for committed love and care merits not only privacy and noninterference but also the "creation of the necessary conditions that will promote and protect the ability of individuals to meet those additional needs and exercise those additional capabilities" (Ball 2003, 106; see 105–12).

Although Macedo's "judgmental liberalism" seeks to steer individuals into choosing better ways of life versus worse ones, his argument for same-sex marriage shares similarities with the arguments of Bamforth and Richards as well as with those of Sullivan and Rauch. Macedo explains, "Homosexual relationships embody many of the same real goods as heterosexual ones: friendship, love, and mutual help and caring stretching over a whole lifetime . . . and this is the moral core of the case for extending privacy rights" (Macedo 1997, 92). The right to conduct one's intimate relationships free from public interference affords, in his words, "the opportunity for gays and lesbians not simply to define themselves or make choices but to pursue the same sorts of basic goods, such as love and intimate friendship, that are so central to heterosexual lives." Despite paying lip service to privacy, Macedo is not subject to the criticism that privacy arguments do not defend the moral value or worth of the activities to be protected. Because people disagree about which activities have value, he says we should afford broad protection to many expressions and activities "for the sake of limiting government's discretion and insuring ample space for valuable expression" (88; see 87–89; Gerstmann 2008, 93). Macedo defends privacy not for its own sake but rather because it can be instrumental to the making of choices he believes to be intrinsically good. Bamforth and Richards (2008) argue that the defense of privacy is often a stand-in for equal respect for persons as moral agents (196), and Macedo's defense of privacy does seem to point toward equal respect in this sense. To make good choices, however, moral agents must possess the autonomy that allows them also to make bad ones. Therefore, I believe that Macedo implicitly invokes the value of autonomy as the right to decide for oneself what kinds of intimate relationships between consenting adults are most congruent with one's self-understanding.

The autonomy argument is also the best approach because the effects of hostile laws and social practices that thwart autonomy objectify, stigmatize, and thereby dehumanize members or perceived members of a targeted group. Bamforth and Richards cite research demonstrating that "laws which regulate lesbian or gay sexuality in a hostile fashion, or which fail to grant appropriate legal protections (including partnership rights), actually *encourage* objectification and disempowerment" (Bamforth and Richards 2008, 214). These effects in turn promote and reinforce moral slavery or disrespect toward classes of people based on dehumanizing stereotypes concerning race, gender, religion, or sexual orientation—stereotypes that themselves stem from a tradition of subordination.

A concrete example of this dynamic is found in Frank's description of the grounds for excluding admitted gays and lesbians from the military that were expressed in the 1993 debates leading to "don't ask, don't tell." The exclusion was necessary, advocates argued, to preserve order and discipline in the armed services. However, no rational explanation was forthcoming with regard to how exclusion accomplishes this objective. The underlying rationale was instead the need to preserve the morality and comfort of heterosexual troops who do not want to be viewed as sex objects by persons of the same sex. "It was circular logic once again," Frank explains. "If the military didn't go out of its way to demonize and bar homosexuality, it would matter far less if someone was suspected of being gay; but the military deployed this fear of being gay to continue to perpetuate anti-gay sentiment and then to insist that that sentiment necessitated gay exclusion" (Frank 2009, 23; see 18–25). The well-known rationale that gays and lesbians are subject to blackmail and are therefore security risks was similarly circular. "Because the policy forbids gays from coming out—indeed requires them to carry a secret and insists that it is shameful—it creates the very security risk that it blames, and punishes, gays for causing" (24; see 18–25). Frank here describes not only an instance of moral slavery, or of policymaking rooted in stereotypes that themselves stem from a tradition of subordination, but also a policy grounded in sectarian reasons, in Richards's terms (1999, 78), meaning reasons peculiar to a particular moral tradition not accessible to all.

Above I note that the sectarian nature of the prohibition on same-sex marriage is one of two reasons why David Richards believes that this ban cannot be justified on compelling and accessible secular grounds. His other reason, mentioned in chapter 1, is that the traditional condemnation of same-sex relationships has in part been based on their perceived "degradation of a man to the passive status of woman," a stigma that itself is premised on ancient assumptions about the degraded nature of women (Richards 1999, 98; see also Richards 2005, 111–12, 137–38; Bamforth and Richards 2008, 223–26). According to Bamforth and Richards, Thomas Aquinas, influenced by Aristotle's perfectionism, conceived of God as "supremely intellectual," without human appetites or the pleasures humans take in them. "What for Aristotle were distinctive human competences (valued by a perfectionist metric) became for Thomas the product of God's creative will for our good and were interpreted accordingly as natural laws" (Bamforth and

Richards 2008, 157). This manner of thinking led not only to the sectarian view of sexuality as an instrumental good oriented purely toward procreation, but also to the bifurcation of human existence into the exclusive alternatives of sexual life and contemplative life. Combining this thinking with Augustine's interpretation that sexual activity apart from procreation represents a loss of control caused by our flawed human nature, Aquinas concluded that ethical values could only be fully realized by a celibate, monastic clergy, as Bamforth and Richards explain. "The final end, in terms of which all such values could alone be understood and ordered, could only be known through the intellectual life that celibacy made possible" (161; see 152–61, 308–20). As Thomas Caramagno observes, however, those in medieval times saw vaginal sexual intercourse within marriage as privileged and ordained, "in the double sense that it is validated by God and, like the priesthood, it provides a direct connection to God by participating in the creation of new life" (Caramagno 2002, 75; see 75–94).

Because a sexual relationship between two men cannot lead to procreation, it represents a loss of control, the triumph of the senses over contemplation, of lust over will. According to Bamforth and Richards, Aquinas sexualized groups who he believed could not participate in the life of contemplation, including Muslims, Jews, and women, particularly reducing women to a passive role just as Aristotle and Augustine did. Like other forms of moral slavery, Bamforth and Richards explain, Aquinas's interpretation rested on unjust stereotypes that view women "as if they lack any moral powers by which they might legitimately make reasonable choices about their public and private lives, including their sexual lives, that are not subordinate to male patriarchal authority" (Bamforth and Richards 2008, 164; see 161–66, 232–36). The new natural lawyers' conception of gender complementarity appears here in a broader context than that of sexual intercourse; it extends to the naturally complementary capacities and inclinations of men and women, which they should be encouraged to fulfill (232–33). Bamforth and Richards undertake detailed analysis of possible alternative Christian interpretations of the new natural law, based on the Bible as well as on the writings of radical abolitionists and Martin Luther King Jr., which neither are patriarchal nor tend toward the moral enslavement of any group. For Bamforth and Richards the ethics of religious belief can play an important role in the public square, "and we would not wish automatically to exclude genuinely *reasonable* Christian interpretations (or reasonable interpretations based upon other religious faiths) from making a contribution to public debate in modern-day constitutional democracies merely because they are

religious. . . . To do so would in itself be illiberal" (342; see 334–70). Because a particular interpretation of Christian doctrine has been ensconced
in Western law, however, Christianity has functioned as a shadow establishment that has itself been illiberal, according to Babst (2002).

From a secular perspective, Okin maintains that the traditional dichotomization of masculine and feminine attributes, roles, and rules of conduct
has promoted not only sexism but also heterosexism. Evidence reveals that
gay and lesbian families are less likely to organize themselves according to a
gendered division of labor than are heterosexual families; from Okin's perspective gay and lesbian families are therefore a good model for heterosexual
families. However, she notes, "even stronger than the conservative fear that
homosexuality threatens 'the family' seems to be the idea that it poses a more
diffuse threat to the whole dichotomization of sex that forms the rationale
for gender inequality" (Okin 1997, 50; see 49–56; Okin 1989, 40, 49). Historically, the resulting maldistribution of opportunity and power that Okin
describes fits the criteria of David Richards's definition of moral slavery:
abridging basic rights for some, followed by rationalizing this abridgment
based on stereotypes produced by the original abridgment. Even if one rejects the argument that points to female degradation, the more widespread
belief in a separate-but-equal dichotomization of attributes and roles is still
a sectarian viewpoint. I agree with Richards's definition of "sectarian": "internal to a moral tradition not based on reasons available and accessible to
all" (Richards 1999, 78).

These observations support the point I make in chapter 1, agreeing with
Cass Sunstein: Same-sex marriages are in part opposed because they unsettle
gender categories in ways that make people uncomfortable (Sunstein 1997,
211). Eskridge also observes that both homophobia and sexism stem from
narcissistic impulses: "Like people of the opposite sex, gay people are viewed
as 'the Other,' a group whose differentness helps the homophobe define
his or her own sexual identity" (Eskridge 1999, 211; see also 214, 223–28,
298). Not everyone agrees however with this parallel between sexism and
heterosexism. For Gerstmann, for example, opposition to same-sex marriage
in particular cannot be equated with gender discrimination. More than half
the states repealed their antisodomy statutes before *Lawrence v. Texas* found
such statutes to be unconstitutional in 2003 (539 U.S. 558 [2003])—a fact
that one would not expect in a climate of fear about male sexual passivity.
If the argument against same-sex marriage shifts to focus on the desire to
uphold traditionally gendered roles within marriage, one finds it difficult to
explain why legal equality within dual-gendered marriage coexists with firm

opposition to same-sex marriage. "The far more straightforward explanation for the same-sex marriage ban is that it has more to do with prevailing attitudes toward gay men and lesbians than it does with prevailing attitudes towards women" (Gerstmann 2008, 64; see 57–68).

Gerstmann instead grounds same-sex marriage on what he views as a fundamental right to marry the person of one's choice. This right does not mean that the state cannot prefer certain forms of marriage to others. It does mean that the burden of proof should be on legislative bodies to defend proposed restrictions on marriage; that is, couples who wish to marry should not be required to demonstrate why they should be allowed to do so (Gerstmann 2008, 73–74). Gerstmann shows that the Supreme Court has increasingly interpreted the ability to marry as a fundamental right. Although space in this book precludes a detailed summary of this trajectory, key cases include *Zablocki v. Redhail* (434 U.S. 374 [1978]) and *Turner v. Safley* (482 U.S. 78 [1987]). *Zablocki* overturned a Wisconsin law requiring that individuals who are under court orders to support minor children must seek judicial permission to marry, so that the state can determine compliance with child support orders. Although the Supreme Court admitted that Wisconsin had a legitimate interest in preventing existing children from becoming public charges, the court, citing *Loving v. Virginia*, asserted that the law in question unnecessarily interfered with the fundamentally important right to marry. "Thus," Gerstmann explains, "the Court drew a line between regulating marriage and excluding people from entering into marriage" (Gerstmann 2008, 88; see 87–88). That is, it is one thing to define and regulate a public institution; it is quite another thing to stipulate who among those desiring to participate may be included and who must be excluded. *Turner* addressed a Missouri state prison regulation that, in the interests of prison security, required permission of the prison superintendent for an inmate to marry and provided for approval only for compelling reasons. Missouri conceded that the right to marry was a fundamental one, but the state argued that it may properly be curtailed for those in prison. The Supreme Court, however, ruled that despite legitimate security concerns that might require reasonable restrictions, the regulation represented "an exaggerated response" (Turner v. Safley, 482 U.S. 78 [1987], at 97–98, as discussed in Gerstmann 2008, 89; see 88–89).

Although these two cases, *Zablocki* and *Turner*, involved a father who was delinquent in paying child support and convicted criminals who were incarcerated, the court affirmed their right to marry as surely as if the context had been a traditional family setting. Particularly in the case of *Turner*, Missouri state prisoners serving sentences cannot produce children and definitely will not rear them in traditional family settings while incarcerated. The court, however, justified inmate marriages as "expressions of emotional support and public commitment," as possible carriers of spiritual significance, as relationships that often form based on an expectation of the inmate's eventual release from prison and full consummation, and as a condition of receiving government benefits (Turner v. Safley, 482 U.S. 78 [1987], at 95–96). Gerstmann (2008) points out that together these cases belie the argument "that the right to marry is a derivative of the right to reproductive freedom or the right to raise children in a traditional setting" (94–95; see also 92–101; Eskridge 1999, 275).

Gerstmann expounds in detail the argument that same-sex marriage should be regarded as a fundamental right. Denial of this right to same-sex couples when it is accorded to opposite-sex couples therefore amounts to the denial of a right that is fundamental. Although I agree with Gerstmann's estimation, as well as with those who believe that sexism contributes to heterosexism, more can be said. Bamforth and Richards suggest that although equality arguments assert that persons or couples deserve the same treatment, they do not explain why such treatment is appropriate in the first place. In the context of same-sex marriage, for example, one way to equalize the treatment of same-sex and opposite-sex couples is to abolish civil marriage altogether. If protections were instead accorded to various combinations of persons in dependency relationships, as Polikoff suggests, no one would need marriage. Although the Supreme Court has indicated that marriage is a fundamental right, one might still ask why it should be such a right. At the beginning of racial integration some southern municipalities closed their swimming pools altogether rather than opening them to African Americans. I do not suggest that access to swimming pools is a fundamental right. I do suggest however that there is more than one way to ensure equality, and we must address the question of why one method is superior to another. Although Gerstmann suggests four criteria for identifying fundamental rights, all four criteria presume a context in which marriage is important to people. Therefore I agree with Bamforth and Richards that autonomy is the underlying value that correctly grounds the rights of consenting adults to have intimate lives of their own choosing, including marriage.

In this respect I follow Will Kymlicka's view that although as humans we possess an "essential interest" in living a good life, a good life is not necessarily a fixed object, like a holy grail; instead it may be "different from leading the life we *currently believe* to be good" (Kymlicka 1991, 10). He identifies two preconditions for fulfilling this essential interest. First, we must "lead our life from the inside, in accordance with our beliefs about what gives value to life," rather than in accordance with others' beliefs about the "correct" account of value. Second, we must "be free to question those beliefs, to examine them in the light of whatever information and examples and arguments our culture can provide," and implicitly to revise them as a consequence of this scrutiny (13). In this view liberals are not skeptics, and their goals are not arbitrary. "Some projects *are* more worthy than others, and liberty is needed precisely to find out what is valuable in life—to question, re-examine, and revise our beliefs about value. . . . Liberty is important not because we already know our good prior to social interaction, or because we can't know about our good, but precisely so that we can come to know our good" (18). Although critics sometimes suggest that liberals advocate freedom for its own sake, Kymlicka suggests (and I agree) that freedom is "a precondition for pursuing those projects and practices that *are* valued for their own sake" (48; see also 50–53; Gill 2001, 13–30).

We do not value given projects, then, because their pursuit affords us freedom. Rather we value freedom because of the opportunity it affords us to pursue projects or goods that we value. In this view liberals do espouse a theory of the good, but what is good is a matter decided by individuals, each for himself or herself, over time. Along similar lines David McCabe suggests that as we form and pursue our conceptions of the good, living life from the inside encompasses a large variety of projects and goals, corresponding to the diversity of human talents and interests. The claim is not that any self-endorsed life is a good one, but rather that any life is more fulfilling if it is self-endorsed. Autonomy cannot be instantiated by the authoritative endorsement of "any particular conception of the good, because what determines whether a life is autonomous is not the particular ideals one is committed to, but is instead the way in which one comes to choose those ideals and to affirm those values" (McCabe 1998, 70; see also 66–67). McCabe appropriately calls this conception one of autonomy-based neutrality because, as I argue in chapter 2, neutrality has meaning in a liberal polity only when it can itself be measured or judged in terms of some standard independent of neutrality. Autonomy-based neutrality emphasizes virtues that do not privilege a specific conception of the good but still, as McCabe explains, "commit the state to some minimal conception of autonomy not just as a potential ideal, but as an ideal that properly extends to the way individuals form and pursue their conceptions of the good" (77).

This conception of autonomy-based neutrality is congruent with Bamforth and Richards's view that neither privacy nor equality can stand on its own as a basis for the rights of adults to intimate lives of their own choosing. Both privacy and equality carry value, but not intrinsically. Rather, like freedom in Kymlicka's interpretation, privacy and equality are preconditions for pursuing goals that in turn are matters of intrinsic value. Therefore, autonomy is the root value here, and respect for consenting adults as autonomous agents should ground acquiescence to the marriages of couples who wish to participate in this institution, whether they are same-sex couples or opposite-sex couples. As we have seen, Polikoff wants to expand the scope of alternative institutions to be more comprehensive than marriage, implying that same-sex marriage in and of itself is a goal that falls short of what same-sex couples and their allies should want. Galeotti, in contrast, suggests that marriage should be an option for same-sex couples not because it is an ideal lifestyle but rather "to provide them with the same opportunity as heterosexuals to pursue their ideal of the good life, within or outside the gay community, in a marriage or in a partnership" (Galeotti 2002, 187; see also 179, 182). In other words, allowing the option of same-sex marriage exemplifies autonomy-based neutrality. Although marriage is not for everyone, David Richards explains, the fundamental right to an intimate life, like the right to conscience, "protects intimately personal moral resources . . . and the way of life that expresses and sustains them in facing and meeting rationally and reasonably the challenge of a life worth living" (Richards 1999, 74; Bamforth and Richards 2008, 197). The publicly recognized right to an intimate life for those who wish to marry plays a role in personal identity akin to a publicly recognized right to pursue a religious or other manifestation of conscientious belief for those with spiritual inclinations. Chapters 4 and 5 draw out this comparison within the framework of the religion clauses of the First Amendment.

CHAPTER 4

Religious Establishment and the Endorsement Test

The confinement of civil marriage to traditional couples at the expense of same-sex couples who wish to marry is analogous to a religious establishment that denies the free exercise of religion. In a persuasive account Gordon Babst argues that the continuing ban on same-sex marriage in most of the United States can be attributed to a de facto "shadow establishment," defined as "an impermissible expression of sectarian preference in the law that is unreasonable in the light of the nation's constitutional commitment to all its citizens" (Babst 2002, 2, emphasis omitted). The prevailing understanding of the value of marriage is in his view a sectarian one, integral to and animated by religious convictions in general. "Nonpreferentialism, customized here as the *shadow establishment*, is also establishment, whereby preference is given to religion, broadly conceived yet narrowly understood as Christian and as opposed to irreligion. Expression of this preference in the law is not a legitimate, publicly justified secular purpose" (57–58).

Babst ranges widely in his explication of the jurisprudence supporting this nonpreferentialism. Sunday closing laws, for example, once were defended as having the secular purpose of providing a uniform day of rest, despite the fact that most Americans, religious or not, regarded Sunday as a family day of rest because of earlier laws that restricted Sunday activities (Babst 2002, 72–76). Babst explains that Sunday closing laws resemble the same-sex marriage ban because "both have successfully hidden the sectarian rationale for their existence behind putatively legitimate governmental purpose" (78). Like Sunday closing laws that lack any truly secular rationale, arguments against same-sex marriage that cite family stability and optimal settings for rearing children as secular reasons are often rooted in convictions that consider only traditional families to be true and "holy." I agree that the genesis of this secular rationale for the same-sex marriage ban, like that for Sunday closing laws, was originally religious or sectarian in the larger sense.

However, others suggest that leaving the question of religious establishment to the majoritarian process, rather than making establishment or nonestablishment a constitutional principle, need not contravene liberal principles. What Daniel Brudney calls "modest noncoercive establishment," for example, protects the free exercise of religious liberty and does not use force (Brudney 2005, 813). It makes only limited use of the public voice and public purse—that is, speech and spending. Any use of these tools to dampen the free exercise of religion because of fears of social ostracism would no longer be modest or noncoercive and would therefore not be compatible with liberal principles. Brudney's overall point is that strict constitutional separation of church and state assumes that all citizens need to have a strong psychological connection to the overall political community. Emphasis on the desirability of this connection, and thus the rejection of modest establishment, he concludes, is grounded in a substantive and disputable conception of the good, and it is therefore potentially not in accordance with liberal principles (Brudney 2005). Brudney's proposed solution, however, places a great deal of weight on the assumption that citizens find it unimportant "to be treated with equal respect *by the state*" (820), and do not value "a sense of connectedness to the political community" (821; see also Gill 2008).

Along related lines, Graham Walker argues that attempts at religious pluralism that reflect both religious and nonreligious views of the public interest represent a vain attempt at a neutral outcome. Because the tenets of diverse religious communities conflict, he explains, "any attempt at an all-inclusive religious pluralism would therefore seem only capable of including those religions whose tenets demand benignity and benevolence, whose doctrines require minimal public validation, and whose view of religion is more individualistic than communal," meaning "religions that are on the Protestant model" (Walker 2000, 115–16). To Walker the preferable alternative is "some form of constitutionally limited religious establishment," or a regime of free exercise combined with establishment, somewhat akin to Brudney's concept of modest noncoercive establishment. "A state can *promote* a given religious orientation without having to go so far as to *require* it; indeed, even while it makes its official preferences plain it can scrupulously remind citizens of their prerogatives of individual nonconformity" (118). Although Walker rejects neutrality in principle, he implies that partial or modest establishment provides greater neutrality in practice than disestablishment does, because it takes seriously the truth claims of all comers, or more specifically it takes seriously both those who advance truth claims and those who do not (121–22). Like Brudney, Walker assumes that citizens do not object if their freely practiced religious beliefs are out of favor with the establishment. In both cases, however, these arrangements may not only exert a chilling effect on some citizens but also convey to the favored group the impression that its status is superior.

Babst, Brudney, and Walker all address different conceptions of religious establishment, suggesting that even regimes that strive for religious neutrality find it elusive. As chapter 2 explains, no state can be completely neutral among rival conceptions of the good or without some limits defining a range of options among which citizens may choose. For William Galston the liberal state is unique because it "rests solely on those beliefs about the good shared by all its citizens, whereas every other state must coercively espouse some controversial assumptions about the good life" (Galston 1991, 93; see also 96–97). If Galston's argument is correct, the distinction between liberal and nonliberal states rests not upon the presence or absence of neutrality but rather on the presence or absence of coercion in the way that the state adopts or espouses its unavoidable assumptions about the good. Genuinely shared assumptions, those realized in a liberal polity, by definition cannot have been coercively espoused or imposed. For Babst, Brudney, and Walker, however, although the institutional arrangements presumably are not imposed, they can significantly disadvantage those who are not in agreement with the dominant consensus. All three suggest that these individuals stand in a different relationship to the state than do those who adhere to this consensus.

The point that every society possesses a particular moral structure and furthermore that it need not apologize for this fact has been famously made by Patrick Devlin. Noting that Christian marriage in England is an integral part of the social structure, he explains, "It is there not because it is Christian. It has got there because it is Christian, but it remains there because it is built into the house in which we live and could not be removed without bringing it down." The majority accepts the Christian institution of marriage as "the only true one. But a non-Christian is bound by it, not because it is part of Christianity but because, rightly or wrongly, it has been adopted by the society in which he lives. . . . If he wants to live in the house, he must accept it as built in the way in which it is" (Devlin 2002, 314; see 313–14). In this view an establishment of religion means not only that the civil institution of marriage is congruent with that of a particular religion, but also that this fact should be accepted as inevitable and unquestionable. Devlin would likely have no patience with the niceties of

Babst's "shadow establishment." The difference between Devlin's view and the view of Babst, which I share, is Babst and I both believe that structural flaws in the house may be perceived, and if that is the case, the house may be remodeled without bringing it down.

With or without a state establishment of religion, every religious arrangement in a political entity rests upon a partial and controversial view of the good. There is always some dominant consensus, not genuinely shared by all, that distinguishes between those who are favored and those who are not. Because this is true even where religious belief and practice are not coerced or made subject to direct compulsion, society must be particularly attentive to its effects. The existence of this dominant consensus can lead those not favored to perceive their opportunities as circumscribed compared to the opportunities enjoyed by those more favored. Similarly, the civil institution of marriage establishes a view of the good. Excluding same-sex couples from this institution parallels an establishment of religion that excludes and hampers the free exercise of those whose understandings draw them to another religion. Therefore, civil marriage, as typically defined, represents a partial and controversial view of the good. Those excluded may feel coerced if they are compelled to choose between traditional marriage, which they cannot affirm, and the foregoing of benefits, both material and nonmaterial, of marriage altogether. Although some may not care whether public policy is inclusive toward individuals situated like themselves, attention should focus on those whose relative deprivation renders them second-class citizens in their own eyes. Neutrality is subject to differing interpretations, and any consensus that favors one interpretation over others will be the predominant one. This dominant position, however, does not entitle it to reign unquestioned by those who may feel excluded.

As chapter 3 explains, the state's accommodation of a practice may constitute permission for but not endorsement of that practice. In the United States, when the state accommodates the practice of different religions, it does not thereby endorse one or some over others. The endorsement test initiated by Justice Sandra Day O'Connor asks whether a law's effect is to endorse one religion over another or religion over nonreligion. According to Mark Strasser "just as the endorsement test in Establishment Clause jurisprudence precludes the state from treating nonadherents of a particular faith as outsiders who are not full members of the community, an endorsement test should preclude the state from denying individuals the right to marry merely because it wants to tell those individuals that they are outsiders who are not full members of the community" (Strasser 2002, 105; see 104–5,

133–45). In his reading of the endorsement test Strasser suggests that without at least an independent, rational basis for treating nonadherents of a faith, or those with an unconventional conception of marriage, as outsiders, the government endorses the practices of insiders. This de facto endorsement suggests that only the insiders are full members of the community, and it thereby violates the establishment clause. He implicitly emphasizes the government's intent, or the message that it wants to convey to those who seek to marry, rather than the perceptions of its recipients. Evan Gerstmann, in contrast, suggests that if a reasonable person can view a government practice or policy, such as allowing religious symbols on public property, as an endorsement of religion, the practice violates the establishment clause, even if other reasonable people can construe the policy as not endorsing religion (Gerstmann 2008, 44–45). His interpretation suggests that endorsement depends not upon the intent of the government but rather on the perception of public policy by those affected by it. Although the subjectivity of this approach may complicate its application, I believe that it is preferable to an approach that dismisses the reactions of those upon whom it bears.

A key problem with establishment regarding either religion or sexuality is its expression of the public inequality of citizens. For Amy Gutmann "Discriminatory exclusion is harmful when it *publicly expresses* the civic inequality of the excluded even in the absence of any other showing that it *causes* the civic inequality in question" (Gutmann 2003, 197). From another perspective Martha Nussbaum suggests that the concept of equality carries ethically substantive content that is lacking in neutrality. "It means that the public realm respects and treats citizens as people of equal worth and entitlement" (Nussbaum 2008, 229). In still another conceptualization Christopher Eisgruber and Lawrence Sager suggest that instead of asking how the government should behave toward religion, we should ask "how government should treat *persons* who have diverse commitments regarding religion . . . and for whom those commitments are important components of identity and well-being." Not only the scope of religious liberty is crucial, but so is its distribution. They explain, "We must not only ensure that people have a fair opportunity to practice their religion, but also prevent the government from favoring or disadvantaging people on account of their religious affiliation (or lack thereof)" (Eisgruber and Sager 2007, 53, 54). The same point can be made regarding sexual orientation.

Civil marriage is of course a public institution, whereas religion in the United States is not. The critical issue, however, is that both the endorsement of some marriage-seeking couples over others and the endorsement of some religious beliefs and practices over others constitute a public expression of civic inequality. Civil marriage is a public institution whose contours are structured by the government. Discriminatory exclusion from its precincts is arguably more harmful than is favoring one religion over others, precisely because the government does not control access to religious membership as it controls access to the institution of civil marriage. That is, government both defines the contours of the public institution we understand as marriage and also decides who will be admitted as participants. Thus its actions may be perceived as doubly exclusionary. People seeking to marry are not requesting an exemption from the rules governing the operation of marriage as a status. They simply want to attain that civil status along with its benefits and burdens.

In this chapter I apply the endorsement test in religious jurisprudence to the issue of same-sex marriage, exploring what this application might mean for those adherents of the varying views of same-sex marriage discussed in chapter 3. A possible objection to this approach argues that because Justice O'Connor, who initiated the endorsement test, has now retired from the Supreme Court, the test is likely to exert less influence over time and may be replaced by Justice Anthony Kennedy's coercion test. I believe that government endorsement is still a fair measure of civic inequality, whatever forthcoming jurisprudence may bring. Writing in 2006, Noah Feldman observed, "O'Connor is the only member of the current Supreme Court who believes both in extending permission for the government to fund religious teaching and also in restricting public displays of religion in the public sphere." Although Feldman himself moves in the opposite direction—arguing to disallow public resources for the support of religion but to relax bans on public displays of religion, as long as these accommodate religious diversity—he nevertheless observes that "O'Connor's endorsement approach has been solidified into law through decisions on both sides of the issue. No longer merely O'Connor's view, the endorsement test . . . is the law of the land shaping the relationship between government and religion," affecting both the definition of establishment and the allowable scope for accommodation of religious preferences in free exercise issues (Feldman 2006, 212; see 211–12, 15–16, 235–49). The law of the land may evolve and change, of course, but meanwhile, we must make judgments based on the present.

Therefore, I first summarize the traditional approach to religious jurisprudence and then discuss Supreme Court cases as vehicles for applying the endorsement approach to same-sex marriage. I then examine the meaning of coercion in this context, arguing that because no approach instantiates an interpretation of neutrality that all can agree is neutral, we should espouse an interpretation that will reduce the public expression of civic inequality. Finally, I consider the civil institution of marriage as a possible instance of speech by the government.

The Endorsement Test: Outsiders and Insiders

Two Supreme Court decisions form the bedrock jurisprudence for contemporary church-state separation. In *Everson v. Board of Education* (330 U.S. 1 [1947]) the court declared that although the establishment clause prohibits aid to one, some, or even all religions, public money might be used to bus children to parochial schools because, like police and fire protection for parochial schools, transportation does not directly support their religious mission. In *Lemon v. Kurtzman* (403 U.S. 602 [1971]) the court found that to be permissible, public expenditures such as supplements to salaries of teachers in parochial schools for teaching secular subjects must have a secular purpose; their primary effect must neither advance nor inhibit religion; and the law must not promote an excessive entanglement of government with religion. The force of these two decisions requires separating the secular impact from the religious impact of public funding, if this support is not to violate the establishment clause.

The *Lemon* test can be difficult to apply. Determining whether a law's primary effect either advances or inhibits religion, for example, may in itself promote an excessive entanglement of government with religion (Wallace v. Jaffree, 472 U.S. 38 [1985], at 109–10). In addressing both purpose and effect, however, *Lemon* focuses on what the government does, not on what observers perceive. Although purpose and effect may appear easier to assess in an objective manner, whether the primary purpose or effect of a law advances or inhibits religion is in itself often a matter of perception, one about which reasonable observers may disagree. Therefore I prefer the endorsement test, which asks whether a law's effect is to endorse one religion over another or religion over nonreligion. Although the presence of endorsement is undoubtedly a matter of subjective judgment, the test is well qualified to weigh the question of whether a law or public policy constitutes a public expression of civic inequality.

Currently most states in the United States ensconce traditional marriage, a particular form of intimacy and family life, as the ideal preferred above all others. Even apart from its reinforcement through legal and economic privileges open on the federal level to married couples alone, traditional marriage is uniquely regarded as "an honorable estate," in the ceremonial words of religious authorities who are also invested with public authority to preside over civil marriages. It seems fair to surmise then that the state in fact endorses the institution of marriage as traditionally conceived. Does including same-sex couples in this institution simply broaden it, without passing judgment on the worthiness of varying types of couples who choose to participate? Or does this inclusion constitute an endorsement of the value of same-sex relationships by elevating them to the level of opposite-sex relationships? This level incidentally posits no qualifications of merit but is open to all traditional couples who meet the legal requirements. Finally, what is the impact of this change on the relationships of those who choose not to marry at all?

In 1984 the Supreme Court held in *Lynch v. Donnelly* (465 U.S. 668 [1984]) that the city of Pawtucket, Rhode Island, had not violated the establishment clause by including a crèche or nativity scene in its annual holiday display in a city park owned by a nonprofit association. The display included a Santa Claus house, reindeer, a Christmas tree, colored lights, and a "Seasons Greetings" sign. Writing for the five-to-four majority, Chief Justice Warren Burger held that given the context of the entire display, the lower courts were in error when they concluded that the primary effect of the crèche, a passive symbol, was to advance or endorse religion (680–81). Any benefit to any religion, he wrote, "is indirect, remote, and incidental" (683). Although the crèche's inclusion appeared politically divisive to some, "this Court has not held that political divisiveness alone can serve to invalidate otherwise permissible conduct" (684).

In a concurring opinion Justice O'Connor argued that the establishment clause may be violated not only by the excessive entanglement of government with religious institutions, but also and more directly by "government endorsement or disapproval of religion. Endorsement sends a message to nonadherents that they are outsiders, not full members of the political community, and an accompanying message to adherents that they are insiders, favored members of the political community" (Lynch v. Donnelly, 465 U.S. 668 [1984], at 688). In O'Connor's view the city of Pawtucket intended neither to endorse Christianity nor to disapprove of other religions. Its secular purpose was simply to celebrate a public holiday through the display of traditional symbols. Moreover, the overall holiday setting ensured not only that viewers would understand this purpose, but also that the effect of the crèche's inclusion was a message conveying neither endorsement nor disapproval of religion (690–94).

In his dissenting opinion, however, Justice William Brennan found that the primary effect of including a nativity scene was indeed to place the city's imprimatur of approval on a particular set of religious beliefs, conferring prestige on a group whose beliefs are uniquely worthy of recognition. He wrote, "It was precisely this sort of religious chauvinism that the Establishment Clause was intended forever to prohibit" (Lynch v. Donnelly, 465 U.S. 668 [1984], at 701). Although the Christmas holiday comprises both secular and sectarian aspects, "to say that government may recognize the holiday's traditional secular elements . . . does not mean that government may indiscriminately embrace the distinctively sectarian aspects of the holiday" (709–10).

If one applies these opinions to the question of endorsement of same-sex relationships, the majority opinion in *Lynch* suggests that inclusion of same-sex couples in the institution of civil marriage does not endorse such relationships. Any additional prestige lent to same-sex couples would likewise be "indirect, remote, and incidental" (Lynch v. Donnelly, 465 U.S. 668 [1984], at 683). O'Connor's opinion can be applied in several ways. If endorsement carries the message that some are outsiders and that others are insiders and favored members of the political community, same-sex couples as current outsiders join the insiders when they are included in the institution of marriage. Because same-sex couples stand in the same relationship to this institution that opposite-sex couples already enjoy, they join the group of favored members, and neither type of relationship is favored over the other. Traditionalist opponents of same-sex marriage, however, compare this scenario to their baseline situation, holding that changing the status of same-sex couples from outsiders to insiders constitutes a second and competing conception of how citizens should conduct their lives. Therefore, the elevation in status of same-sex couples does in fact constitute an endorsement of their relationships, in the traditionalist view.

Finally, people who are in relationships but are skeptical about marriage remain outsiders, as do polygamists and other combinations of individuals who traditionalists fear might clamor for inclusion (Richards 1999, 36; Strasser 2002, 124–25; Babst 2002, 95–99; Richards 2005, 92, 139; Gerstmann 2008, 105–11). Comparatively, the inclusion of same-sex couples constitutes an endorsement of same-sex relationships, as long as there remain excluded individuals who want their own types of relationships similarly recognized. Brennan's dissent in *Lynch* also suggests that the inclusion of same-sex couples signifies endorsement by putting the imprimatur of approval on same-sex relationships and traditional ones alike, at the expense of those ineligible for marriage by law or by choice. However, if same-sex and opposite-sex relationships are analogous to two different religious traditions, neither is deemed uniquely worthy of recognition, unlike the crèche in Pawtucket, because some states do recognize both kinds of relationships. Overall, the application of *Lynch* to the issue of endorsement of same-sex relationships results in a mixed conclusion, depending on one's basis for comparison.

Five years after *Lynch*, in 1989, the Supreme Court ruled in *County of Allegheny v. ACLU* (492 U.S. 573 [1989]) that the holiday display of a crèche in the county courthouse violated the establishment clause, but that a menorah paired with a Christmas tree outside a city-county office building did not. Writing for the court in an opinion joined in various parts by four other justices, Justice Harry Blackmun noted that the definition of governmental endorsement of religion has been interpreted to mean "that religion or a particular religious belief is *favored or preferred*," or, alternatively, promoted (593). Both the majority and minority in *Lynch* in fact agreed, Blackmun argued, that a government imprimatur of approval renders its use of religious symbolism unconstitutional; the divergence in *Lynch* centered on whether the particular display in Pawtucket had in fact conveyed this approval (597). In the *Allegheny* case, Blackmun argued, the prominent crèche display by itself in a public building cannot help but convey a religious message (598–601). The menorah display alongside the Christmas tree, however, did not constitute an endorsement of both Christianity and Judaism; the display simply suggested that there are various ways to observe the winter holiday season (613–22).

In a concurring opinion joined in part by three other justices, Justice O'Connor argued that whereas the inclusion of a crèche as part of a larger display in *Lynch* did not suggest "an effort to advocate a particular religious message," here the crèche alone on the grand staircase at the county courthouse "conveys a message to nonadherents of Christianity that they are not full members of the political community, and a corresponding message to Christians that they are favored members of the political community" (County of Allegheny v. ACLU, 492 U.S. 573 [1989], at 624, 626). Justice Kennedy, in a dissent advocating the legitimacy of both the crèche and the menorah as passive symbols, contended that recognizing only the secular aspects of the Christmas holiday suggested not neutrality but rather "an unjustified hostility toward religion," "a callous indifference toward religious faith," and "a pervasive intent to insulate government from all things religious" (655, 664). He concluded "therefore that the endorsement test is flawed in its fundamentals and unworkable in practice" (669).

O'Connor responded that the endorsement test embodies "the essential command of the Establishment Clause, namely, that government must not make a person's religious beliefs relevant to his or her standing in the political community" by conveying favoritism or preference for particular religious beliefs or religion in general, something that may be accomplished without government proselytization or outright coercion (County of Allegheny v. ACLU, 492 U.S. 573 [1989], at 627–28; see also Wallace v. Jaffree, 472 U.S. 38 [1985], at 68–70). The role of religion may be acknowledged without being endorsed, she argued, and "religious liberty . . . is protected, not impeded, when government avoids endorsing religion or favoring particular beliefs over others" (631). Finally, in yet another dissent joined in part by two other justices, Justice Brennan wanted neither display. Although O'Connor argued that the display of the menorah with the Christmas tree "sends a message of pluralism and freedom to choose one's own beliefs" (634; see also 635), Brennan countered that O'Connor's argument simply implies that "governmental promotion of religion is acceptable as long as one religion is not favored" (644). That is, in Brennan's view O'Connor's opinion may promote neutrality among religions, but not between religion and nonreligion.

Ironically, Kennedy's and O'Connor's conflicting opinions in *Allegheny* both suggest that with two variants of the institution of marriage—one involving opposite-sex couples and the other involving same-sex couples—neither appears to be endorsed by the government, just as a display including both a menorah and a Christmas tree suggests no religious preference. Liberal advocates of same-sex marriage favor this interpretation, because it means that same-sex couples can have the option of marrying and their relationships can enjoy equal status with those of opposite-sex couples. Confining marriage to its traditional form is analogous to displaying the crèche alone; it indicates a preferred way of life, and participation in it heightens one's status in the community at the expense of all others. Traditionalist opponents of same-sex marriage of course prefer this latter scenario, because they regard traditional marriage as the uniquely desirable model. However, Brennan's dissent can be applied to suggest that although the recognition of same-sex marriage promotes neutrality between the two variants of marriage, it prefers or endorses marriage in general over the maintenance of single status, just as the display of the menorah along with the Christmas tree suggests an endorsement of religion itself over nonreligion. Traditionalist proponents of marriage as inclusive and expected of all committed couples, in this view, therefore endorse this interpretation, whereas skeptics about the institution of marriage reject this seeming pressure to conform. Just as the meaning of the display of religious symbols depends upon the context in which they appear, the question of whether the government endorses same-sex relationships by recognizing same-sex marriage is affected by the context within which this recognition takes place.

In 1995 in *Capitol Square v. Pinette* (515 U.S. 753 [1995]), the Supreme Court upheld the rulings of lower courts in requiring the Capitol Square Review and Advisory Board to issue a permit it had originally denied, allowing the Ku Klux Klan to set up an untended cross during the Christmas season on the statehouse plaza in Columbus, Ohio. Writing for the court in a split decision in which six justices joined in various parts, Justice Antonin Scalia reviewed the board's contention that although this plaza had hosted varying public speeches and gatherings, its proximity to the statehouse might cause an observer "to mistake private expression for officially endorsed religious expression." Therefore, its seemingly content-based restriction on religious expression stemmed not from disagreement with the political message conveyed by the cross, but instead from the state's desire to avoid endorsing sectarian religion (763). Scalia argued, however, that if endorsement means promotion of or favoritism toward particular viewpoints, giving even a religious display access to a public forum enjoyed by others hardly constitutes endorsement. "And as a matter of Establishment Clause jurisprudence, we have consistently held that it is no violation for government to enact neutral policies that happen to benefit religion" (764).

Moreover, Scalia continued, this case differed from *Lynch*, where the religious expression was attributed to the government itself, and from *Allegheny*, where the government discriminated in favor of private religious expression by allowing a crèche in a location not open to all. Where the establishment clause forbids government speech endorsing religion, the free speech and free exercise clauses do protect private speech endorsing religion (Capitol Square v. Pinette, 515 U.S. 753 [1995], at 765). Scalia asserted, "It has radical implications for our public policy to suggest that neutral laws are invalid whenever hypothetical observers may—*even reasonably*—confuse an incidental benefit to religion with state endorsement" (768). The question of endorsement does not even arise, he concluded, when religious expression is purely private and occurs in a designated public forum (770).

In a separate concurrence, joined by Justices David Souter and Stephen Breyer, Justice O'Connor argued that endorsement considerations might indeed be at issue "where private religious conduct has intersected with a neutral government policy providing some benefit" (Capitol Square v. Pinette,

515 U.S. 753 [1995], at 774). She observed that Scalia himself applied the endorsement test in suggesting that private speech in a public forum, unlike government speech, is benign with respect to the establishment clause. Moreover, O'Connor continued, when a reasonable observer can view a particular practice as endorsing religion, "it is our *duty* to hold the practice invalid" (777). Even without intending to do so, governmental action may have the effect of conveying a message of endorsement. O'Connor rejected, however, Scalia's conception of the observer as a casual passerby whose perceptions cannot be anticipated, instead favoring a hypothetical reasonable observer who is more likely to be aware of the nature of the forum in which a religious display may appear (778–82). Therefore, she concluded that the display of the Klan cross, with a posted disclaimer of government endorsement, did not violate the establishment clause.

In a different concurring opinion Souter agreed with O'Connor that if a religious display in a public, government-owned forum might be interpreted by a reasonable observer as an endorsement of religion, the absence of such intent is irrelevant, as with the crèche in the county courthouse in *Allegheny* (Capitol Square v. Pinette, 515 U.S. 753 [1995], at 787–88). Rather than applying a standard test to argue that religious expression cannot violate the establishment clause even in a public forum if the expression is private, as Scalia did in the plurality opinion, Souter emphasized the necessity of contextual judgment of the particular circumstances, agreeing with the plurality because of the possibility of posting a disclaimer of government endorsement (784, 788–89). Otherwise, "By allowing government to encourage what it cannot do on its own, the proposed . . . rule would tempt a public body to contract out its establishment of religion, by encouraging the private enterprise of the religious to exhibit what the government could not display itself" (792). Finally, Justice John Paul Stevens in dissent suggested that different reasonable observers could receive different messages from a Klan cross (797–98). Even with a disclaimer the placement of something on another's property conveys at least an indirect message of endorsement (806). "For a religious display to violate the Establishment Clause," he wrote, "I think it is enough that *some* reasonable observers would attribute a religious message to the State" (807).

The heart of Scalia's plurality opinion is his assertion that religious speech that is both private and uttered in a public forum cannot violate the establishment clause. If one applies this idea to the recognition of same-sex marriage, one can conclude that the institution of marriage is a private commitment that is contracted as a matter of public record. Imagining the public space as a designated public forum for marriage, the endorsement question should not arise, ironically, with regard to whether the government is promoting or favoring particular viewpoints or types of relationships. If one applies O'Connor's perspective, however, the addition of same-sex marriage to traditional marriage could represent that point at which "private . . . conduct has intersected with a neutral government policy providing some benefit" (Capitol Square v. Pinette, 515 U.S. 753 [1995], at 774). Sanctioning same-sex marriage may then carry the effect of endorsement even without this intention. However, a hypothetical reasonable observer would probably recognize, to paraphrase O'Connor, the distinction between marriages the government supports and marriages the government allows. Again, however, O'Connor here referred to "a place that traditionally has been open to a range of private speakers" (782), whereas the civil institution of marriage has historically been open only to traditional marriage. The presence of a second variant of marriage either could function like the display of both the Christmas tree and the menorah in *Lynch*, meaning that neither is publicly endorsed, or could require some kind of "posted" disclaimer concerning same-sex marriage. Overall, the justices agreed that the impact on observers is the key factor; their disagreement centered on what observers might conclude.

In *Van Orden v. Perry* (125 S. Ct. 2854 [2005]), one of two cases in 2005, the Supreme Court upheld the lower courts in ruling that a large monument inscribed with the Ten Commandments—one of many commemorative monuments on the Texas state capitol grounds—did not violate the establishment clause. The monument, like many similar installations around the country, had been donated, in this case, by the Fraternal Order of Eagles, a civic and patriotic group. In his opinion for a four-justice plurality, Chief Justice William Rehnquist wrote that given the many acknowledgments of the role of God in the nation's heritage, the monument's religious connotations were but one aspect of its meaning. The monuments on the capitol grounds also represented political and legal history. Therefore, "The inclusion of the Ten Commandments monument in this group has a dual significance, partaking of both religion and government. We cannot say that Texas' display of this monument violates the Establishment Clause of the First Amendment" (2864). In a separate concurrence Justice Clarence Thomas argued that a return to the original meaning of religious establishment—the "coercion of religious orthodoxy and of financial support by *force of law and threat of penalty*" (2865)—would simplify decisions in both this and other establishment cases faced by the court. Concurring in the judgment to form a majority, Justice Breyer emphasized the Eagles's interest in "the Commandments' role in shaping civic morality as part of that organization's efforts to combat juvenile delinquency" (2870). Such an interest implicitly qualifies as a secular purpose, whose primary effect does not include advancing religion.

However, in his dissent Justice Stevens, joined by Justice Ruth Bader Ginsburg, observed that the disputed monument displayed the text of only one version of the Ten Commandments. Even though a number of religious traditions subscribe to its injunctions, he argued, the principle of separation "is based on the straightforward notion that governmental promotion of orthodoxy is not saved by the aggregation of several orthodoxies under the State's banner" (Van Orden v. Perry, 125 S. Ct. 2854 [2005], at 2875–76; see also 2881). Moreover, past cases have "reaffirmed the principle that the Establishment Clause requires the same respect for the atheist as it does for the adherent of a Christian faith" (2876). Although the Fraternal Order of Eagles is a nonsectarian organization, membership is based on belief in a supreme being. Combating juvenile delinquency "through biblical teachings injects a religious purpose into an otherwise secular endeavor" (2878; see also 2885–86; Wallace v. Jaffree, 472 U.S. 38 [1985], at 105, 113). "Fortunately, we are not bound by the Framers' expectations. . . . As religious pluralism has expanded, so has our acceptance of what constitutes valid belief systems." Overall, Stevens concluded, the court's plurality here "makes a mockery of the constitutional ideal that government must remain neutral between religion and irreligion" (Van Orden v. Perry, 125 S. Ct. 2854 [2005], at 2890). Also dissenting was Justice Souter, joined by Stevens and Ginsburg; he wrote, "It would . . . be difficult to miss the point that the government of Texas is telling everyone who sees the monument to live up to a moral code because God requires it, with both code and conception of God being rightly understood as the inheritances specifically of Jews and Christians" (2893). Justice O'Connor, for the reasons given in Souter's opinion, also dissented.

Finally, in *McCreary County v. ACLU of Kentucky*, also in 2005 (125 S. Ct. 2722 [2005]), the Supreme Court upheld the rulings of lower courts that displays of the Ten Commandments in two county courthouses lacked a predominantly secular purpose, despite two later efforts by each county to integrate other documents such as the Magna Carta and Declaration of Independence into their displays. Writing for the five-to-four majority, Justice Souter emphasized the importance of neutrality between religions as well as between religion and nonreligion (2742). In a concurring opinion Justice O'Connor argued that "voluntary religious belief and expression may be as threatened when government takes the mantle of religion upon itself as when a government directly interferes with private religious practices. . . . Allowing government to be a potential mouthpiece for competing religious ideas risks the sort of division that might easily spill over into suppression of rival beliefs" (2742).

Justices Rehnquist, Thomas, and Kennedy joined Justice Scalia in part in a dissenting opinion in *McCreary*. Arguing that unlike many European countries, the United States has never pretended to be a secular nation, Scalia asked how the court can "*possibly* assert" that the First Amendment requires neutrality between religion and nonreligion and forbids any purpose that favors a general adherence to religion (McCreary County v. ACLU of Kentucky, 125 S. Ct. 2722 [2005], at 2750). Accommodation of religious organizations by exempting them from varying burdens and prohibitions "surely means to bestow a benefit on religious practice" (2751). Moreover, publicly honoring the Ten Commandments honors the deity who is central to "the three most popular religions in the United States, Christianity, Judaism, and Islam" (2753; see also 2762). Referring to Justice Stevens's dissent in *Van Orden*, Scalia argued that far from marginalizing alternative belief systems, various historical acknowledgments of God express "the interest of the overwhelming majority of religious believers in being able to give God thanks and supplication *as a people*, and with respect to our national endeavors" (2756). Moreover, Scalia argued, the court had shifted the requirement that a governmental action have a secular purpose by adding "the heightened requirement that the secular purpose 'predominate' over any purpose to advance religion" (2757). Whatever the two counties' original motivations, he noted, a plaque next to the displays indicated that the documents play significant roles in the foundation of our system of government.

Both *Van Orden* and *McCreary* focused on context. For both the plurality or majority and also the minority in each case, differences centered on how the displays balanced religious and secular elements and on how they might be interpreted by observers. Most interesting is the dialogue we may infer from comparing Stevens's dissent in *Van Orden* with Scalia's dissent in *McCreary*. Where Stevens asserted that governmental neutrality requires that religion in general not be favored over irreligion, Scalia responded that both history and law support his contention that neutrality requires only that some religious traditions not be favored—or endorsed—over others. If one applies Scalia's viewpoint to same-sex marriage, simply recognizing same-sex marriage does not mean that government endorses either same-sex marriage or opposite-sex marriage over the other. But recognition of same-sex marriage alongside opposite-sex marriage does endorse marriage in general over intimate relationships outside of marriage, possibly including civil unions and domestic partnerships. Traditionalist opponents of same-sex marriage would dislike this inference, because it raises same-sex couples to the same level as traditional couples. For the same reason, traditionalist proponents would approve of this interpretation. If Scalia believes that religion may be favored as an institution as long as we do not prefer one religion over another, marriage might logically be favored as an institution as long as we allow diversity among the types of couples who may marry.

Stevens's dissent in *Van Orden* may also be interpreted to favor the recognition of same-sex marriage. When viewed from the perspective of potentially an entire universe of types of intimate relationships, his dissent suggests that government must be neutral between marriage and other types of relationships. Skeptics about marriage may be favorably disposed toward this inference. In contrast, if one applies his point about the framers' expectations, the thrust of his argument opens up the institution of marriage beyond that which conforms to earlier expectations. If "our acceptance of what constitutes valid belief systems" has expanded in the area of religion (Van Orden v. Perry, 125 S. Ct. 2854 [2005], at 2890), so also has our notion of what constitutes valid qualifications for marriage. The recognition of same-sex marriage recognizes nontraditional qualifications as also appropriate for marriage. This recognition does not favor or endorse one set of qualifications over another, just as a broader interpretation of religion does not favor some religious beliefs or practices over others. Both traditionalist and rights-based advocates of same-sex marriage, therefore, might welcome this interpretation of Stevens's dissent in *Van Orden*.

In these cases, whether or not the government is endorsing a particular tradition, viewpoint, or set of beliefs depends both on the context and on the baseline assumptions of the viewer or observer. However, rather than joining Justice Kennedy in *Allegheny* in concluding that the endorsement test is therefore flawed and unworkable, I refer back to Chai Feldblum's view of law and morality discussed in chapter 2. In her view, when the government enacts antidiscrimination laws that protect an unpopular group or way of life, in one sense the government is morally neutral because it is not indicating that this way of life is either good or bad compared with other ways of life. When, however, the government refuses to pass such antidiscrimination laws or to allow access to marriage by same-sex couples, Feldblum says, it "has decided that a homosexual or bisexual orientation is not morally neutral, but rather may legitimately be viewed by some as morally problematic" (Feldblum 2008, 132; see 131–32; Galeotti 2002, 14–15, 73, 100–105, 175–77, 194–95).

Put differently, although both the enactment of antidiscrimination laws and the refusal to enact such laws express or imply the government's prior moral assessments regarding the harmfulness of particular ways of life, and because therefore neither position is or can be neutral from a metatheoretical perspective, only the enactment of antidiscrimination laws is neutral within a range of identities or ways of life. Moreover, such laws are neutral because of the context in which they exist and the baseline assumptions of those whom they affect. In these circumstances the government's failure to act by recognizing same-sex marriage signifies a public expression of civic inequality between ways of life that implicitly fall within the range of ways of life that are not morally problematic. In failing to recognize same-sex marriage, viewed in Justice O'Connor's terms, public authority itself distinguishes between outsiders and insiders, between those who are not full members of the political community and those who are full members and are therefore favored by the political community. The endorsement test captures this asymmetry in ways that apply both to religion and to sexuality. It demonstrates that civic equality requires the inclusion of same-sex couples in the civil institution of marriage.

The Issue of Coercion

Earlier in this chapter I note Galston's view that because no state can be completely neutral among rival conceptions of the good, the distinction between liberal and nonliberal states rests upon the presence or absence of coercion in the way the state adopts or espouses its unavoidable assumptions about the good. Whether the government endorses some religious views over others, endorses religion over nonreligion, or endorses nonreligion over religion, the endorsement test cautions against distinguishing between outsiders and insiders, between flawed and favored members of the political community, even when legal sanction or coercion is not at issue. The other test currently applied in establishment jurisprudence is the coercion test, which is often associated with Justice Kennedy.

Brudney's conception of a modest, noncoercive establishment rests on the assumption that as long as citizens enjoy the free exercise of religion, they do not object to outsider status or to the public expression of civic inequality that such an establishment connotes. Although coercion is an elusive concept, F. A. Hayek's definition is serviceable: "Coercion implies both the threat of inflicting harm and the intention thereby to bring about certain conduct" (Hayek 1960, 134). Prohibitions against murder threaten to impose punishment and thereby intend to discourage such actions. Like endorsement, coercion is not always a straightforward or objective matter of fact, independent of the perceptions or feelings of the one coerced. An example might be the subjective perception of coercion experienced by those who find the range of opportunities extended to them limited by democratically enacted legislation, compared to the range extended to others in the community. From this perspective exclusion from civil marriage by those who wish to participate, as well as exclusion from the material benefits of marriage by those in partnerships or relationships of dependency who are not in a position to marry, can be experienced as harmful and coercive. This point is important because some, like Kennedy, reject the endorsement test. I accept the endorsement test, but even without it, the exclusion of same-sex couples from civil marriage may be regarded as coercive.

In *Allegheny* Kennedy argued in his dissent for the legitimacy of both the crèche and the menorah on public property, suggesting that the establishment clause allows latitude to the government "in recognizing and accommodating the central role religion plays in our society" (County of Allegheny v. ACLU, 492 U.S. 573 [1989], at 657). Although the line between accommodation and establishment is a narrow one, two limiting principles exist. Kennedy explained, "Government may not coerce anyone to support or participate in any religion or its exercise; and it may not, in the guise of avoiding hostility or callous indifference, give direct benefits to religion in such a degree" as to establish or tend to establish a religious faith (659). In Kennedy's view some degree of coercion, even if it is subtle, is a necessary condition of establishing a religion, "be it in the form of taxation to supply the substantial benefits that would sustain a state-established faith, direct compulsion to observance, or government exhortation to religiosity that amounts in fact to proselytizing" (659–60). In allowing the placement of both the crèche and the menorah in this case, "the government's act of recognition or accommodation is passive and symbolic," meaning that any intangible benefit to religion does not risk establishment (662; see also 664). The endorsement test requires the court not only to jettison many historical practices that recognize religion but also to judge, among other matters, the context of a display and the majority or minority status of religions and for all practical purposes "to sit as a national theology board" (678; see 669–79). Although Kennedy defined coercion broadly, endorsement did not in his opinion meet the conditions of material benefit to religion, compulsion to religious observance, and proselytization that are central to coercion. As put by Nussbaum, for Kennedy the government may endorse, but it may not proselytize (Nussbaum 2008, 267).

In his majority opinion in *Allegheny*, however, Justice Blackmun argued that proof of coercion is not a necessary grounding for an establishment clause violation. The nation has too often taken actions that have endorsed Christianity specifically. If the establishment clause means anything, he explained, "it certainly means at the very least that government may not demonstrate a preference for one particular sect or creed," as the prominent display of the crèche alone on the grand staircase of the county courthouse suggested (County of Allegheny v. ACLU, 492 U.S. 573 [1989], at 604; see also 601). Moreover, the concept of accommodation, Blackmun continued, should not even be in play. Religious accommodations "are permissible when they remove burdens on the free exercise of religion" (601), a point reiterated by Justice O'Connor in her concurrence in this case (632). Because Christians can display crèches in many other settings, domestic and religious, Blackmun noted, prohibiting this particular display simply "deprives Christians of the satisfaction of seeing the government adopt their religious message as their [its] own," a policy that "is precisely what the Establishment Clause precludes" (601).

Traditional marriage has historically been accompanied by substantial material benefits and tax advantages accruing only to married couples. These benefits could be viewed as sufficient to render traditional marriage an establishment—the first of Kennedy's three conditions for the coercion that may "sustain a state-established faith" (County of Allegheny v. ACLU, 492 U.S. 573 [1989], at 659–60). Although his second condition, direct coercion to participate in traditional marriage, does not exist, President George W. Bush favored a federal constitutional amendment restricting marriage to heterosexual couples; as chapter 3 describes, his administration supported policies to encourage marriage that were akin to proselytizing, meeting Kennedy's third condition. If opposition to same-sex marriage represents a preference for one faith over others, marriage promotion also suggests a preference for religion over nonreligion. Traditional marriage is akin to the crèche on the grand staircase of the county courthouse in *Allegheny*, favored among religions (that is, other types of marriage) and also over nonreligion (that is, over relationships that do not include marriage). In reference to Blackmun's point that accommodations are permissible in removing burdens on the free exercise of religion, traditional marriage does not need to be favored as an accommodation with the purpose of removing a burden, because marriages may be religiously solemnized in settings apart from any civil imprimatur. If civil marriage did not exist, traditional and same-sex couples would be similarly situated in seeking religious solemnization alone. Currently, however, advocates of traditional marriage in most states have the satisfaction of seeing the government adopt their views about marriage as its own, a hallmark of religious establishment and also, in my view, of marital "establishment." Religion, of course, is privately organized, whereas civil marriage is a public institution. When the government creates a status that confers material benefits and proselytizes to induce individuals to seek this status, yet simultaneously bars some from taking it up, the government not only expresses but also creates or establishes civic inequality. Therefore, historical support for traditional marriage and the exclusion of same-sex marriage arguably fits Kennedy's coercion test as well as the broader endorsement test.

Thus, in Hayek's terms same-sex couples are subject to coercion in two ways. First, they suffer the tangible harm of being deprived of benefits available to traditional couples, plus the intangible harm of being deprived of the recognition afforded to traditional couples. Any individual may of course marry a partner of the opposite sex. But for those who experience same-sex attraction, this "solution" is akin to converting to an established religion that one cannot conscientiously affirm to avoid the legal disabilities and harms of belonging to a religion that is not recognized. Second, if the threat of inflicting harm is meant to bring about some kinds of conduct and to exclude others, most current public policy seems to discourage the formation of stable same-sex unions—even though this is an unintended effect, a point recognized by traditionalist proponents of same-sex marriage. Because the state holds a monopoly on the benefits of civil marriage, both tangible and intangible, Hayek suggests that to prevent the exercise of coercive power such a monopolist should be required "to treat all customers alike, i.e., . . . insist that his prices be the same for all and to prohibit all discrimination on his part" (Hayek 1960, 136). In any case, choices are available to some "customers," or traditional couples, that are unavailable to other customers, or same-sex couples.

Along similar lines Kenneth Henley persuasively argues that changes in matrimonial law concerning the equal status of the spouses and no-fault divorce with the right to remarry have greatly diminished the institution's existence as a religiously based status and have rendered it almost entirely a matter of contract. "Only the Cheshire cat smile remains. But the smile is only bestowed upon heterosexual couples" (Henley 2008, 135; see 134–35).

In Henley's view the legal essence of marriage is now akin to the state enforcement of private contracts, which, if discriminatory, can be viewed as coercive state action violating the Fourteenth Amendment. State action is more directly involved in marriage than in, for example, the enforcement of racially discriminatory restrictive covenants, because the state itself defines the obligations and benefits of this status. Although being excluded might not appear to coerce same-sex couples, Henley disagrees. With respect to Hayek's definition of coercion, same-sex couples are deprived both of benefits and of equality before the law, and thus harm is inflicted. Regarding the intention of eliciting particular conduct, Henley argues that although legal marriage historically incorporated Christian sexual ethics and child rearing, these ethics are no longer enforced, despite Devlin's point that Christian marriage is the way the house is built. Therefore, Henley believes it is irrational to retain the one traditional and coercive element of confining marriage to traditional couples. He explains, "The vestigial coercive marriage regime does not directly coerce same-sex couples, but the coercive institutional arrangements deprive same-sex couples of an opportunity that is directly provided by the state." Because any secular purposes that the state might pursue are no longer directly pursued through marriage, Henley concludes that "the only remaining imaginable coercive intent is to enforce a particular religious conception of marriage, even though extremely attenuated. That intent is illegitimate in a state recognizing religious liberty" (142; see also 138–43; Laycock 2008, 201–7; Babst 2002). Put differently, traditional marriage in its current form is analogous to an establishment of religion.

Another court case also demonstrates the coercive element in the exclusion of same-sex couples from civil marriage. In 1992 the Supreme Court ruled in *Lee v. Weisman* (505 U.S. 577 [1992]) that the school-sponsored inclusion of an invocation and benediction by a rabbi at a public secondary school graduation in Providence, Rhode Island, constituted an establishment of religion. In his opinion for the court Justice Kennedy noted that although government may accommodate the free exercise of religion, "the government may not coerce anyone to support or participate in religion or its exercise, or otherwise act" in ways that tend to establish religion. In an overt religious exercise sponsored and supervised by public authority, "subtle coercive pressures exist . . . where the student has no real alternative which would have allowed her to avoid the fact or appearance of participation" (587, 588). Although common ground may be found on which disparate faiths can express "the shared conviction that there is an ethic and a morality which transcend human invention," and the government should not stifle prayers that do so, the First Amendment does not "permit the government to undertake that task for itself" (589). What originates as "a tolerant expression of [government] religious views" may evolve into an orthodoxy that indoctrinates and coerces (592).

In Kennedy's estimation, a formal prayer supervised by a public entity may coerce, whereas the passive symbol of the crèche on the grand staircase in *Allegheny* cannot coerce. In the case of commencement prayer, he explained, both public and peer pressure induce the students to stand or "maintain a respectful silence during the invocation and benediction. This pressure, though subtle and indirect, can be for adolescents as real as any overt compulsion." Standing or remaining silent is an implicit expression of participation and approval, and this expression cannot be distinguished from mere respect for others' views, either in the eyes of "a reasonable dissenter" or in the estimation of others (Lee v. Weisman, 505 U.S. 577 [1992], at 593; see also Nussbaum 2008, 248–52, 309). "Attendance may not be required by official decree, yet it is apparent that a student is not free to absent herself from the graduation exercise in any real sense of the term 'voluntary,' for absence would require forfeiture of those intangible benefits which have motivated the student through youth and all her high school years." The importance of the event that induced the majority's desire for recognition of its spiritual significance is precisely the reason that students must not be forced "to choose between compliance or forfeiture" (595; see 595–99).

Justice Blackmun, in a concurrence joined by Justices Stevens and O'Connor, noted that although government coercion is not a necessary condition for finding an establishment clause violation, "it is sufficient. Government pressure to participate in a religious activity is an obvious indication that the government is endorsing or promoting religion" (Lee v. Weisman, 505 U.S. 577 [1992], at 604; see also Nussbaum 2008, 236–38, 243). Justice Souter, in a separate concurrence joined by Stevens and O'Connor, presented extensive historical evidence as to why he believed that the First Amendment rejects nonpreferential state promotion of religion and prohibits the preferential treatment of religion in general over nonreligion. Although a finding of coercion is necessary in a free exercise violation, endorsement is sufficient to find an establishment clause violation. Otherwise, he concluded, the framers meant the establishment clause "simply to ornament the First Amendment" (Lee v. Weisman, 505 U.S. 577 [1992], at 621; see 609–31). Justice Scalia in his dissent, however, objected that the court was wrong not only in its finding in this case of state-induced coercion but more importantly in "making violation of the Establishment Clause hinge

on such a precious question. The coercion that was a hallmark of historical establishments of religion was coercion of religious orthodoxy and of
financial support *by force of law and threat of penalty*," including required
attendance at the state church and the imposition of civil disabilities on
dissenters (640–41). For Scalia the crucial issue was not whether frustrat-
ing the desire of the religious majority to join in voluntary prayer should
be preferred to "'imposing psychological coercion,' or a feeling of exclusion,
upon nonbelievers. Rather the question is *whether a mandatory choice in favor of the former has been imposed by the United States Constitution*" (646; see
645–46). Where Blackmun and Souter concurred because they believed that
the school district was endorsing religion, whether or not it was narrowly
coercive in its method, Scalia dissented because he thought that the court
was defining coercion too broadly.

Kennedy's argument that students who object to prayers at graduation
are forced to choose between compliance or forfeiture is on point when
applied to same-sex marriage. No one is forced to marry. Given the respect
that has traditionally been accorded to the institution of marriage and those
who participate in it, however, those who do not qualify for marriage under
current matrimonial law, as well as those who are skeptical about marriage as
an institution overall, are in Kennedy's terms not free to "absent" themselves
"in any real sense of the term 'voluntary'" (Lee v. Weisman, 505 U.S. 577
[1992], at 595). Although they need not marry, they indirectly participate
in a legal order that has established a sort of "religion" from which they are
excluded, or one they cannot conscientiously support. This is a religion,
moreover, that connotes participation in a so-called honorable estate that
historically has been equated with full citizenship in the polity. According
to Brudney's conception of modest noncoercive establishment, the key potential difficulty posed by religious establishment is the possibility that those
not of the established religion may feel themselves demeaned and excluded,
not full members of the political community. But although modest noncoercive establishment affirms the superiority of the established religion over
nonestablished religion, "such disrespect is a significant harm only if citizens
find it important to be treated with equal respect *by the state*." This is the
case "only if one values a sense of connectedness to the political community"
(Brudney 2005, 820, 821). In John Rawls's view, one's self-respect partly
depends upon securing the respect of others. But this dependence, Brudney
maintains, "does not entail that it depends on respect from the state" (823).
The argument that alienation from the polity harms self-respect is a controversial and disputed premise upon which not all agree, and it thus represents

a failure of neutrality. Therefore, Brudney rejects a complete constitutional separation of church and state in favor of a possible majoritarian choice of a modest noncoercive establishment in light of the particular empirical context of a society.

Brudney's modest noncoercive establishment is noncoercive in the sense that it does not require adherence to the tenets of a particular faith tradition as a condition of full citizenship, unlike Scalia's conception of establishment. As Brudney suggests, self-respect may not in fact depend upon respect from the state. Additionally, if citizens may freely exercise their own beliefs, and if there is no religious test for receipt of any direct public benefit (Brudney 2005, 817), might one not argue that the state does in fact respect them? Why in fact *should* society value citizens' strong identification with the polity? First a polity is healthier if citizens feel they have a stake in a common project. If some feel alienated or, in O'Connor's terms, feel like outsiders, they are less likely to perceive the existence of this stake. Second, when some feel demeaned by the continued force of laws and practices that recognize others at their own expense, they may feel both alienated and coerced if even indirect public benefits that are accessible to others are inaccessible to them. This is especially true in a model such as Walker's constitutionally limited establishment, according to which a state can promote a particular religious orientation without requiring it (Walker 2000, 118). Although this model does not coerce religious observance, it does not exclude the possibility of material benefits, and it might well be interpreted as proselytization—both of which are components of Kennedy's definition of coercion in *Allegheny*. Both factors therefore point to the coercion necessary in his view to find an establishment clause violation, as well as to find the endorsement sufficient for such a violation in Souter's opinion.

Moreover, even if one disregards the material benefits denied to same-sex couples either by states in which they cannot marry or by the federal government even in states where they can marry, these couples are also made to subsidize indirectly, through taxation, the tax advantages that accrue to married couples—relationships in which they may not themselves take part. This participation in an establishment they cannot support parallels the situation of the graduating students in *Lee v. Weisman*, whose standing or silent attention during government-sponsored prayer connoted participation and approval of a policy from which they may dissent, in the eyes of the court. Indirect subsidization through taxation qualifies as the financial support by force of law and threat of penalty that Scalia argued is one of the constitutive conditions of the sort of coercion he identifies with establishment. Most crucially, insofar as the present institution of marriage constitutes a partial establishment, many people of varying opinions about marriage seem to care very much about identifying who are insiders and outsiders and overall about experiencing a strong psychological connection to the political community. Traditionalist opponents of same-sex marriage claim that if couples whom they believe are unworthy are allowed to participate in this institution, the polity will as a result disrespect traditional marriage and its participants. Skeptics about marriage are alienated at the prospect of marginalization as more couples marry. Thus people of all viewpoints care about what the state thinks.

Same-sex couples and their allies want these couples to be treated with equal respect not only by their fellow citizens but also by the state. Because matrimony confers benefits, both material and psychological, the exclusion of same-sex couples from the civil institution of marriage because they are same-sex couples imposes a kind of religious test on those who seek such benefits. Rightly or wrongly, civil marriage is held out by many as a goal to which to aspire. The inability to make this commitment, not only "in the eyes of God and this congregation" but also in the eyes of the state, or the hypothetical assemblage of one's fellow citizens, can thwart individuals' free exercise of their conscientious beliefs. Whether or not same-sex couples desire religious solemnization of their unions, what they often want is the solemnization of their unions in civil terms, in the eyes of the state. Their religious, moral, or ethical beliefs may impel them to participate in the institution of marriage not—or not only—to attain conventionally religious legitimacy but also to attain civil legitimacy, the full seal of approval. In sum, even a limited or modest noncoercive establishment may shade into proselytization of an orthodoxy with coercive effects.

Eisgruber and Sager argue that religious displays or endorsements carry a social meaning with "a special charge or valence," valorizing some beliefs and their adherents and thereby implicitly disparaging those who do not share them. "In the United States, religion plays a major role in defining civic identity" (Eisgruber and Sager 2007, 126; see 124–30). So also does marriage, as chapter 1 demonstrates. Although the government cannot avoid conveying some message about religion, whether by a limited establishment, nonpreferentialism, or disestablishment, that does not mean that solutions are out of reach. Similarly, in my view, the government cannot avoid conveying some message about marriage, whether by upholding traditional marriage exclusively, by including same-sex couples, or by disestablishing marriage as a civil institution altogether. Some may interpret opening civil marriage to same-sex couples as disparaging the special status of traditional marriage. As Eisgruber and Sager observe concerning religion, however, "if insistence on equal status offends a group of persons because it demotes them from a superior status, their taking offense . . . is not what we would or should regard as a constitutionally cognizable harm" (130). The same, I argue, is true of marriage.

Government Speech

In *Lee v. Weisman* Justice Kennedy also contrasted the ways in which the First Amendment protects speech and religion, pointing out that although the government is to embrace no religious view, the object of political speech is to persuade the government to adopt as its own the views expressed (Lee v. Weisman, 505 U.S. 577 [1992], at 591–92). The government itself speaks through the formation of public policy. Those advocating both for and against including same-sex couples in the institution of civil marriage care what the state thinks, and the varying parties want the government to speak in ways that support their own views. Some, in fact, disagree with the distinction Kennedy drew in *Lee* between the protection of religion and the protection of speech. Brudney, for example, rejects the common objection that governmental speech and spending, even when merely persuasive, are actually coercive because they are funded by coercively extracted taxes. The use of public funds to subsidize some kinds of farmers but not others may disappoint those who miss out, but they do not find the decision an illegitimate exercise of the majority's sincere beliefs about what best promotes the public welfare. "So why is one subsidy morally sanitary and the other not?" Brudney asks (Brudney 2005, 816; see 815–16).

In 1991 the Supreme Court ruled on the legitimacy of government speech in *Rust v. Sullivan* (500 U.S. 173 [1991]). In this case it upheld public funding for a family planning program that was contingent on private social service providers' silence about abortion as an option, ruling that "the government can, without violating the Constitution, selectively fund a program to encourage certain activities it believes to be in the public interest, without at the same time funding an alternative program which seeks to deal with the problem another way" (193). Although I oppose what is sometimes called the abortion gag rule, the point stands. Public authority may, with democratic input, determine the scope of public purposes and may even make public funding and in-kind support contingent upon recipients' conducting their programs in accord with these purposes. This point is consistent with the general prohibition of discrimination on the basis of race, religion, national origin, and sex, for example, in government-funded programs.

This finding may also, however, be interpreted to facilitate giving aid to religion. According to Michael McConnell, the strict separation of church and state constitutes a partial view of the good that denigrates religious belief in the public sphere. A constitutional framework in which individuals and groups bring to bear their competing perspectives and worldviews results in a neutral outcome, he argues, because the laws reflect the judgments of both religious and nonreligious parties about the public interest. Although secularists might argue that laws grounded on religious arguments demean the status of nonbelievers, "the pluralist would respond that no citizen is demeaned by laws that he disagrees with, so long as he has an equal right both to advocate for laws he deems just and to disagree with arguments he does not find persuasive" (McConnell 2000, 105; see 100–105).

Although McConnell's pluralist approach does not support even a modest, noncoercive establishment, his point is similar to Brudney's: Within limits, the majority should be able to instantiate its view of morality at the expense of outsiders, even if the latter feel denigrated by the dominant consensus. Just as the government always conveys some message about religion, a dominant social consensus always exists. Those of a minority religion or sexual orientation may, in some circumstances, have little likelihood of successfully influencing this consensus. In these cases the right to advocate for alternative laws and to disagree with majority arguments may carry little value. If, as Eisgruber and Sager suggest, religious endorsements of the dominant consensus by the state—to which I add endorsements concerning sexual orientation—possess a high valence or significance in defining one's civic identity, those not part of the dominant consensus are likely to feel excluded despite their ability to advocate for changes in the law. This likelihood does not mean that governmental speech is never appropriate. It does call for careful consideration of context.

In 2009 the Supreme Court decided *Pleasant Grove City v. Summum* (129 S. Ct. 1125 [2009]), a case with implications for both government speech and religious establishment. A small religious group called Summum sought to install a monument in a city park in Pleasant Grove City, Utah; the monument was to be inscribed with Seven Principles of Creation, or Seven Aphorisms, which Summum believes were handed down on tablets from God to Moses on Mount Sinai (Liptak 2008a; *New York Times* 2008). The park displays privately donated monuments, including historical artifacts, a

September 11 memorial, and, most notably, a Ten Commandments monument donated by the Fraternal Order of Eagles. Pleasant Grove City rejected the application, explaining that its existing monuments either related to the city's history or came from groups with long-standing community ties. Summum sued on the grounds that because Pleasant Grove City had accepted the Ten Commandments monument, it must also accept theirs. Although the district court denied Summum's request for a preliminary injunction, the Tenth Circuit Court of Appeals ruled that the Seven Aphorisms would be private speech in an open public forum and that therefore the city should erect the monument.

Writing for the Supreme Court in an opinion in which seven other justices joined and with which Justice Stevens concurred separately, Justice Samuel Alito ruled against Summum, holding that although parks are traditional public forums for speech and other transitory forms of expression, the acceptance of a permanent monument renders its placement government speech. As a result, the Summum claim of denial of free speech was incorrect. The Summum group, he explained, was wrong to think that a monument conveys only one meaning or message. "The thoughts or sentiments expressed by a government entity that accepts and displays such an object may be quite different from those of either its creator or its donor." The government may accept a monument such as the Ten Commandments donation without necessarily endorsing the meaning, in this case religious, that the donor attributes to it (Pleasant Grove City v. Summum, 129 S. Ct. 1125 [2009], at 1136). Because public parks generally can accept a limited number of enduring monuments, Alito implied that a government might be selective in deciding what message it wishes to convey.

In a concurrence joined by Justice Ginsburg, Justice Stevens expressed doubt about the merits of "the recently minted government speech doctrine to uphold government action." He stated that rather than classifying a permanent display as government speech, the court could have arrived at the same conclusion simply by deeming the placement of the proposed monument "an implicit endorsement of the donor's message" (Pleasant Grove City v. Summum, 129 S. Ct. 1125 [2009], at 1138–39). This was consistent with his earlier dissent in *Capitol Square v. Pinette*, which dealt with a display that was merely temporary. In a concurrence joined by Justice Thomas, however, Justice Scalia argued that Pleasant Grove City did not need to hesitate to classify its permanent monuments as government speech. The court had agreed in *Van Orden v. Perry* that although the Ten Commandments monument on the Texas state capitol grounds was indeed government speech, it conveyed a permissible secular message and therefore did not raise establishment issues. Therefore, Pleasant Grove City, Scalia explained, "ought not fear that today's victory has propelled it from the Free Speech Clause frying pan into the Establishment Clause fire" (1139–40). In his own concurrence Justice Breyer reminded the court that classifications of government speech must not unduly restrict freedom of expression (1140–41). In yet another concurrence Justice Souter cautioned that to prevent government speech from discriminating between religious groups, the court should "ask whether a reasonable and fully informed observer would understand the expression to be government speech" in determining whether speech is private or government speech (1141–42). Souter thereby implicitly returned to the endorsement test.

Although Summum brought this suit as an instance of the denial of free speech, hanging over the case is the specter of the establishment clause, despite Scalia's remarks to the contrary. This implication could explain why Alito took pains to explain that a display may convey different meanings to different individuals and that the government may accept a monument without endorsing the meaning intended by its donor. Pleasant Grove City had already installed a Ten Commandments monument. If the meaning that the government attributed to this monument was not necessarily a religious one, then the resulting government speech was not an endorsement of religion. Therefore, the choice not to accept the Summum monument could not be seen as preference for one religious tradition over another, or of classifying those following the Judeo-Christian tradition as insiders while classifying the followers of Summum as outsiders.

Chief Justice John Roberts recognized the tension in this position in the case's 2008 oral argument session before the court. He observed to Jay Sekulow, who represented the city, "'You're really just picking your poison, aren't you? . . . The more you say that the monument is government speech' to avoid the free speech clause problem, . . . 'the more it seems to me you're walking into a trap under the establishment clause'" (quoted in Liptak 2008b). Reactions to the case both before and after the decision implied that it should have been resolved under the establishment clause rather than the free speech clause. Following oral argument the *New York Times* (2008) editorialized, "Public property . . . must be open to all religions on an equal basis—or open to none at all." Following the decision, the Reverend Barry W. Lynn of the religious liberty watchdog group Americans United for Separation of Church and State stated, "No one expects that a community would be required to erect every symbol it is given. The question lurking below the surface is why government should have the right to display religious symbols and signs at all" (quoted in Americans United 2009). Rather than adding the Summum monument to the park, this perspective suggested, the city should instead have been required to withdraw the Ten Commandments monument.

To apply this ruling to same-sex marriage, proponents of traditional marriage who do not want marriage adulterated by same-sex couples could argue that the institution of civil marriage as traditionally conceived is an instance of government speech. Although same-sex couples, like opposite-sex couples, may interpret marriage as a public symbol of their enduring bond, the government might interpret it as the foundation of a secure home for the rearing of children who are a couple's biological offspring. If the institution of marriage is compared to a public park, the marriage contracted by a couple ideally stands as a permanent monument, not a temporary display. Therefore, those who seek to participate in the institution are not applicants for admission to a public forum. If couples are permitted to marry by the state, their relationships become instances of government speech. According to *Pleasant Grove City v. Summum*, then, the government cannot and need not accept every sort of relationship that presents itself for acceptance under the rubric of marriage. The government actually sponsors and subsidizes the institution, and it may be selective both in choosing what relationships to accept and in choosing what message it intends to convey by doing so. To paraphrase *Rust v. Sullivan*, the government can encourage activities that it believes to be in the public interest without also encouraging alternative activities that arguably also promote the public interest but in another way. Traditionalists might even recast Stevens's concurrence to argue that because the inclusion of same-sex couples implicitly endorses same-sex relationships, the government can simply maintain their exclusion without deeming the institution of marriage to be government speech.

Both Breyer's and Souter's concurrences, however, concerned the possible curtailment of free expression that might result from exclusive government policies based on declarations of government speech. Souter's concern in particular suggests that the test of whether civil marriage constitutes government speech depends on whether a reasonable, fully informed observer would interpret the inclusion of same-sex couples as conveying government approval or endorsement of their relationships. Libertarians and skeptics about marriage might agree with Americans United for Separation of Church and State that rather than adding new monuments, or types of marriage, to the "park," the government should disestablish marriage altogether as a civil institution. Both traditionalist and liberal proponents of same-sex marriage, as well as libertarians and skeptics, might be wary of the government's ability to set policy simply by arguing that the policy is an instance of government speech. If monuments become government speech simply by being accepted, and if (as Alito stated) the government need not endorse the donor's meaning but may implicitly select its own meaning, this combination approaches the Mad Hatter's assertion that a word may mean anything one wants it to mean.

In February 2009 the federal government launched a $5 million national media campaign directed at people between the ages of eighteen and thirty to extol the benefits of marriage. Ads, videos, or spots began appearing in magazines and on social media, radio talk shows, public transit displays, and even a new website. According to Paul Amato, a sociologist and adviser to the National Healthy Marriage Resource Center, which led the effort, the campaign is not telling people to marry but is rather saying, "Don't underestimate the benefits of marriage" (quoted in Jayson 2009). This campaign goes beyond the mere acceptance of monuments (that is, marriages) in the "public park" of the institution of marriage. It represents proselytization in favor of the placement of more monuments. More important, however, the government is proselytizing in favor of—indeed, will only accept—monuments in the form of traditional marriage. That is, traditional marriages are like the Ten Commandments monument in the Pleasant Grove City park. Same-sex couples wishing to marry are like the Summum group who wants to add its monument to the park.

I agree with the *Pleasant Grove City* court that government speech is a legitimate category of speech. I also grant that just as the government cannot accept every monument donated, it need not accept every type of marriage that individuals desire to contract, a point that chapter 5 discusses in regard to polygamy. I believe, however, that the proselytization of marriage as a desirable status combined with the exclusion of same-sex couples who want only to be included on the same terms as traditional couples resembles an establishment of religion. Such an establishment of traditional marriage disadvantages same-sex couples, just as the establishment of a mainstream or majority religion disadvantages those whose beliefs and practices appear distasteful and illegitimate to others. If marriage were entirely disestablished, or if it never existed as a civil institution but were manifested only through private contracts or religious solemnizations that did not directly involve the government, this tension would not exist. However, because the government maintains and in fact promotes marriage as a civil institution, it should be open to all who are willing to participate on the terms that the government defines.

Applying Justice Souter's concurrence in *Pleasant Grove City v. Summum*, one can conclude that "a reasonable and fully informed observer" indeed can conclude that marriages, as currently permitted and promoted, are instances of government speech. Souter warns, "The government could well argue, as a development of government speech doctrine, that when it expresses its own views, it is free of the Establishment Clause's stricture against discriminating among religious sects or groups. Under this view . . . it would be easy for a government to favor some private religious speakers over others by its choice of monuments to accept" (Pleasant Grove City v. Summum, 129 S. Ct. 1125 [2009], at 1142). This scenario is exactly what is happening in most jurisdictions regarding marriage, most notably in federal marriage policy through the 1996 Defense of Marriage Act regarding the exclusion of same-sex couples. If one compares couples who want to marry to private religious speakers, the government is accepting the monuments of some over those that others want to install, thereby favoring traditional couples as insiders who alone are full members of the political community.

The intersection of government speech and private speech in a landmark equal access case can be found in *Rosenberger v. Rector* (515 U.S. 819 [1995]). In this 1995 case, decided on the same day as *Capitol Square v. Pinette*, the Supreme Court overturned the University of Virginia's refusal to authorize payments from its student activities fund to the printer of *Wide Awake*, the student newspaper of an independent evangelical Christian organization. The university's student activity fund guidelines ruled out funding for religious activities, which the university defines as any activity that "primarily promotes or manifests a particular belief in or about a deity or an ultimate reality" (quoted at 825). Nonetheless, Justice Kennedy, joined by Justices Rehnquist, O'Connor, Scalia, and Thomas, ruled that the university had engaged in unconstitutional viewpoint discrimination. Kennedy argued that because the university does allow philosophical inquiry into comprehensive bodies of thought such as religion, it "does not exclude religion as a subject matter but selects for disfavored treatment those student journalistic efforts with religious editorial viewpoints" (831; see also 829–30). Because the university found the perspective, not the subject matter, to be problematic, it had engaged not in content discrimination but in viewpoint discrimination. Although the government can regulate the content of its speech to ensure that its message is accurately transmitted, as the court found in *Rust v. Sullivan*, in *Rosenberger* the government had, through the public university's student activity fund, created a program to encourage private speech in presumably diverse forms (833).

In considering establishment clause issues, Kennedy noted that the court had long recognized that the government must not withhold general benefits from citizens, regardless of religion, in overzealous efforts to avoid establishment problems. The program in question did not fund government speech that endorses religion; it funded only private speech, which, in this particular case, would have endorsed religion (Rosenberger v. Rector, 515 U.S. 819 [1995], at 841; see also 837–46). Furthermore, to avoid funding student speech that contains prohibited religious material, the university would be forced to scrutinize material and censor writings and publications that did not "meet some baseline standard of secular orthodoxy," Kennedy observed (844). In a concurrence O'Connor noted that student organizations were independent of the university, for several reasons: Financial assistance was paid not to organizations but directly to service providers such as the printer; assistance was provided to a variety of student publications with widely divergent viewpoints; and students selected qualifying recipients for funding. Because student organizations were independent, O'Connor concluded, the university would not be understood as endorsing the religious perspective of *Wide Awake* (849–52).

However, in a dissent joined by Justices Stevens, Ginsburg, and Breyer, Justice Souter declared that "the Court today, for the first time, approves direct funding of core religious activities by an arm of the State" (Rosenberger v. Rector, 515 U.S. 819 [1995], at 863). *Wide Awake* was a proselytizing publication, he explained, "a straightforward exhortation to enter into a relationship with God as revealed in Jesus Christ, and to satisfy a series of moral obligations derived from the teachings of Jesus Christ" (867). Souter noted that James Madison's *Memorial and Remonstrance against Religious Assessments*, written to oppose a Virginia tax assessment to support churches, was directed against just this sort of establishment supported by public funds (868–76). Maintaining the distinction between content and viewpoint discrimination, Souter argued that university guidelines prohibited the funding of any activity that "primarily promotes or manifests a particular belief in or about a deity or an ultimate reality," whether it is Christian, Muslim, Jewish, Buddhist, agnostic, or atheist (895–96). The distinction required the university "not to deny funding for those who discuss issues in general from a religious viewpoint, but to those engaged in promoting or opposing religious conversion and religious observances as such" (898). That is, Souter interpreted the university guidelines as prohibiting funding of material with evangelical and proselytizing content, not the discussion of religion altogether.

The distinction between content discrimination and viewpoint discrimination in *Rosenberger* is a crucial one with applicability to same-sex marriage. Content discrimination may be permissible to preserve the purposes intended in a limited public forum. If the institution of civil marriage is analogous to a public forum such as a park, as I argue, then one possible interpretation says the government may limit what is displayed there because permanent displays become instances of government speech, about which the government may be selective. In Kennedy's view, however, because the government does not exclude marriage as a civil institution but in fact sanctions it and bestows benefits on those who participate in it, the exclusion of same-sex couples arguably constitutes viewpoint discrimination. If the government believes, for example, that supporting civil marriage encourages the founding of secure families for the rearing of children, the exclusion discriminates against same-sex couples in committed relationships who can and already do provide stable homes for children. Although couples' commitments could be regarded as private speech that becomes government speech if or when they are permitted to marry, the government's evangelism on behalf of marriage could certainly be regarded as a program to encourage this sort of private speech.

Kennedy's point about establishment concerns is also applicable here. Although he warned that the government must not try to avoid establishment problems by withholding general benefits from citizens of any religion, in civil marriage the government in most jurisdictions already bestows benefits on citizens of one religion yet withholds them from those of another. Extending these benefits to those of a different religion or persuasion not only avoids viewpoint discrimination, as Kennedy defines it, but also avoids an establishment of one religion at the expense of another. Similarly, in light of O'Connor's concurrence, the close association of the government with civil marriage leaves no doubt that the government is endorsing the commitments of traditional couples at the expense of others. From this perspective the government should neither fund benefits for some kinds of families over others nor engage in government speech about its preferences in this regard. To both traditional and liberal proponents of same-sex marriage, this promotion equates to favoritism toward one religion despite the fact that adherents to another religion want recognition also. Recognition of this favoritism is explicit in a 1995 Canadian Supreme Court ruling that discrimination against unmarried couples was unconstitutional: "Discrimination on

the basis of marital status . . . touches the individual's freedom to live life
with the mate of one's choice in the fashion of one's choice. . . . Discrimination on the basis of marital status may be seen as akin to discrimination on
the ground of religion, to the extent that it finds its roots and expression in
moral disapproval of all sexual unions except those sanctioned by the church
and state" (Miron v. Trudel, 2 S.C.R. 418 [Canada 1995], at 420, quoted in
Polikoff 2008, 111–12).

This use of *Rosenberger v. Rector* may seem inapposite because its subject was the public funding of religious speech, not symbolic recognition
in the public square. However, marriage carries both material and symbolic significance. Both factors play a role in my argument that same-sex
couples who wish to marry should be able to do so. Maintaining an exclusive public institution that historically has excluded same-sex couples who
want to be included on the same terms as traditional couples is analogous
to an establishment of religion that favors one faith over another. The
relative importance of material and symbolic benefits to religious believers is a matter of dispute. Noah Feldman, for example, wants to combine
greater latitude for religious discourse and symbolism in the public square
with greater restrictions on public funding for religious institutions and
activities, although in both areas this recommendation goes against recent
trends. Though coercion regarding religion would still be prohibited in his
vision, endorsement of religion would no longer be problematic. Feldman
believes that if all citizens and groups have the right to speak, "no one
group or person should be threatened by the symbolic or political speech
of others, much as they may disagree" (Feldman 2006, 238; see 14–16,
235–49; see also Nussbaum 2008, 273–75). Money, however, is finite. Although both money and speech are used to allocate value, money is subject
to political competition over the relative worth of competing purposes,
whereas speech and symbols are theoretically unlimited.

Eisgruber and Sager believe Feldman is unrealistic to think that greater
latitude for religious symbolism will lower tensions in a diverse population.
Although more and different kinds of speech and symbols may in theory
be added to make public displays more inclusive, public authorities may
refuse some manifestations of religious expression and have been upheld
by the courts in doing so. Eisgruber and Sager find in Feldman's view, "ultimately, a moral judgment: people *ought* not to care as much as they do
about public sponsorship of religious symbols" (Eisgruber and Sager 2007,
155; see 152–58). Feldman argues that "it is largely an interpretive choice
to feel excluded by the fact of other people's faith, and the atheist can just as

easily adhere to his own views while insisting on his citizenship" (Feldman 2006, 142). Eisgruber and Sager reply, "Of course, what is at issue is not 'the fact of other people's religion,' but the fact of government sponsorship and support of it" (Eisgruber and Sager 2007, 306n50). As Nussbaum similarly observes, "Even the bare knowledge that the state has expressed a message that demeans a given class of citizens can reasonably be thought to affect those people's standing in the community, whether they view the message or not" (Nussbaum 2008, 252), at least in the eyes of others, whether or not they care themselves.

This last point resonates on the subject of marriage as fully as it does in the area of religion. One can argue that same-sex couples should not care whether their relationships carry the title of "marriage." If they are granted legal status such as civil unions and domestic partnerships, it is "an interpretive choice," in Feldman's words, to feel excluded by the fact that traditional couples can marry when in most jurisdictions same-sex couples cannot (Feldman 2006, 142). Same-sex couples can choose to be proud of their own identities and relationships despite their exclusion from the status of marriage. As Eisgruber and Sager observe, however, the problem is that marriage is a public institution. Its civil incarnation is sponsored and supported by the government. Courts in several states have agreed with same-sex couples and their advocates that even where civil unions or domestic partnerships carry the same material benefits for same-sex couples that civil marriage does for traditional couples in those states, "the dissimilitude between the terms 'civil marriage' and 'civil union' is not innocuous; it is a considered choice of language that reflects a demonstrable assigning of same-sex, largely homosexual, couples to a second-class status" (*In re* Opinions of the Justices to the Senate, 440 Mass. 1201 [2004], at 1207). The California Supreme Court agreed: "We conclude that the distinction drawn by the current California statutes between the designation of family relationships available to opposite-sex couples and the designation available to same-sex couples impinges upon the fundamental interest of same-sex couples in having their official family relationships accorded dignity and respect equal to that conferred upon the family relationships of opposite-sex couples" (*In re* Marriage Cases, 43 Cal. 4th 757 [2008], at 846–47).

Moreover, just as unconventional religious beliefs that may have been scorned in the past are now more readily respected, so too are unconventional personal relationships. In the words of the Connecticut Supreme Court, marriage has long been a basic civil right in the state, and "our conventional understanding of marriage must yield to a more contemporary appreciation of the rights entitled to constitutional protection" (Kerrigan

v. Commissioner of Public Health, 289 Conn. 135 [2008], at 262). If, as
Eisgruber and Sager suggest, religion carries a special valence or significance
according to which it plays a major role in civic identity, so too does the status of couples who wish to marry, whether or not they ought to care about
their eligibility for this status. Marriage as traditionally administered is akin
to an establishment of religion, and exclusion from not only its material
benefits but also its symbolic benefits constitutes a public expression of civic
inequality.

CHAPTER 5

Free Exercise and the Right to Conscience

In chapter 4 I argue that confining civil marriage to opposite-sex couples performs a function akin to religious establishment. It promotes a particular vision of intimate relationship and family as the preferred model for all, privileging those who participate in it to the exclusion of those who adhere to a different vision. Although denial of the material benefits accompanying civil marriage is a tangible expression of civic inequality, what is equally if not more crucial is the symbolic distinction between insiders and outsiders that this exclusion promotes. Just as the display of the religious symbols of only one religion in the public square sends a message that its adherents are favored members of the political community, so also does the public recognition of only one kind of intimate relationship. Although the perception that one is an outsider may seem to be "an interpretive choice" (Feldman 2006, 142), this exclusion not only functions as a public expression of civic inequality, but also serves to confirm and entrench the dominant consensus. Because both religion and sexuality have significance that accords each a major role in civic identity (Eisgruber and Sager 2007, 126), public favoritism has no place in a liberal democratic polity. Public policy may be government speech that legitimately reflects its viewpoint, but this category of speech can easily expand to favor some religious or sexual orientations over others, which is all the more troubling in the absence of a compelling public interest to support this move.

It is one thing, however, to argue that the singular status of traditional marriage in most jurisdictions constitutes an establishment akin to an establishment of religion. It is quite another to show that the denial of civil marriage to same-sex couples is analogous to a denial of the free exercise of religion. My claim does not necessarily rest on traditional conceptions of religion as adherence to established or recognized creeds. Instead, it rests on a broader conception of conscientious belief that is more individualistic in nature. Moreover, this claim does not simply request from public authority exemptions or accommodations that allow believers to follow their consciences unimpeded. Rather, it requires positive action on the part of government to broaden the scope of a public institution to include those traditionally deemed ineligible to participate.

It is not enough simply to allow individuals to engage in acceptable but unpopular practices quietly or in closeted fashion, so that they avoid disturbing the comfort of the dominant consensus. Drawing in part on the work of Martha Nussbaum and Andrew Murphy, in this chapter I argue for an expanded conception of conscientious belief, maintaining that its protection not only may require the removal of barriers to practices flowing from it but also may need positive action if legitimate but unpopular practices are to receive the same civic respect as majority ones. Then I discuss three landmark Supreme Court cases concerning gay rights in light of conscientious belief. Finally, I make the case for including same-sex couples in civil marriage as an extension of the free exercise of conscientious belief.

Sexuality, Religion, and "Moral Strangers"

David A. J. Richards's conception of moral slavery, addressed in chapter 3, encompasses both an abridgment of human rights in a group and also the rationalization of this abridgment based on dehumanizing stereotypes that themselves reflect a culture of abridgment. Individuals subject to moral slavery, that is, cannot define their own identities because they are culturally constructed by the dominant culture, a form of intolerance that Richards equates with a violation of the right of conscience, or "the free exercise of the moral powers of rationality and reasonableness in terms of which persons define personal and ethical meaning in living" (Richards 1999, 18). With regard to sexuality, Richards argues, the fundamental right to an intimate life, like the right to conscience, "protects intimately personal moral resources . . . and the way of life that expresses and sustains them in facing and meeting rationally and reasonably the challenge of a life worth living" (74; Bamforth and Richards 2008, 197). Historically, even reasonable discussion of homosexuality has been considered "a kind of ultimate heresy or treason against essential moral values" (Richards 1999, 90), akin to the disrespect shown toward traditionally despised religions such as Judaism. With regard to the imperatives of both denigrated religions and sexual orientations, individuals have been expected to either convert or remain silent about their unorthodox allegiances. This sort of expectation is for Richards a sectarian form of moral orthodoxy (Richards 1999, 70, 90–93; Richards 2005, 107–9, 118–19; Bamforth and Richards 2008, 226–27; Richards 2009, 222–23).

In a critique of the new natural lawyers, David Erdos concurs that because both sexual and religious expression carry deep meaning for many individuals, "human sexual expression and human religious expression can both be considered specific forms of a more general category, namely, intimate self-expression" (Erdos 2005, 21). Because even contemporary natural lawyers differ in their views on the proper scope of the political community, Erdos suggests, paternalistic approaches may justify intervention in people's sexual lives as well as their religious lives, insofar as the state might determine that both their sexual and religious practices are grounded on false reasoning or reflect false beliefs. "State attempts to extinguish a person's right to an intimate sexual life rest . . . on a perfectionist understanding of the state which in its logic undermines not only sexual freedom but also other freedoms including religious freedom" (22; see 19–23). Erdos notes that although natural lawyer John Finnis does not seek to criminalize consensual sexual acts between adults that are carried out in secret (Erdos 2005, 20), this stance is akin to the traditional silencing of both religious and sexual practices on the part of the dominant consensus, which Richards rightly condemns. Both religious and sexual expression may be curtailed when this is justified by compelling social needs, but society should not pressure individuals to closet permissible religious and sexual practices.

The analogy between freedom of intimate association and freedom of religion and expression is also made by Karen Struening. Although she rejects the essentialist notion that sexual orientations or practices fix or standardize individuals' identities, she argues that the process of forming our own judgments in these areas is a central constituent of self-definition. For her "The regulation and repression of non-coercive and consensual sexual practices between adults is a direct assault on moral pluralism" (Struening 1996, 509; see 507–9). As John Stuart Mill recognized, the dominance of social convention sacrifices our ability to determine both what we do and who we are or what we become. In Will Kymlicka's view, we sacrifice not only our capacity to pursue self-endorsed lives but also our capacity to examine, question, and reaffirm or revise our current projects and goals (Kymlicka 1991, 10, 13, 18). Struening explains, "Sexuality, like religious and moral beliefs, is our own in the sense that without it our ability to be self-determining and self-defining is seriously compromised" (Struening 1996, 521–22; see also 513). Given that Struening agrees with Mill regarding the harms perpetrated by the dominance of social convention, she may agree with Richards and Erdos that discussion of unpopular sexual practices, like that of unpopular religious practices, should not be silenced by the dominant consensus.

Not all agree with this argument, however, even among those who believe that one's sexuality belongs to oneself and should not be legally repressed. Some suggest that by insisting on equal respect for dissenters, rights-based liberals too often conflate toleration with approval. Steven Kautz, for example, asserts that liberals tend to demand not only permission but also esteem, not only toleration but also respect and praise, for unpopular ways of life. But Kautz argues this tendency teaches citizens what to think, in effect denying that private choices and pursuits are indeed private. Although he does not explicitly address the issue of sexual orientation and practice, his argument fits this issue well. For him, one of the "most splendid achievements" of liberal politics is its protection of liberal individualists who are "moral strangers" to the community, even when they are neither understood nor admired. These individuals should reciprocate by not demanding more than grudging tolerance, instead honoring ordinary citizens "by refusing to repay this respectable generosity with contempt" (Kautz 1993, 624; see also 620; Kautz 1995, 52–57, 63, 67–68, 72–75). Some ways of life may be privately tolerated or even admired, Kautz says, without being openly praised (Kautz 1993, 629; see also 614).

Kautz may appear simply to be arguing against extremes of political correctness, suggesting that liberal individualists or so-called moral strangers do not need praise, only permission. A community that offers only grudging tolerance "is consistent with self-respect though not a right to equal respect" (Kautz 1993, 628). Any feelings of denigration experienced by moral strangers is, in Noah Feldman's terms, an interpretive choice (Feldman 2006, 142). Kautz expressed his views before same-sex sodomy was decriminalized. However, his views are compatible not only with Finnis's opinion that sexual practices subject to disapprobation should not be penalized when they are closeted, but also with the idea that retaining rarely enforced antisodomy regulations is compatible with permission for closeted sexual expression. Stated more emphatically regarding same-sex marriage, same-sex couples, who are moral strangers to the traditional conception of marriage, should not "repay this respectable generosity" of grudging tolerance for same-sex couples "with contempt" by demanding the right to participate in the institution of civil marriage (Kautz 1993, 624).

A stance of grudging toleration, however, implies that individuals who choose or affirm unpopular ways of life, as well as their supporters, should simply be grateful for this modicum of toleration and should withhold demands for measures to end public discrimination and possibly prevent private discrimination. The hard work of liberal citizenship, as Jeff Spinner-Halev terms it, requires the equal and civil treatment of others in the public square, whatever our private sentiments. For example, although citizens of a liberal democracy can expect some acculturation by new ethnic and religious groups, citizens must also be willing to accept ways of life that they dislike as long as these are not illiberal. "The liberal state cannot demand that people think of everyone as equal; it can merely demand that citizens treat each other equally in public institutions" (Spinner 1994, 47; see also 37–38, 45–48, 74–76; Gill 2001, 111–14). Spinner-Halev notes that Margaret Thatcher, as prime minister of the United Kingdom, stated that people of varied faiths and cultures would be welcome and respected in Great Britain and that this was completely compatible with maintaining Great Britain's own identity. From Spinner-Halev's perspective, Thatcher "allowed non-Christians to have a place in Britain, but she did not want them to challenge the fundamental identity of Britain as a Christian state. As long as this attitude prevails, non-Christians will not have full citizenship in Britain" (Spinner 1994, 75). Similarly, if individuals who experience same-sex attraction must remain nominally closeted to expect equal treatment in the public square, this expectation constitutes a public expression of civic inequality in the service of heteronormativity. Those who are different, whether in religion, culture, or sexuality, should not be pressured to conform by their silence any more than by their behavior. Individuals should be recognized or respected as whole persons even when their practices are disliked, and they should not be encouraged or pressured to sacrifice the conditions of their own autonomy for the comfort of the majority.

Kautz, in contrast, argues that from a strategic standpoint, culture wars can be avoided only if dissenters from the dominant consensus refrain from attempting to instantiate a liberal orthodoxy grounded in moral autonomy or equal respect (Kautz 1995, 11–13, 56, 68). Kautz argues that protecting unpopular practices legitimates them, and publicly legitimating them praises them. In sum, he believes that civil peace requires a degree of hypocrisy. Ordinary citizens and nonconformists should collude in a settlement in which dissenters exchange silence for toleration with the unspoken acquiescence of both parties. A specific example of this logic existed in the "don't ask, don't tell" policy of the United States armed forces, repealed in 2010. Before the United Kingdom lifted its own ban on openly gay military service, researchers noted that the difficulty in effecting change there was not military but political. Nathanial Frank explains, "Prejudice had become a justification, once again, for continuing itself. . . . The self-image of the British military, its members' sense of entitlement to preserve a way of life they saw as besieged, and to carry things out in the way they saw fit—these were the currency of the debate" (Frank 2009, 143). In the United States, he observes, "Much of the opposition to gay service, particularly from religious conservatives, remains grounded in the objection that the government should not force people to accept homosexuality (never mind that the current ban is, among other things, precisely an expression of public beliefs about homosexuality)" (164). The same is true of opposition to same-sex marriage.

Although every political community ranks some values above others, the essential question lies in how this hierarchy is determined. Communally determined notions of worth and merit too easily allow society to judge individual worth primarily in terms of how well one upholds these apparently constant norms, which in turn are grounded "within the dominant understanding of a particular community's traditions" (Lund 1993, 587). William Lund argues that reliance on current norms suggests that "we treat people as equals when we hold their beliefs and conduct up to currently accepted understandings of our traditions and shared purposes." This practice raises, "perhaps to prohibitive levels, the costs of citizens revising their conceptions of the good away from a recognized consensus." This practice also makes it "difficult for the community as a whole to have enough experience with, or to hear arguments about, alternatives that might cause it to revise or even reject its current understanding" (588). In other words, enshrining the current consensus, whether about gay military service or same-sex marriage, discourages critical reflection on individual or collective projects and goals.

These observations reveal a contradiction in views such as those Kautz espouses. His worry is that claims to equal concern and respect call on the community to teach citizens what to think. That is, if public policies mandate equal treatment for those who adhere to unpopular beliefs and practices, the community thereby inculcates values that promote equal respect. Yet the policy of exchanging toleration for silence also teaches citizens what to think, in this case inculcating and reinforcing dominant understandings of traditions. This policy inculcates values that can be used to measure the legitimacy of private beliefs and desires against the communal consensus, eliciting and rewarding some beliefs and practices but discouraging and stigmatizing others. Kautz cannot have it both ways. As it is, he conveys the impression that teaching citizens what to think is abhorrent when the process inculcates equal respect for beliefs and practices repugnant to the majority.

But teaching citizens what to think is apparently acceptable and desirable when it promotes beliefs and practices that reinforce the current consensus on these matters. When "don't ask, don't tell" was in force, for example, the prohibition against openness about one's same-sex attraction not only exchanged toleration for silence but also conveyed the unspoken message that heterosexuality was a superior status.

A kernel of truth does exist, however, in concerns such as Kautz's. As chapter 2 describes in discussing the work of Chai Feldblum and Anna Elisabetta Galeotti, the existence of antidiscrimination laws does suggest that particular beliefs and practices are legitimate as part of the so-called normal range of options viable in a liberal society and that they should be treated as such. In William N. Eskridge Jr.'s terms they are benign variations (Eskridge 1999, 10, 293). Although Kautz correctly recognizes that protecting unpopular practices in a sense legitimates them, he fails to recognize that reinforcing the dominant consensus is also nonneutral, just in the opposite direction. The recognition of a varied range of options as legitimate, moreover, is less likely to teach citizens what to think than is the continued inculcation of a dominant consensus combined with grudging tolerance of those who are different. Objections to gay military service again illustrate this point. Military opponents of reform in Britain claimed that reform would constitute "coercive interference in their way of life," whereas American opposition has been grounded in the idea that people should not be forced to accept homosexuality (Frank 2009, 143, 164). "Forced" here means being compelled to work alongside known gays or lesbians. It does not mean being forced personally to accept the legitimacy of same-sex attraction, any more than being required to work alongside someone of a different religion means being forced personally to acknowledge that this individual's religion is on par with one's own. In the 1993 congressional hearings on gays in the military, some opponents mentioned that some service members find serving with gays morally and religiously unacceptable, as well as believing it to infringe on their religious rights, as Frank summarizes (89, 106–7). We do not, however, have religious rights against being forced to work alongside those who are different regarding either religion or sexual orientation. As Spinner-Halev asserts, we do not have to think everyone is equal; we need only to treat them equally in public institutions, whether the armed forces or the institution of civil marriage.

This dynamic suggests a behavioralistic approach to the formation of attitudes. As liberal citizens, we must treat people as equals in the public square, whatever our private opinions, but over time our behavior can

influence our opinions. L. A. Kosman recalls that in Aristotle's moral philosophy virtues are dispositions toward feelings as well as toward actions. We
may initially decide to act virtuously in a particular situation for prudential
reasons, without the proper moral disposition, but in time this sort of action
may become habitual. Although we do not directly or deliberately choose
our feelings, Kosman says, "a person may act in certain ways that are char-
acteristically and naturally associated with a certain range of feelings, and
through these actions acquire the virtue that is the disposition for having the
feelings directly. Acts are chosen, virtues and feelings follow in their wake"
(Kosman 1980, 112). Some of the hard work of liberal citizenship, then, is
accomplished by behaving as liberal citizens should behave, regardless of our
current feelings. As Spinner-Halev states, "Habituated to treat others equally
or at least civilly, liberal citizens may begin to look upon others equally or
civilly" (Spinner 1994, 48).

Kosman's and Spinner-Halev's accounts suggest that public policy that
focuses on individuals' behavior does indirectly, on some level, teach people
what to think. Individuals do not form, revise, or affirm their existing beliefs
in a vacuum; they do so within a particular context. A context in which a
range of options concerning religion or sexuality is recognized as legitimate
will shape people's convictions as well as their behavior; so also will policy
that reinforces the dominant consensus, combined with grudging tolerance
of dissenting beliefs and practice. However, if I am correct in arguing that
neither strategy is neutral, we must pick the type of nonneutrality that we
believe to be most congruent with the ideals of a liberal democratic society.
To me, this nonneutrality means recognition and equal respect for a diversity of beliefs, practices, and ways of life that society has deemed permissible,
whether or not these are in favor with the majority. Insisting on the recognition and respect that constitute civic equality does not repay generosity with
contempt. Rather, it reflects the intuition that liberal democratic citizens
should not be divided between insiders and outsiders, a distinction that is
surely a public expression of civic inequality.

Consigning benign sexual variation, as Eskridge calls it (1999, 293),
to a regimen of "don't ask, don't tell" is unworthy of a liberal democratic
polity. In the next two sections I consider the nature of conscientious belief and argue that its protection may not only require the removal of barriers to practices that flow from it, but also require positive action through
public policy.

The Right of Conscience

The extent to which religious and arguably sexual expression carry deep meaning for individuals is well expressed by Nussbaum. In her view, the religion clauses of the First Amendment protect a tradition not only of liberty of both belief and conduct, but also of the equal liberty necessary for civic equality or equal standing in the community. She explains, "The argument for religious liberty and equality in the tradition begins from a special respect for the faculty in human beings with which they search for life's ultimate meaning." This faculty is conscience. Because it is both precious and vulnerable, it "needs a protected space around it within which people can pursue their search for life's meaning (or not pursue it, if they choose). Government should guarantee that protected space" (Nussbaum 2008, 19; see 18–25, 52–53; Nussbaum 2000, 342). Nussbaum draws heavily on Roger Williams's idea "that all human beings are of equal worth in virtue of their inner capacity for moral striving and choice, and that all human beings, whoever and whatever they are, are owed equal respect" (Nussbaum 2008, 45). Although the seventeenth-century charter for Williams's new colony of Rhode Island prohibited civil disturbance emanating from the violation of others' rights or from breaches of public order and morality, it also nullified the applicability of laws to individuals in cases where it threatened their religious liberty (49–50). Williams believed that conscience, in Nussbaum's words, might be "damaged and crushed." Persecution is equivalent to imprisonment when it denies individuals the breathing space to act according to their consciences, and it is what Williams called "soule rape," for, as Nussbaum explains, "it goes inside a person and does terrible damage" (53–54; see 53–58). Because conscience is a precious faculty in every human being, it deserves equal respect in all, orthodox and unorthodox believers alike.

Nussbaum observes that Williams believed the individual conscience, not organized religion, to be responsible for personal salvation. Summarizing Williams, Nussbaum explains that "peace is in jeopardy only to the extent that churches overstep their boundaries and start making civil law, or interfering with people's property, livelihood, and liberty" (Nussbaum 2008, 60; see 59–68, 91–97; Feldman 2006, 36–37). Nussbaum's interpretation implies that an establishment of religion, whether single or nonpreferential, is problematic not only for the usual reason that civil authority is likely to favor some citizens over others. It can also give religious authorities and their communities undue influence over civil law, thereby violating the consciences of those who must obey laws with which they disagree. Absent establishment, conscience is guarded by the protected space that constitutes equal liberty for all, that is, the free exercise of religion. Feldman explains that the First Amendment eventually required two clauses "because the framers understood that there was a difference between making somebody do something against his will and stopping him from doing something he wanted to do" (Feldman 2006, 49–50). The influence of religious authority on the exercise of civil power can compel individuals in both the positive and negative senses that Feldman describes.

"In short," Nussbaum says, "for Williams the civil state has a moral foundation, but a moral foundation need not be, and must not be, a religious foundation" (Nussbaum 2008, 64). Like others of his time, "he favored laws against adultery and other so-called morals laws. Not, however, on religious grounds" (49–50). Williams's conception of equal liberty, or space for discernment exercised by the individual conscience, goes beyond many historical understandings of the free exercise of religion. First, his perspicacity compares favorably with later notions that morality derives only from religion. Feldman explains that the common schools that developed in the nineteenth-century United States were premised on the conviction that the schools should teach moral values and espouse nonsectarianism, "the claim that there were moral principles shared in common by all Christian sects, independent of their particular theological beliefs" (Feldman 2006, 61; see 57–92). Viewed by Roman Catholics as "sectarian Protestantism in disguise," in Feldman's words (63), the theory of nonsectarianism denied any reliance on particular religious values, yet propounded a supposedly nonsectarian faith as a necessary grounding for civic morality. "Nonsectarianism, in other words, was an ideology of inclusiveness that was fully prepared to exclude" (85; see also 83). The dominant but unstated assumptions that animate American secularism have historically been Protestant. Concerning the regulation of sexuality, Janet Jakobsen and Ann Pellegrini observe, "the secular state understands itself to be doing so not in the name of religion per se, but in the cause of a universal morality. And yet, time and again, particular religious interpretations provide the state's last best defense for its policies concerning sex" (Jakobsen and Pellegrini 2004, 22; see also 13, 21–22, 31, 47, 104, 109–14).

The controversy over nonsectarianism is instructive in the context of same-sex marriage. Although religious solemnization of marriage became optional as the government extended its regulatory arm over the institution, in 1646 the Massachusetts Puritans prohibited clergy from officiating altogether, flouting the Anglican establishment in favor of civil magistrates. Although clerical authority was restored in 1691, civil marriage remained an option unknown in England, one that spread to other colonies. "With the rise of nonsectarian ideology, however, . . . the same government that taught morals through nonsectarian religion in the public schools could be said to uphold the morals of a good Christian life through the institution of marriage." The quasi-religious character even of civil marriage exemplifies Gordon Babst's "shadow establishment," as "words like 'sacred' increasingly attached to the legally sanctioned institution, not to the formal religious solemnization of marriage," Feldman explains. "If marriage was a moral bulwark for republican society, then it had a religious component, even if it could be administered by a justice of the peace or a city clerk" (Feldman 2006, 105; see 101–5). This mélange of sacred and civil elements allowed the courts to prohibit Mormon polygamy, despite its essentially religious character, as antithetical to the civil contract as the government envisioned it. The exclusion of polygamy (discussed in detail later in this chapter) and of same-sex couples from the institution of civil marriage illustrates Feldman's point about the importance of the free exercise clause. That is, despite the fact that couples are not compelled to do anything against their wills, they are prohibited from doing something that they want to do. Although civil marriage is supposed to be a nonsectarian institution, through the "shadow establishment" of its quasi-religious elements it is still "fully prepared to exclude" (85; see also 83).

A second noteworthy point about Williams lies in a key distinction between him and John Locke concerning religious accommodation. Although Locke wrote that a church or religious body may rightly expel individuals at odds with its religious principles, he said that "no private Person has any Right, in any manner, to prejudice another Person in his Civil Enjoyments, because he is of another Church or Religion. All the Rights and Franchises that belong to him as a Man, or as a Denison [denizen], are inviolably to be preserved to him. These are not the Business of Religion" (Locke 1689, 31). However, despite Locke's advocacy of civil toleration for diverse religious practices, for him the line between the civil and the religious is subject to civil determination rather than conscientious belief. Locke asserted that with a government directed toward the public good, the situation should seldom arise, yet an individual who is commanded by the magistrate or government to do something concerning worldly or civil matters that offends his conscience may "abstain from the Action that he judges unlawful." Nevertheless, "he is to undergo the Punishment, which it is not unlawful for him to bear. For the private judgment of any Person concerning a Law enacted in Political Matters, for the publick Good, does not take away the Obligation of that Law, nor deserve a Dispensation" (Locke 1689, 48; see 48–50; McClure 1990, 373–81). That is, Locke said, society does not need to tolerate practices that are forbidden in civil law just because they have a religious justification. Animal sacrifice, for example, should not be forbidden as a religious rite if animals may be killed for food. However, if a magistrate were to forbid the killing of cattle for secular reasons, such as species endangerment, "who sees not that the Magistrate, in such a case, may forbid all his subjects to kill any Calves for any use whatsoever?" (Locke 1689, 42; see also Nussbaum 2008, 60–61, 67, 122). The prohibition here is not religiously based; it is a political or civil regulation that happens to affect religious practice.

For Williams, in contrast, religious liberty trumps the application of law and custom. Nussbaum explains his view: "If a law says that people have to testify on Saturday, and your religion forbids this, then that law is inapplicable in your case. . . . Laws of general applicability have force only up to the point where they threaten religious liberty (and public order and safety are not at stake)" (Nussbaum 2008, 50; see also 60–61, 66–67). When religious conscience is at stake, then generally individuals should neither be compelled to act against their wills nor be prohibited from acting in accordance with their wills. Nussbaum observes that "the difference between Locke and Williams on this point anticipates the difference between Justice [Antonin] Scalia and former Justice [Sandra Day] O'Connor (and others) over the issue of a judicial role in mandating accommodations" that facilitate the free exercise of religion (67). From Locke's perspective, a generally applicable measure forbidding the consumption of alcohol, such as Prohibition in the United States, should not allow exceptions for wine used in religious sacraments. Although Prohibition was enacted for secular reasons and reflected no animus toward religious practice, without the religious exemption it would have affected this practice nonetheless. Williams's approach, in contrast, is sensitive to the imperatives of both belief and practice.

Although Williams provides religious exemptions where Locke does not, what is admirable about both Williams and Locke is that both eschew partiality toward the dominant religion and support equal liberty for many of those whose beliefs and practices are unpopular. Religious or sexual practices that appear strange or morally objectionable to the majority are too often banned or penalized under the rationale that they threaten civil order. If civic equality is to be achieved, equal liberty does not require boundless accommodation for the free exercise of religion, but rather evenhandedness in the accommodations that are granted. Moreover, although Nussbaum observes that the First Amendment "does make religion (whatever that includes) special for the purposes of the Free Exercise Clause, fair or unfair," the phrase "whatever that includes" opens the door to a broader interpretation of liberty of conscience (Nussbaum 2008, 102; see also Marcosson 2009, 137–42). If the argument for religious liberty and equality is grounded on "respect for the faculty in human beings with which they search for life's ultimate meaning" (Nussbaum 2008, 19), this faculty may pertain to more than what we think of as conventionally religious values.

Spinner-Halev speculates that exemptions in support of people's core beliefs and practices might be extended to ethnic groups and other kinds of associations. "If we treat religion as a special source of exemption, why not other groups?" Although religious believers' convictions that they will go to hell if they act against their conscientious beliefs suggest drastic consequences, nonbelievers may also experience internal trauma if forced to act against their consciences (Spinner-Halev 2000, 207–14; Eisgruber and Sager 2007, 100–104). In contrast, Brian Barry says that cultural or religious exemptions from generally applicable laws simply result from pressures by special interest groups that politicians find irresistible. "Usually, . . . either the case for the law (or some version of it) is strong enough to rule out exemptions, or the case that can be made for exemptions is strong enough to suggest that there should be no law anyway" (Barry 2001, 39). Overall, it is by no means obvious that religion as conventionally understood is special—or that *only* religion as conventionally understood is special.

Nussbaum's interpretation of equal liberty focuses on equality between mainstream religions and those not accepted on the same terms as others. Christopher Eisgruber and Lawrence Sager are more attuned to self-defining commitments that may not be conventionally religious. They take issue with the paradox that under the dominant interpretation of the separation of church and state, the Constitution simultaneously confers special benefits and imposes special burdens or disabilities on religious practice. Christians could use wine in religious sacraments during Prohibition, for example, but religious enterprises have traditionally been deprived of public funding accessible to secular enterprises with similar purposes. Eisgruber and Sager's conception of equal liberty, on the contrary, "denies that religion is a constitutional anomaly, a category of human experience that demands special benefits and/or necessitates special restrictions" (Eisgruber and Sager 2007, 6). We often arrive at wrong answers about religious freedom, they suggest, because we ask the wrong questions. Where standard interpretations of separation "ask how government should behave toward religion," their version of equal liberty "asks how government should treat persons who have diverse commitments regarding religion (including, in some cases, a commitment to reject religion) and for whom those commitments are important components of identity and well-being" (53). The constitutional rights of individuals to follow their consciences, Eisgruber and Sager maintain, should not "vary according to the spiritual foundations of their beliefs. This result seems unjust on its face, and it also seems at odds with the essence of religious freedom in that it imposes a test of religious orthodoxy as a condition of constitutional entitlement" (11; see 8–14, 54–56). The same can be said of individual conscience in the face of sexual orthodoxy.

However, Eisgruber and Sager do not seek to create equal liberty for those with diverse commitments by lowering the ceiling or clamping down on constitutional protection for those whose motivations are traditionally religious. They prefer, rather, to lower the floor, or to institute a lower threshold of protection for the unconventionally religious or the nonreligious than is currently typical. Like Nussbaum they argue "that minority religious practices, needs, and interests must be as well and as favorably accommodated by government as are more familiar and mainstream interests" (Eisgruber and Sager 2007, 13). Where Nussbaum might favor conventionally religious requests for accommodation but not those rooted in altruistic but secular motivations, Eisgruber and Sager want to accommodate either both or neither. For them religious practice should be neither benefited nor burdened simply because it is conventionally religious. They believe that this policy will increase both the equality and liberty of those with diverse commitments that are central to their identities. Individuals who feel conscientiously unable to comply with particular laws face similar civil sanctions, whether their objections are religiously or secularly derived. Eisgruber and Sager conclude, "Equal Liberty's nondiscrimination principle requires that the state show equal regard for the religious and nonreligious needs of citizens when it distributes these burdens—by which we mean the burdens of civil law, the only burdens that the state has any power to impose" (104).

If one takes Nussbaum's lesson that equal liberty should be accorded to unpopular as well as mainstream religious practices, combined with Eisgruber and Sager's lesson that equal liberty should apply to all conscientious commitments, conventionally religious or not, complications remain. Neutrality always requires a context. Here conscientious commitments are advantaged over desires that are not thus grounded. In *Thornton v. Calder* (105 S. Ct. 2914 [1985]), for example, the Supreme Court struck down a Connecticut statute that guaranteed to sabbath observers a weekly entitlement of one day off on their sabbath. The court believed that the law unfairly advantaged sabbath observers over nonobservers, because only the former could select a coveted weekend day for their guaranteed day off. In *Sherbert v. Verner* (374 U.S. 398 [1963]), however, the court overruled the denial of state unemployment compensation to a Seventh-Day Adventist for refusing to work on her sabbath, which is Saturday. As Michael Sandel observes, a state attending to sabbath observance does not in this view violate neutrality but rather enforces it in the light of religious differences. To force workers to choose between their religious convictions and their means of support would advantage those without religious duties over those with duties whose exercise may conflict with secular expectations (Sandel 1987, 88–90; see also Nussbaum 2008, 135–40).

These two cases, *Thornton* and *Sherbert*, exemplify alternative meanings of freedom of conscience. In Kirstie McClure's terms, as discussed in chapter 2, the set of social facts grounding *Thornton* classifies sabbath observance as a choice; therefore, according more freedom to observant workers than to nonobservant workers in selecting a day off is not a civilly benign practice but is civilly injurious to people with less choice: that is, those who cannot claim religious observance as a justification for choice. The set of social facts grounding *Sherbert*, however, classifies sabbath observance as a duty; thus, allowing observant workers to refuse to work on their sabbath without forfeiting unemployment benefits is civilly benign across the board. Although applicants must accept available work to be eligible for benefits, sabbath work is not available in the sense that observant workers may choose to perform it. In view of these social facts it is civilly injurious to penalize sabbath-observant workers, who have less choice than do the nonobservant, who can accept available work at any time.

Central here is that under either interpretation of these cases, somebody loses. Why, nonobservers wonder, should sabbath beliefs be privileged through exemptions granted for practices flowing from them, when other types of deeply held beliefs are not? An individual who believes life means nothing without Sunday football games exhibits a practice rooted in a deeply held belief—but not a belief rooted in conscience. Even if all conscientious beliefs are accorded equal treatment, in the end the "magistrate," in Locke's terms, often influenced by a dominant consensus, must still determine what is and is not an instance of conscientious belief. Equal liberty exists only within a context that defines the circumstances or situations that require equal treatment. David Richards, with whom I agree, says that the traditional viewpoint about the unacceptability of same-sex relationships is a violation of the right of conscience, of "intimately personal moral resources" that are among central constituents of identity (Richards 1999, 74). As a citizen of a liberal polity, I argue that the ban on civil marriage for same-sex couples in most jurisdictions denies to those who want to marry a moral entitlement to make the same public commitment that is already available to countless numbers of traditional couples. I do not claim that this stance is neutral. I do claim that permitting civil marriage to same-sex couples, like permitting the free exercise of religion to practitioners of unconventional religions or no religion, is a necessary component of civic equality.

Identity Politics, Religion, and Sexuality

Equating sexual orientation and its expression with religious allegiance and its practice does not lack controversy. Andrew Murphy argues that Richards's "expansive view of toleration and conscience" equates conscience with personal autonomy and therefore requires a much broader conception of the private sphere than traditional interpretations of toleration require (Murphy 2001, 29; see also 33–37, 41, 43). Murphy explains that claims of conscience by New England dissenters such as Williams and Anne Hutchinson were rooted in theological individualism and did not necessarily implicate a more general liberty of conscience. Matters with religious roots might also affect public order, as shown in Nussbaum's expansive interpretation of Williams's philosophy. Thus, Murphy concludes, "disputes fall within either the sphere of conscience *or* the civil sphere, and issues having a deleterious effect on civil peace leave the realm of conscience in their very essence" (52). Historically, tolerationists simply desired the negative liberty of noncoercion and state neutrality. "They did not praise autonomy for its own sake," Murphy explains, "but only in contexts in which it enabled one to act in religiously responsible ways to secure the ultimate good of personal salvation," or in which it created "a public space in which individuals and groups of differing persuasions could live out their own conceptions of religious truth and the demands it placed on human life" (240, 242).

Central to the meaning of toleration are historically competing views of the meaning of conscience or of conscientious belief. To the Massachusetts Puritans who expelled Roger Williams, explains Murphy, only individuals who are afflicted, or persecuted, for objectively correct beliefs truly experience persecution. If one is mistaken even sincerely, one is not righteous and therefore is not truly persecuted, meaning afflicted for the sake of one's objectively righteous views (Murphy 2001, 49–50; see also 111, 227–28).

Early tolerationists such as Williams, Locke, and William Penn, however, increasingly adhered to a subjective understanding of conscience, according to which even the affliction of objectively false beliefs or practices constituted persecution. Murphy summarizes, "Since conscience was a faculty of the understanding and not of the will, it could not be coerced into believing one thing or another" (228; see also 112). In the colonies liberty of conscience thus became grounded in religious voluntarism, or the conviction that one should not only worship correctly but also do so voluntarily. Moreover, "voluntarism is not the same thing, strictly speaking, as *choice*: in other words, tolerationists did not claim that one *chose* one's beliefs, but rather that the understanding was persuaded, inexorably so, of the truth of a given faith" (229; see also 254).

Murphy's conscience paradigm both extends the notion of conscience to nonreligious standards of morality and also includes its increasingly subjective character. "For all its change over the years, then, conscience remains a term denoting the belief structures (whatever their source or foundation) by which individuals decide upon and judge their actions" (Murphy 2001, 278). Despite changes "conscience-based politics boils down to the claim that states must recognize individuals' beliefs and values about truth and the good . . . as sacrosanct. . . . Within the parameters of civil peace and social order, government must grant liberty to act on those values, as a necessary corollary to the free workings of the human mind" (279). This conception of conscience is broad enough, I believe, to encompass not only religious convictions but also other core facets of moral personality such as culture and sexuality.

Murphy argues that contemporary issues concerning race, gender, and sexual orientation belong under the rubric of identity politics rather than liberty of conscience. Where the conscience paradigm requires equal treatment before the law and the removal of barriers implicit in the concept of negative liberty, identity politics "instead argues for a positive commitment to equal respect between social groups and even the affirmation and celebration of difference *per se*" (Murphy 2001, 281). He suggests that the concerns for authenticity and respect that characterize identity politics, often grounded in ascribed characteristics, do not fit well into a conscience paradigm based on freedom to believe (282). The conscience paradigm valorizes neither neutrality nor the pursuit of self-respect "but instead the promotion of a pacific public space in which citizens can live out their deepest beliefs" (287).

However, Murphy admits that because beliefs about ultimate truth, religious or not, are foundational in one's sense of self, "conscience contains within it at least a latent notion of identity" (Murphy 2001, 281), although the two concepts imply distinct sociopolitical agendas. He wrote in 2001 that the then potential reversal of the Supreme Court's decision to uphold Georgia's criminalization of sodomy, *Bowers v. Hardwick* (478 U.S. 186 [1986]), would represent a minimal baseline of toleration from which further discussion about the requirements of liberal citizenship might proceed (288). In 2003 this reversal occurred in *Lawrence v. Texas* (539 U.S. 558 [2003]). Therefore, I maintain that the desire of same-sex couples to participate in the institution of civil marriage comprises both the search for tolerance rooted in conscience politics and also the search for recognition and equal respect that Murphy associates with identity politics.

Although Murphy suggests that the emphasis on ascribed characteristics that often describes identity politics is ill suited to the conscience paradigm based on religious voluntarism, he also states that religious voluntarism should not be interpreted to denote one's choice of beliefs, but rather one's understanding that a particular set of beliefs is true. A fault line exists here that pertains to discussions of both religious belief and sexuality. Same-sex attraction is understood by most scholars as an innate and unchosen predisposition (e.g., Stein 1999, 258–74), and in this sense it functions as an ascribed characteristic. Sexual orientation suggests a particular type of attraction and a corresponding disposition to engage in certain kinds of behavior. For Feldblum, as chapter 2 explains, certain practices flow from given religious beliefs or sexual orientation—practices that are necessary to bring meaning to these facets of identity (Feldblum 2008, 142–43, 123–24). Whether individuals experience opposite-sex attraction, same-sex attraction, or both, they may choose either to act upon or not to act upon the attraction they experience or their understanding of their sexuality. Babst goes even further, maintaining that heteronormativity, or the idea that heterosexuality is the norm, misleads us to assume that the world is divided into two kinds of people. He suggests instead that heterosexuality's alternative is human sexual pluralism, premised on the assumption "that human beings are sexual beings, not types of sexual beings" (Babst 2009, 185; see 183–90). Either way, like the human capacity for religious experience, the human capacity for sexual intimacy typically takes different forms for different individuals.

Considering individuals who choose a celibate life may elucidate the relationship between sexuality and behavior. Although celibacy may be a function of circumstance, as seen in the loss or absence of a partner, it may also result from choice, as seen in decisions to join certain religious orders or to foreswear intimate relationships for any number of personal reasons. But the decision to live a celibate life does not indicate that these individuals possess no capacity for sexual intimacy. They may simply hold other values in higher regard. Although their capacity for sexual intimacy is an innate and objective condition, their deployment of this orientation is a matter of choice. When individuals do not opt to live celibate lives, in contrast, their behaviors and practices flow from their capacity for sexual intimacy, whether their specific attraction is to persons of the opposite sex, the same sex, or both. In Murphy's terms their understandings are inexorably persuaded of the truth that one type of expression of this capacity, not another, defines that aspect of their selfhoods. In his dissent in *Bowers v. Hardwick*, Justice Harry Blackmun suggested that when we protect rights to family relationships, we do so because they are so central to individual life and happiness. "The fact that individuals define themselves in a significant way through their intimate sexual relationships with others suggests, in a Nation as diverse as ours, that there may be many 'right' ways of conducting these relationships, and that much of the richness of a relationship will come from the freedom an individual has to *choose* the form and nature of these intensely personal bonds" (Bowers v. Hardwick, 478 U.S. 186 [1986], at 204–5).

This point may invite an interpretation that militates against my overall comparison of religion and sexuality as central facets of identity that individuals should be able to own publicly. Some conservative Christians regard acting on same-sex attraction as a sinful choice. As Andrew Sullivan notes, in 1986 the Roman Catholic church through Cardinal Joseph Ratzinger, now Pope Benedict XVI, acknowledged that because same-sex attraction is an innate predisposition or unchosen condition, it cannot be a sin, and the dignity of individuals who experience it should be protected (Sullivan 1996, 38–40). For the Catholic church, nevertheless, the tendency toward a morally evil practice is itself an "objective disorder." Thus, although the Catholic church now recognizes nonmajority sexual orientation as a central constituent of human identity, those who experience same-sex attraction must still eschew same-sex relationships to remain in its good graces. As Sullivan explains, the church asks us "to love the sinner more deeply than ever before, but to hate the sin even more passionately" (40; see 38–43). When I suggest that a person may be persuaded of the truth of certain religious beliefs or of a particular sexual orientation as constituents of identity, but also that acting on one's beliefs or sexual orientation is a matter of choice, religious conservatives may seize upon this distinction to encourage celibacy, or at least the closet as Finnis suggests, for those who experience same-sex attraction.

I categorically reject this gloss, as my thrust is in the opposite direction. That is, although those with unconventional religious beliefs or minority sexual orientations can certainly decide not engage in the religious or sexual practices that typically flow from these beliefs or orientations, or to engage in them only in the closet, absent direct harm to assignable others the civil authorities should not saddle them with these expectations, either explicitly or implicitly. Even without the overt persecution that Williams likened to imprisonment and "soule rape," legal or even moral pressure can affect the context within which individuals live out their religious, and I would add sexual, identities. If practice is necessary to bring meaning to core facets of identity, pressure to renounce or strictly circumscribe legally acceptable practices makes a mockery of what purports to be acceptance.

As an example, the military policy of "don't ask, don't tell" purported to target not status or orientation, but only conduct or practice. In its application, however, once an individual's status was known, he or she was deemed to have a propensity to engage in same-sex relationships, interpreted as a likelihood that this activity would occur. Although the individual had an opportunity to rebut this presumption, the burden was on the service member essentially to prove a negative, because military officials were directed not to accept a member's simple assurance that he or she was unlikely to engage in sexual activity with those of the same sex. Frank concludes, "While lawyers can argue that 'don't ask, don't tell' targets only conduct, it clearly targets status" (Frank 2009, 177; see 173–78). Similarly, although the Roman Catholic church objects only to conduct, not to orientation, it nevertheless deems the tendency or propensity toward this conduct to be an objective disorder and the actions that flow from it therefore to be blameworthy. This interface between status and conduct is ironic in view of the emphasis that religion typically places on practice as well as belief. As Jakobsen and Pellegrini explain, "For both individuals and communities . . . religion is never a matter solely of text and belief, but crucially involves—one could even say is instantiated by—practice" (Jakobsen and Pellegrini 2004, 99; see also 99–101; 125–26; Eskridge 1999, 296–97; Feldblum 2008, 142–49).

These examples demonstrate that as core aspects of identity, neither religious belief and practice nor sexual orientation and conduct can be separated as readily as one may assume. If human religious expression and sexual expression are both forms of intimate self-expression (Erdos 2005, 21), the acceptance of unpopular but benign manifestations of this expression is a necessary component of civic equality. My point about religious practice and sexual conduct being choices is intended not to facilitate the imposition of straitjackets, but on the contrary to enable those experiencing same-sex attraction to exercise autonomy and to resist essentializing pressures, such as those that often face women. Women must possess the ability to reject traditional roles and self-definitions. But they must also be able to affirm traditional roles if they so choose, after questioning and examining them in a context that presents them with genuine alternatives. Those experiencing same-sex attraction must have similar choices. Like heterosexuals they may decide to eschew committed relationships, to remain unpartnered, or even to practice celibacy. But they must also be able to sustain committed relationships through civil unions or domestic partnerships or to marry, if they choose, on the same terms as committed traditional couples. Patricia Boling suggests, "Assuming an essentialized identity based on intimate affiliations or decisions . . . renders the diversity of people's experiences invisible and places normalizing pressures on different or dissenting group members" (Boling 1996, 79).

As with religion, one's understanding may be inexorably persuaded, in Murphy's terms (2001, 229), that opposite-sex attraction, same-sex attraction, or bisexual attraction describes one's capacity for sexual intimacy. One then affirms this understanding by acting on it. This conduct, however, is still a matter of choice because one could have acted otherwise. Nevertheless, because one's choices of religious practice or sexual conduct, whatever they may be, flow from central constituents of identity, thwarting them without compelling reasons may indeed be equated with the "soule rape" of which Williams speaks, as described by Nussbaum. Choice need not mean choosing from a menu of ice cream flavors from which one is detached. Instead, choice is the outcome of an understanding of identity of which one is inexorably persuaded, whether in the realm of religion or of sexuality.

The tension that Murphy highlights between choice and understanding resonates with a key distinction made by Sandel. To Sandel, autonomy theorists, who often appear to view the individual as an unsituated, autonomous chooser, impoverish the self by emphasizing the voluntarist dimension of human agency, "in which the self is related to its ends as a willing subject to the object of choice," at the expense of the cognitive dimension, "in which the self is related to its ends as a knowing subject to the objects of understanding" (Sandel 1982, 58; see 57–58). Because we are "subjects constituted in part by our central aspirations and attachments" (172), human agency requires the self not only to choose but also to reflect, "to turn its light inward upon itself, to inquire into its constituent nature, to survey its various attachments and acknowledge their respective claims . . . to arrive at a self-understanding less opaque if never perfectly transparent, a subjectivity fluid if never finally fixed, and so gradually through a lifetime, to participate in the constitution of its identity" (153). Because the self is made up of past reflections and experiences, it cannot experience freedom from constitutive ends and interests without being disempowered and actually dissolved, in Sandel's estimation.

This simply means that we cannot constantly start afresh as we approach life decisions, uninfluenced and unencumbered by past reflections and experiences (Gill 2001, 19, 37). But past reflections and experiences are not dispositive in our decisions. Rational scrutiny and self-examination may lead us as autonomous persons to affirm our past convictions in light of current developments, or the current developments may induce us to review our long-standing convictions and to act differently. Either way, we act from reasons that are authentically ours. When Sandel's self looks inward, surveys its constituent attachments, and acknowledges their respective claims, this rational scrutiny is performed by a self influenced by past experiences, but also with a reality apart from its apparently constitutive ends. Otherwise, its attachments would be fixed and unable to be ranked and ordered. Thus even Sandel's self is autonomous in itself. The voluntarist and cognitive dimensions of agency are not competitive then, as Sandel sometimes implies (Sandel 1982, 58), but complementary, necessary both to individual self-definition and the individual exercise of human moral powers. Moreover, the two dimensions of agency reinforce each other. If preferences and traits, projects and goals, have been endorsed or affirmed by an agent, they have in some sense been chosen. Yet, once affirmed, they become constitutive of the agent, although potentially subject to reexamination, and thus become the ground or standpoint from which subsequent choices are made.

Therefore, although it is generally agreed that gender identity and sexual orientation can be physically embedded in a way that cultural identity and religious orientation are not, I believe our self-interpretation of our sexual identities, like that of our cultural and religious identities, is in many contexts worthy of positive protection as a manifestation of conscientious belief. Arguing for the extent to which the categorization of sexual desire is socially constructed, Nussbaum notes that social construction "is far less adequate as an account of how particular social actors come to inhabit the categories they do inhabit" (Nussbaum 1997, 30; see 25–31). That is, something about sexual desire cannot be reduced to social or cultural construction, although it is influenced by society and culture. Georgia Warnke, in contrast, maintains that conflicted legal and social understandings of what makes individuals men or women—whether genes, hormones, secondary sexual characteristics, or ostensibly characteristic behaviors—indicate that gender identity is far less fixed than we tend to imagine (Warnke 2007, 27–48, 169–79). Either way, although the individual is situated within a particular context that provides background conditions for the exercise of agency, the individual's existence diminishes neither the centrality of agency in realizing core features of moral personality nor the need for positive protection for some of its manifestations.

Because sexual expression, like religion, may in Murphy's terms implicate personal beliefs about truth and the good, it also fits under the rubric of conscience-based politics. As voluntary organizations, religious groups may decide for themselves which unions to celebrate. The Roman Catholic church, for example, does not preside at the marriages of divorced persons unless they have first secured annulments through the church. However, the state, by depriving same-sex couples of the ability to participate in the civil institution of marriage when opposite-sex couples may do so, confers on same-sex couples a mark of second-class citizenship through its selective abridgment of the free exercise of conscience. Moreover, if freedom of conscience means freedom of belief and generally of practice, it also implies freedom to be open about what one's beliefs and practices are. As Kenji Yoshino argues, "So long as there is a *right to be* a particular kind of person, I believe it logically and morally follows there is a *right to say what one is*" (Yoshino 2007, 70).

Some view same-sex marriage as a kind of assimilation, because it makes same-sex couples more like straight couples. For this reason traditionalist proponents of same-sex marriage support it, whereas queer and feminist skeptics and some libertarians oppose it, as chapter 3 explains. For Yoshino, however, advocating for or participating in same-sex marriage can be a type of flaunting, an assertion that same-sex couples can publicly claim the same rights as traditional couples (91; see also 18; Hull 2006, 69–77, 142–51). Whatever one's internal motivation for attempting to marry, I argue that the public commitment represented by civil marriage is the ultimate act of "saying what one is." This point is more crucial because by endorsing marriage, the public's agent, the state, confers civil meaning and status on what would otherwise be a private commitment even if concluded in public.

Marriage is also an instance of what Ingrid Creppell terms "public privacy" (Creppell 1996, 226). She recalls that when Locke became convinced that the implementation of religious toleration would mitigate rather than exacerbate the dangers of religious identification, he suggested that God should be publicly worshiped through the public presentation of one's private beliefs before the larger community, despite the fact that the community witnessing this presentation was not unified in terms of belief. Such a practice would legitimate an individuation of belief by protecting public presentation from interference and by creating a buffer zone between the purely private and purely public that combines communal expression and recognition with distance and protection (Creppell 1996, 227–29).

Similarly, the participation of same-sex couples in the civil institution of marriage is—as it is for straight couples—a public presentation of identity, belief, and commitment. Marriage creates a buffer zone that shields couples, absent abuse, from interference in their private relationships, but it does so through the public affirmation of commitment in the eyes of the community. As Warnke explains, "Civil marriage entails a publicly recognized right to an involvement in one's partner's life and to protection from state interference into the relationship, short of protecting the individuals within it from violence and coercion" (Warnke 2007, 203; see 198–213). Public recognition is a precondition, in this view, for the protection of the private aspects of religious belief and practice, and this protection can be extended to sexual orientation and practice. However, when the state's protection is limited to majority expressions of conscientious belief, whether religious or sexual, equal citizenship is impossible. The protection that most jurisdictions offer only to traditional couples is an expression of heterosexism and heteronormativity, in that it excludes the conscientious commitments of same-sex couples. Therefore, given the state's recognition of traditional marriage, an evenhanded public privacy requires positive action by the state that recognizes the "public presentation" of same-sex couples if civic equality is to be achieved (Creppell 1996, 228).

If, as I argue, the deployment of one's sexuality may be considered a matter of adhering to one's conscientious beliefs, how much more so is the personal decision to undertake the ideally lifelong commitment of matrimony? Typically, one's understanding is persuaded, "inexorably so" in Murphy's terms, of the truth that only life with another particular person will fulfill life's ultimate meaning, will sustain one in the challenges of a worthwhile life, and will allow one to live out one's values about truth and the good. The religious significance of marriage has been recognized by the Supreme Court, which has noted that "many religions recognize marriage as having spiritual significance; for some . . . , the commitment of marriage may be an exercise of religious faith as well as an expression of personal dedication" (Turner v. Safley, 482 U.S. 78 [1987], at 96). The religious significance of marriage is certainly endorsed by opponents of same-sex marriage, many of whom argue against it on the grounds of traditional marriage's divine design, its universality as a human institution, or its compatibility with natural law (Kohm 2003; Gallagher 2003; George 2003). For same-sex couples, conventionally religiously inclined or not, the desire to participate in marriage as a civil institution may reflect a desire to exercise freely their religious or broader conscientious beliefs—free exercise that they view as denied by those who want to maintain traditional marriage as an exclusive institution. In typical, conscience-based politics, dissenters wish to practice religious beliefs that are different from those enshrined in and endorsed by the dominant consensus. Here, however, the dissenters wish to practice their beliefs in exactly the same way that the majority does. If the conscience paradigm promotes "a pacific public space in which citizens can live out their deepest beliefs" (Murphy 2001, 287), the quest for same-sex marriage qualifies as conscience-based politics. Benign sexual variation deserves the same recognition as benign religious variation.

Philosophical and Legal Issues: *Bowers, Lawrence,* and *Romer*

Arguing for a right of conscience to participate in marriage as a civil institution may seem problematic to some. Proponents of same-sex marriage rely on conscience as a basis for their claims, but this grounding cuts both ways. Traditionalist opponents can also maintain that their consciences force them to oppose inclusion in what they see as a time-honored, traditional institution limited to one man and one woman. However, it is one thing to maintain that my conscience impels me to live in accordance with particular convictions. It is a different matter to argue that my conscience impels me to pressure or to force others to live in accordance with them. As Mill pointed out in 1859, religious zealots often harbor "a determination not to tolerate others in doing what is permitted by their religion, because it is not permitted by the persecutor's religion," or "a belief that God not only abominates the act of the misbeliever, but will not hold us guiltless if we leave him unmolested" (91; see also 10–11). David Richards argues that the abridgment of rights of conscience must be "justified on compelling secular grounds of protecting public goods reasonably acknowledged as such by all persons," or on "a compelling public reason, not on grounds of reasons that are today sectarian (internal to a moral tradition not based on reasons available and accessible to all)" (Richards 1999, 18, 78). That is, religious grounds should not count as grounds for abridgment simply because they are religious. If they were to count as such grounds, giving more weight to your religious objections than to my own practice of conscientious beliefs implies that your religious beliefs somehow trump my own. However, the individual right of conscience as a basis for same-sex marriage can indeed comprise not only religious grounds but secular ones as well.

Traditionalist opponents of same-sex marriage argue, as chapter 3 describes, that traditional marriage as a social institution serves a public purpose that cannot be well served by same-sex marriage. They contend that a public good indeed exists, one that the state should protect by confining marriage to traditional couples. This contention makes the unwarranted assumption that a traditional interpretation of the value of marriage serves public purposes and should therefore be protected as a public good, to the exclusion of other interpretations of these purposes or goods.

I argue, however, that same-sex couples' participation in the institution of marriage is not only an expression of conscientious belief but also a public good that should be acknowledged and protected. Most agree that marriage represents the intention of making a long-term commitment to another person, animated by common interests and goals that typically include, but are not limited to, the satisfaction of sexual desire. Critics too often assume, as Richards observes, "that homosexuality, unlike heterosexuality, is exclusively about sex. It is this assumption that is, I believe, the basis for the wounded sense of outrage surrounding even the suggestion of the legitimacy of extending the humane values of the institutions that protect the dignity of heterosexual intimate life to homosexuals. Homosexuals, on this view, can no more marry than animals" (Richards 1999, 159; see also 168, 183–84, 186, 188, 192; Richards 2005, 110–11, 133, 140). In Richards's view the assumption that same-sex attraction is almost exclusively about sex also accounts for its portrayal as a consumerist model, in which individuals choose among sexual acts as they would among brands of soap, rather on the basis of the "longing and moral competence for loving and being loved that dignify the intimate lives among heterosexuals in all their variegated moral complexity" (Richards 1999, 192). Therefore, society must move from the negative liberty to conduct same-sex relationships without interference to a positive right to participate in the civil institution of marriage.

Bowers v. Hardwick, in which the Supreme Court upheld the Georgia statute criminalizing sodomy, exemplifies divergent ways to frame the debate about public purposes and a community's shared conceptions of the good. Relying on the shared goods of family relationships and of acquiescence in long-standing majority beliefs, Justice Byron White framed the issue for the court as that of whether the Constitution confers "a fundamental right to engage in homosexual sodomy" (Bowers v. Hardwick, 478 U.S. 186 [1986], at 191; see 190–96). Because *Bowers* seemed to involve none of the fundamental rights recognized in previous cases concerning family relationships, marriage, or procreation, White concluded that the defense of sodomy was not warranted under the rubric of a fundamental right. In a short concurrence Chief Justice Warren Burger alluded to the historical condemnation of sodomy in Western civilization, noting, "condemnation of these practices is firmly rooted in Judaeo-Christian moral and ethical standards" (196). However, in his dissent, Justice Blackmun suggested that we need to look not only at the types of rights that have been classified as fundamental but also at the reasons why these practices have been so designated. When the state protects rights to family relationships, it does so neither because they directly contribute to the public welfare nor because we prefer traditional households, but rather because these rights are so central to individual life and happiness. Blackmun argued that the centrality of sexual intimacy suggests that in a diverse nation "there may be many 'right' ways of conducting these relationships, and that much of the richness of a relationship will come from the freedom an individual has to *choose* the form and nature of these intensely personal bonds" (204–5; see 204–6). Blackmun explained that we need to look not simply at what rights and practices have been protected, but also at the broader purposes that these values might serve in ways previously unrecognized because of social prejudice. Moreover, historical and traditional condemnations of sodomy do not justify using the law to endorse private biases (210–12). Overall, he argued, "Depriving individuals of the right to choose for themselves how to conduct their intimate relationships poses a far greater threat to the values most deeply rooted in our Nation's history than tolerance of nonconformity could ever do" (214).

Despite their agreement with the thrust of Blackmun's dissent in *Bowers*, some commentators view it as timid or anemic. Sandel, for example, agrees with the dissent, but he argues that specific practices are better defended for their "intrinsic value or social importance" than as instances of privacy, autonomy, and individual choice (Sandel 1996, 93; see also Macedo 1990, 194–96). One might argue not only that intimate associations should be matters of individual choice, but also "that much that is valuable in conventional marriage is also present in homosexual unions. On this view, the connection between heterosexual and homosexual relations is not that both are products of individual choice but that both realize important human goods" (Sandel 1996, 104). Both provide opportunities for mutual support and self-expression in ways that other relationships do not. Sandel concludes that a neutral or autonomy-based argument is inadequate. First, the voluntarist or choice-based justification "is parasitic—politically as well as philosophically—on some measure of agreement that the practices protected are morally permissible." Second, precisely because they are not based on substance, voluntarist justifications of choice may secure merely "a thin and fragile toleration. A fuller respect would require, if not admiration, at least some appreciation of the lives homosexuals live" (107).

Agreeing with Sandel, Feldblum notes that when people who say they disapprove of same-sex relationships nevertheless support a civil rights bill that prohibits discrimination based on sexual orientation by private employers, landlords, and business owners, they often indicate that their opinions stem from a sense of fairness. Although they may not realize it, Feldblum argues, they must have undergone a shift in their moral assessment, at least "to the position that gay sexual activity is not so morally problematic that employers may justifiably use that activity as the basis for granting or withholding job opportunities" (Feldblum 2009, 211; see 205–11; Feldblum 2008, 131). Feldblum believes that extending the discussion of gay rights to the area of moral values facilitates more open communication and greater respect among those with different substantive moral views. In this context she alludes to the 2004 election exit polls that indicated the predominance of so-called values voters who emphasized moral values—defined as opposition to abortion and same-sex marriage—over economic and foreign policy issues in their voting decisions. "The reality is that social conservatives have been incredibly successful with promoting *their* moral values (as moral values) in the public discourse" (Feldblum 2009, 212). Feldblum concludes that supporters of gay rights, including supporters of same-sex marriage, therefore need to claim these values in terms of their meaning for the equality of gay, lesbian, bisexual, and transgender persons.

I agree with Feldblum's point that traditionalists should not and do not hold a monopoly on moral values. However, casting equality and the free exercise of one's conscientious beliefs in terms of substantive moral values may also work against gays, lesbians, and bisexuals who do not want to undertake long-term commitments. Although the range of justifications for a given practice may expand if its "intrinsic value or social importance" can be demonstrated, as Sandel describes, we might correspondingly withhold or withdraw social acceptance from a legal practice with no perceived value (Sandel 1996, 93). If the value or importance of something is rooted in the dominant understanding of a particular community's traditions, that understanding will be used to measure the legitimacy of individuals' private beliefs and desires, protecting them in some instances but leaving them vulnerable in others. Moreover, a community whose shared conceptions of the good are circumscribed by the dominant understanding will have little incentive to rethink this understanding and possibly to interpret accepted human goods in new ways. Those who lose out in the search for approval on substantive grounds will lose their claim to equal respect.

William Lund argues, "Grounding coercive or even merely hortatory legislation on contested accounts of what is 'intrinsically good' inevitably puts into play a publicly backed appraisal of citizens and their conceptions of the good. In the absence of various liberal constraints, those will be used to justify unequal distributions of the opportunities and costs of various lives, and they will be so used whether or not those who are penalized actually accept the worth of the 'good' in question" (Lund 1993, 595; see also Jakobsen and Pellegrini 2004, 27–29, 34; Snyder 2006, 139–42). That is, we cannot be completely constituted or shaped by today's community values without losing the possibility of critical purchase as we ponder, both individually and collectively, what values we want the community to embody tomorrow (Gill 2001, 198–202). Although Sandel's and Feldblum's exhortations to appeal to substantive moral values have merit, this move works only if the majority is open to new definitions or interpretations of what constitutes moral values.

For example, as Bonnie Honig points out, Sandel's approach grants equal respect—and by extension, civic equality—only to those who want to enter committed relationships and who therefore most closely resemble the heterosexual majority. Sandel argues that "a fuller respect would require . . . at least some appreciation for the lives homosexuals live" (Sandel 1996, 107). For Honig "this fuller respect could be accorded only to some, to those whose homosexual relationships are intimate in ways that are recognizable to 'us' and can be likened to those 'we' value as a culture. . . . Sandel's new economy of toleration and respect . . . includes some homosexuals on the basis of their likeness to a standard set by a dominant heterosexual and heterosexist culture" (Honig 1993, 190; see 186–95). In other words, toleration of sexual relationships and expressions varies directly with the extent to which these resemble heterosexual marriage. Although Sandel compares same-sex relationships favorably to the enjoyment of obscene materials, for Honig this comparison means only that he upholds intimacy rather than marriage or reproduction as the new test of acceptable sexual behavior, still relegating the consumer of pornography to the status of other, one who is therefore outside the communitarian ideal (191–92; see also 171). This process may mean narrowing the definition of deviancy, as it were, in that behavior formerly regarded as deviant is no longer so regarded. But the category still exists, and it functions to exclude some individuals as alien or other, because they attempt to participate in the community on terms that community will not accept.

Like Honig, Babst is wary of Sandel's communitarian defense of same-sex relationships. "The entire gay and lesbian community may not wish to be represented in the [court] majority's terms of choice"; that is, they may not want to be portrayed in the way Sandel believes is best calculated to influence a court majority favorably on their behalf (Babst 1997, 153; see 147–57). Because Sandel's approach purports to represent the interests of all gay, lesbian, bisexual, and transgender persons, Babst argues that this approach "is a refusal to see gays & [sic] lesbians on their own terms (e.g., subject to other desires), not objects of a stealthy juridical and moralizing discourse that occupies the site of normativity, which makes citizenship less valuable for them" (155; see also Pierceson 2005, 44–48). For Babst as for Honig, therefore, an emphasis on rights rather than on communally shared goods better serves the interests of any marginalized group.

Because I argue for same-sex couples' right to marry, giving attention here to the interests of those of minority sexual orientations who question this focus may seem counterproductive. I disagree. Same-sex couples who want to marry presumably regard marriage as the public expression of a conscientious belief in the value they themselves accord to the long-term commitment that this civil institution represents. This expression of their own belief is why they should be accorded the right to marry. With respect to religion, many do not espouse religious beliefs and have no interest in religious practice. Yet, within a broad latitude, we guarantee the free exercise of religion because religious belief and practice are core constituents of identity for those who hold them as central to their lives, not because a congruence exists between communally shared values and particular religious beliefs and practices. The law attends to the conscientious convictions of those whose religious beliefs and practices appear to carry no social benefit and even of those whose beliefs and practices are neither conventionally religious nor religious at all. It is one thing to permit within broad limits the free exercise of religious or sexual practice because this exercise is congruent with a community's current values. It is quite another to accord this freedom because it carries intrinsic value for individuals, whether or not the community favors some of its manifestations. These reasons are not mutually exclusive, and

Sandel is correct to point out that the value of same-sex relationships can be comparable to marriage. Like Honig and Babst, however, I am wary of defenses of sexual practice that rely upon community approval alone. A facile identification of public purposes with conventional values can too easily lead to public expressions of civic inequality.

In *Lawrence v. Texas* the Supreme Court recognized the weakness in the *Bowers* court's focus on a narrow right to homosexual sodomy. In *Lawrence* Justice Anthony Kennedy specifically criticized *Bowers's* narrow interpretation of same-sex relationships. "To say that the issue in *Bowers* was simply the right to engage in certain sexual conduct demeans the claim the individual put forward, just as it would demean a married couple were it said that marriage is just about the right to have sexual intercourse" (Lawrence v. Texas, 539 U.S. 558 [2003], at 567). Although protection of same-sex sodomy is not deeply rooted in this nation's history and traditions, protection of individual relationships and expressive associations has indeed been deeply rooted (Gill 2001, 197–204). More to the point, same-sex marriage does concern family relationships, marriage, and procreation or child rearing, the very issues that the *Bowers* court had declared to be unrelated to same-sex relationships. If the relevant distinction for that court was implicitly between committed and uncommitted relationships, rather than between traditional and same-sex ones, then *Bowers* not only did not contravene claims to the legitimacy of same-sex marriage but might even be viewed as supporting them. Although the value of intimate relationships is in my view based on their meaning for the individuals involved, the fact that these relationships may support or enhance activities also valued by the community is all to the good.

Condemnation of same-sex relationships, Kennedy wrote in *Lawrence*, has historically been based on conventional but profound convictions about religion, morality, and the status of the traditional family. The issue before the court, however, "is whether the majority may use the power of the State to enforce these views on the whole society through operation of the criminal law. 'Our obligation is to define the liberty of all, not to mandate our own moral code'" (Lawrence v. Texas, 539 U.S. 558 [2003], at 571, quoting Planned Parenthood of Southeastern Pa. v. Casey, 505 U.S. 833 [1992], at 850). Kennedy cited *Planned Parenthood of Southeastern Pa. v. Casey*, among other decisions relating to contraception and abortion, to support offering constitutional protection to personal decisions concerning marriage, procreation, family relationships, and child rearing. The *Casey* court had stated, "These matters, involving the most intimate and personal choices a person may make in a lifetime, choices central to personal dignity and autonomy, are central to the liberty protected by the Fourteenth Amendment," crucial to which is "the right to define one's own concept of existence, of meaning, of the universe, and of the mystery of human life. Beliefs about these matters could not define the attributes of personhood were they formed under compulsion of the State" (Planned Parenthood of Southeastern Pa. v. Casey, 505 U.S. 833 [1992], at 851, cited in Lawrence v. Texas, 539 U.S. 558 [2003], at 574). Whether or not particular personal relationships merit formal legal recognition, Kennedy wrote in *Lawrence*, "when sexuality finds overt expression in intimate conduct with another person, the conduct can be but one element in a personal bond that is more enduring. The liberty protected by the Constitution allows homosexual persons the right to make this choice" (*Lawrence*, at 567). Partly because *Lawrence* did "not involve whether the government must give formal recognition to any relationships that homosexuals persons seek to enter" (578), such as marriage, the present generation should "see that laws once thought necessary and proper in fact serve only to oppress" (579). As Struening later summarized, for Kennedy "the liberty interest at stake in *Bowers* and *Lawrence* is not the right to engage in homosexual sodomy but the right to exercise autonomy in intimate relationships" (Struening 2009, 25; see 24–28, 41–43).

In her concurring opinion in *Lawrence*, Justice Sandra Day O'Connor maintained a narrower equal protection justification for striking down the Texas law, because, unlike the Georgia law upheld in *Bowers*, the Texas law applied only to same-sex conduct, not to opposite-sex conduct. She also opined that the state of Texas could not assert a legitimate state interest in retaining the law, "such as national security or preserving the traditional institution of marriage. Unlike the moral disapproval of same-sex relations—the asserted state interest in this case—other reasons exist to promote the institution of marriage beyond mere moral disapproval of an excluded group" (Lawrence v. Texas, 539 U.S. 558 [2003], at 585; see also 583).

In his dissent, however, Justice Antonin Scalia suggested that a legitimate state interest in "'preserving the traditional institution of marriage' is just a kinder way of describing the State's *moral disapproval* of same-sex couples" (Lawrence v. Texas, 539 U.S. 558 [2003], at 601). Although perceptions of morality do change over time, persuading one's fellow citizens to change the law is much preferable to imposing judicial fiat (603). Alluding to Kennedy's observation that liberty of sexual expression may be but one element in an enduring personal bond, Scalia wondered, "What justification could there possibly be for denying the benefits of marriage to homosexual couples exercising 'the liberty protected by the Constitution'?" (605). That is, if the sexual expression of same-sex couples is worthy of judicial protection as a part of a potentially enduring relationship, as the court ruled, *Lawrence* left no ground for continuing to deny civil recognition of such a relationship, or marriage, to these couples.

Lawrence, like Blackmun's dissent in *Bowers*, has elicited mixed reviews from advocates for the rights of same-sex couples. Like Scalia, some commentators argue, albeit with enthusiasm rather than dismay, that *Lawrence* not only removed the criminal and social stigma from same-sex intimacy but also laid the groundwork for same-sex marriage. Jo Ann Citron and Mary Lyndon Shanley note that Kennedy's opinion repeatedly cited, in "respectful" tones, examples of the due process liberty interest in consensual sexual conduct represented by prior cases involving contraception and the privacy of the marital relationship (Citron and Shanley 2005, 219; see 217–23). "As a legal opinion," they observe, "*Lawrence* stands for the proposition that the due process clause protects a person's liberty interest in exploring identity through sexual practices undertaken in private with other consenting adults *no matter what these practices look like.* . . . The liberty of the person . . . protects not just what a person does, but who a person *is*; not just association, but *autonomy*; not just conduct, but *identity*." Citron and Shanley nevertheless remark that *Lawrence* still promoted heteronormativity by "making gay relationships look like marital ones" and "by eliding the differences between the 'insiders' and the 'outsiders'" (222), a concern that Honig and Babst shared regarding *Bowers*. Alternatively, Joe Rollins points out that although *Lawrence* removed the stigma from same-sex intimacy, "marriage is further elevated and venerated, granted to heterosexuals; homosexuals are left branded with the stigma of exclusion" (Rollins 2005, 181).

On a different note, Anna Marie Smith maintains that in most privacy-based decisions, the rights bearer is treated as a lone individual who qualifies for a privacy right to choice free from governmental intrusion. The rights bearer is not simultaneously treated as a member of a historically disadvantaged group that is engaged in a collective struggle and that should be categorized as a suspect class. Smith explains, "Being 'homosexual' is like preferring spicy food or choosing . . . to take a bath instead of a shower. From this perspective, being 'homosexual' has very little in common with being Catholic—that is to say, with being a member of a social group that is protected from discriminatory law by an elevated level of judicial scrutiny" (Smith 2005, 193; see 186–203). Therefore, Smith says, "We ought to applaud the Court for striking down *Bowers* and yet criticize it for the way it achieves that goal by perpetuating its neoconservative individualism" (199). In other words, where privacy claims may be satisfied by a negative liberty to pursue the activities in question without interference, historically disadvantaged groups often require a positive right as such to be included in activities or institutions from which they have previously been excluded.

However, Andrew Koppelman, suggesting that *Lawrence* does address the subordination of gays as a group, argues that at least one clear rule emerges: "*If a state singles out gays for unprecedentedly harsh treatment, the Court will presume that what is going on is a bare desire to harm, rather than mere moral disapproval*" (Koppelman 2005, 154; see 152–55; see also Erdos 2005, 27–28). This is a presumption the *Romer* court already recognized in 1996. Laws about morals may be permissible, Koppelman explains, but those carrying the effect of encouraging prejudice toward individuals within a particular group "diminish the weight that is given to the state's purposes when the Court balances those purposes against the burden the law imposes" (Koppelman 2005, 152; see also Gerstmann 2008, 45). In some contexts the social meaning of laws may be such that their existence amounts to an invitation to discriminate. Provisions in the law that operate unequally on members of different groups can confirm citizens in the comfort of their existing prejudices. As Justice Kennedy observed in *Lawrence*, "When homosexual conduct is made criminal by the law of the State, that declaration in and of itself is an invitation to subject homosexual persons to discrimination in both the public and in the private spheres" (Lawrence v. Texas, 539 U.S. 558 [2003], at 575; see also Koppelman 2005, 152).

Both *Bowers* and *Lawrence* focused on the appropriateness of affording individuals the freedom from interference or negative liberty necessary to conduct same-sex relationships. In *Lawrence* both Kennedy for the court and Scalia in dissent implicitly agreed that the issue turned on the propriety of using the law to enforce a conventional or majority conception of sexual morality. Insofar as such enforcement hinders the free exercise of a core feature of moral personality on the part of those with unconventional identities, allegiances, and conscientious beliefs, it is akin to enforcement that hinders the free exercise of unpopular religious practices.

Although it does not address sexual practices directly, a more explicit analogy between sexuality and religion appears in *Romer v. Evans* (517 U.S. 620 [1996]), in which the Supreme Court declared unconstitutional Colorado's Amendment 2. The amendment had prohibited the enactment, adoption, or enforcement of antidiscrimination legislation protecting any nonmajority sexual orientation. In his majority opinion Justice Kennedy ruled that the rights against discrimination withheld under Amendment 2 were not special rights but rather "are protections taken for granted by most people either because they already have them or do not need them; these are protections against exclusion from an almost limitless number of transactions and endeavors that constitute ordinary civic life in a free society" (631; see 630–31). Amendment 2 imposed a broad disability on one particular group, the reasons for which seemed "inexplicable by anything but animus toward the class it affects," therefore failing to meet even the test of a rational relationship to legitimate state interests (632). The state of Colorado had argued that without Amendment 2, the freedom of association of employers or landlords with objections to homosexuality would be threatened. Kennedy countered that in reality "Amendment 2 classifies homosexuals not to further a proper legislative end but to make them unequal to everyone else. This Colorado cannot do. A State cannot so deem a class of persons a stranger to its laws" (634–35; see also Eskridge 1999, 298).

In his dissent Justice Scalia maintained that although Colorado was among a number of states that had repealed its antisodomy laws, "the society that eliminates criminal punishment for homosexual acts does not necessarily abandon the view that homosexuality is morally wrong and socially harmful" (Romer v. Evans, 517 U.S. 620 [1996], at 643; see also 636–39, 641–42). The state, in his view, may properly deny what he viewed as favored status to individuals experiencing same-sex attraction. In the portion of his dissent most relevant for this discussion, Scalia noted that the constitutions of five states singled out a sexual practice by prohibiting polygamy. Four of them had done so because Congress required it as a condition of statehood, and the fifth did so as a territory when the Supreme Court upheld a statutory provision depriving polygamists of the franchise. "Thus, this 'singling out' of the sexual practices of a single group for statewide, democratic vote—so utterly alien to our constitutional system, the Court would have us believe—has not only happened, but has received the explicit approval of the United States Congress" (649; see 647–51). Overall, Scalia concluded, the court should not take sides in this culture war, in which "Amendment 2 is designed to prevent piecemeal deterioration of the sexual morality of a majority of Coloradans. . . . Striking it down is an act, not of judicial judgment, but of political will" (653). In sum, the issue in *Romer* was whether those with conventional or majority views might use the power of the state to enforce these views—not as in *Bowers* and *Lawrence* by curtailing negative liberty through criminalizing particular conduct, but rather by prohibiting positive political action.

The government's interest in prohibiting polygamy, however, comprised not only intimate relationships but also the character of state government itself. In his majority opinion in *Romer*, Kennedy distinguished between laws prohibiting polygamy, which he attributed to a legitimate governmental interest, and laws that Congress had passed denying Mormons, polygamists, and advocates of polygamy the right to vote. There is some evidence that the court's concern in *Reynolds v. United States* (98 U.S. 145 [1879]) was also political rather than religious. As Nancy Rosenblum explains, rather than operating as a small, separatist community, such as the Old Order Amish, the rhetoric of contemporary Mormon leaders indicated the desire for an expanding theocratic empire within the United States (Rosenblum 1997, 75–76; Feldman 2006, 99–102). The practice of polygamy as a point of comparison is discussed in greater detail below. Denial of the franchise based on the views one advocates, however, is no longer constitutional (Romer v. Evans, 517 U.S. 620 [1996], at 634–35). Kennedy countered that engaging in criminalized conduct is one thing; but membership in a group that advocates such conduct, or mere advocacy of such conduct without membership in that group, is something else. Thus, even if sodomy had not been decriminalized in Colorado before 1996, it would be constitutionally illegitimate to pass measures forbidding the passage of antidiscrimination laws that might result from this advocacy. In his dissent, however, Scalia retorted that the right to vote has been declared a fundamental right (650). In other words, although no one was advocating that individuals participating in same-sex relationships be disenfranchised, the democratic process might legitimately be used to forbid the instantiation of what he viewed as favored status for these individuals (646).

Although the subject of *Romer* is the legitimate use of the political process, the decision resonates on a number of levels with the contention that opposition to same-sex marriage is based on conventional notions about religion, morality, and family that are sectarian in nature. As David Richards notes, although a compelling state interest might justify banning conduct that is a conscientious expression of a right to intimate life, such as polygamy or sodomy, "it did not follow that their [those experiencing same-sex attraction] public claims and lives as gays and lesbians could for that reason be the subject of discrimination." That is, a religious practice might be banned, but its advocates cannot be penalized through deprivation of a basic right such as voting or political advocacy (Richards 2005, 92; see also Richards 2009, 117). *Lawrence* found antisodomy laws to be unconstitutional. Yet the conscientious expression of a right to the publicly acknowledged intimate life that civil marriage represents is still widely opposed. Although Richards writes about *Romer* and antidiscrimination laws, what he says is also applicable to same-sex marriage: "The ground for discrimination against gay and lesbian conscience, thus understood, is sectarian religious convictions—sectarian in that the sense that they rest on perceptions internal to religious convictions, not on public arguments reasonably available in contemporary terms to all persons. . . . The expression through public law of one form of sectarian conscience against another form of conscience, without compelling justification in public arguments available to all, is constitutionally invidious, and therefore constitutionally suspect, religious intolerance" (Richards 2005, 117). Such intolerance, Richards suggests, both burdens the free exercise of some manifestations of conscience and establishes other, majoritarian manifestations.

Furthermore, in *Romer* Kennedy stated that for some, antidiscrimination laws constitute "protections against exclusion from an almost limitless number of transactions and endeavors that constitute ordinary civil life in a free society" (Romer v. Evans, 517 U.S. 620 [1996], at 631). Because a great many benefits accompany entrance into the civil institution of marriage, barring same-sex couples excludes them from many "transactions and endeavors" that opposite-sex couples take for granted. Some object that because these civil benefits are unrelated to religious belief, the free exercise of conscience is not thwarted by excluding same-sex couples. The relevant point here, however, is that same-sex couples are excluded and deprived of these benefits because of the sectarian beliefs of others. Observant Jews do not consume pork, for example, but few would agree that it should therefore be prohibited to all (Nussbaum 2010, 141, 144–45). When Kennedy stated that the disability imposed by Colorado's Amendment 2 seemed "inexplicable by anything but animus toward the class it affects" and that "a State cannot so deem a class of persons a stranger to its laws" (Romer v. Evans, 517 U.S. 620 [1996], at 632, 635), he was suggesting that a rational case had not been made, and perhaps could not be made, that would justify depriving those experiencing same-sex attraction of the ability to protect themselves through the passage of antidiscrimination laws. This deprivation, moreover, had an impact not only on those who directly benefit from such laws but also on their allies, such as relatives, friends, and any others who conscientiously believe that passing laws targeting discrimination based on sexual orientation is a matter of justice. Similarly, I suggest that a dispositively rational case has not been made that justifies excluding same-sex couples from the institution of marriage.

According to Jonathan Chait, for example, the National Organization for Marriage tells activists that when people ask who gets harmed if same-sex couples can marry, they should answer, "The people of this state who lose our right to define marriage as the union of husband and wife, that's who." In Chait's view, this assertion simply means that "expanding a right to a new group deprives the rest of us of our right to deny that right to others," thereby devaluing the right by making it less special (Chait 2009, 2). The same dynamic appeared in some arguments for California's Proposition 8, which in 2008 rescinded the right to marry that same-sex couples had been granted months earlier. Supporters of the proposition declared that it would simply preserve marriage as historically defined and would not harm the rights and protections of gays and lesbians, to whom domestic partnerships would still be available under California law. As Feldblum notes, however, a key secondary argument "was that providing access to marriage for gay couples would *reduce* the rights available to *others*," such as those of parents who wish to shield their children from knowledge of same-sex relationships. "From this vantage point, an essential selling point of Proposition 8 was that it would *protect* people from the excesses of extending rights to gay couples" (Feldblum 2009, 222; see also 221–28; Nussbaum 2010, 141–50). Feldblum thinks we should be forthright in acknowledging that the extension of marriage rights to same-sex couples may burden the conscientious beliefs of those who resist such change. However, to consider these burdens as equal or superior to those on same-sex couples who are denied the right to marry is grossly disproportionate. Absent a rigorous and compelling case, reserving marriage for a particular group of couples while excluding others is not only a public expression of civic inequality; it is also a quintessential example of a "special right."

Along related lines, Scalia in his dissent in *Romer* implied that Coloradans who sought through Amendment 2 to prevent the "piecemeal deterioration" of the sexual morality they favored had an equal claim to enact their wishes into the state constitution as did those experiencing same-sex attraction and their allies who wished to protect individuals from discrimination (Romer v. Evans, 517 U.S. 520 [1996], at 653; see 646). Those who favor legislation or constitutional amendments to limit marriage to opposite-sex couples are implicitly making a similar argument. That is, they imply that "protecting" the institution of marriage through such measures is at least as legitimate as measures to include same-sex couples in the civil institution of marriage. As Jakobsen and Pellegrini note, however, Scalia's characterization of antidiscrimination laws as instances of special rights "effectively repositions those who would exclude gay men, lesbians, and bisexuals from American democracy as the ones most in need of legal protection. In other words, the people . . . whose rights are already recognized and enforced are the ones treated as if their rights are endangered" (Jakobsen and Pellegrini 2004, 42–43; see also 39).

Similarly, traditionalist opponents of same-sex marriage use laws and constitutional amendments to reposition themselves as the group needing legal protections, despite the fact that their own rights to marry are well recognized and enforced. However, in matters of faith or sexuality that are central to individual self-definition, I believe that regulation or prohibition exerts a greater impact on those directly or principally concerned than the lack of it exerts on those offended by particular manifestations of faith or sexuality. Once again, as Mill cautioned, "There is no parity between the feelings of a person for his own opinion, and the feelings of another who is offended at his holding it; no more than the desire of a thief to take a purse, and the desire of the right owner to keep it" (Mill 1859, 84).

Mill also criticized the theory of collective or social rights, according to which it is one's right that every other person "act in every respect exactly as he ought." To those who suggest that sexual orientation is a private matter that should be kept private, Mill today might respond that as a doctrine of social rights, "so monstrous a principle . . . acknowledges no right to any freedom whatsoever, except perhaps to that of holding opinions in secret, without ever disclosing them" (Mill 1859, 89). That is, although people experiencing same-sex attraction possess the negative liberty to participate in intimate relationships without direct interference, they had best lie low, so to speak, even after *Lawrence.* If they are open about this core feature of moral personality, they may suffer discrimination against which they might properly be deprived of legal recourse, according to Scalia's dissent in *Romer.* Furthermore, if they wish to enter the public commitment of civil marriage, their opponents may engage in preemptive legal strikes to forestall attempts to empower them to do so. In other words, if those who share Scalia's opinion have their way, people experiencing same-sex attraction would be deprived of the liberty to improve their situation, which in turn lessens the value or worth of their liberty to engage either in intimate relationships or in politics.

At the time *Romer* was argued, Jeffrey Rosen suggested that "in some ways, Amendment 2 is a civil, statewide version of 'Don't Ask, Don't Tell.' It recognizes that homosexuals exist, even tolerates their private lives, but refuses to grant them any public recognition as equal citizens." Equal rights are fine, "as long as the rights aren't demanded too obviously. It's the anti-discrimination law that dare not speak its name" (Rosen 1995, 25). Similarly, the law currently recognizes that same-sex couples exist, tolerates their private relationships, and in some jurisdictions even grants them the public status of civil unions or domestic partnerships. Let them demand the gold standard of civil marriage, however, and suddenly these couples are in most jurisdictions unworthy of the positive protection and the signification of equal citizenship that marriage represents.

According to T. M. Scanlon, a public policy of true toleration not only requires an institutional equality of legal and political rights but also extends to "the informal politics of social life," which involves the right to participate in defining the social ethos, or influencing what it is that people value (Scanlon 1996, 229; see 229–30). Unlike private associations where the meaning of particular goods depends upon the acceptance of certain beliefs, as with religious sacraments, he suggests that the goods of the larger society "do not lose their meaning if they are extended to people with whom we disagree about the kind of society we would like to have, or even to those who reject its most basic tenets" (233).

The institution of marriage is a good in the eyes of many, although the reasons vary. It carries a particular meaning for those who adhere to religious traditions; for some of them, marriage is a sacrament. This institution will not lose this religious meaning, however, if the opportunity to participate is extended to same-sex couples, some of whom may value it both as a civil institution and as a religious rite. Everyone in a society should have access to the same opportunities to shape the culture in which they live, despite the risk to one's preferred form of social ethos. *Romer* did not mandate the passage of antidiscrimination laws. It only allowed proponents to attempt their passage. Similarly, rejecting current measures to exclude same-sex couples from marriage does not automatically mandate their inclusion. Such decisions do, however, prohibit efforts to make it more difficult for some groups to attempt to shape the contours of their society.

In his *Romer* dissent Scalia argued that if a state might criminalize sexual conduct, as *Bowers* then permitted, "surely it is constitutionally permissible for a State to enact other laws merely *disfavoring* homosexual conduct," especially because, for him, Amendment 2 disfavored no conduct but simply prohibited the bestowal of special protections (Romer v. Evans, 517 U.S. 620 [1996], at 641; see 641–42, 636–39; Gerstmann 1999, 68–69). Although same-sex intimacy is no longer criminal in any state, following *Lawrence*, traditionalist opponents of same-sex marriage may agree with Scalia that the denial of civil marriage, like the denial of antidiscrimination laws, merely disfavors same-sex intimacy. Nevertheless, we should not force fellow citizens to pay reparations for our so-called generosity through the back door for costs that we do not extract through the front door. That is, we should not force people to pay through second-class citizenship just because we have lifted criminal penalties from behaviors that are no longer against the law. On the contrary, we should afford to same-sex couples not only the material benefits that accompany marriage, many of which attach to civil unions and domestic partnerships, but also the title of the status of marriage. Otherwise, the ostensible moral superiority of traditional couples over same-sex couples is enshrined in the law as a clear public expression of civic inequality, a point on which several state courts in recent marriage cases agree.

For example, after the Supreme Court of Massachusetts approved the civil status of marriage for same-sex couples in 2003 (Goodridge v. Department of Public Health, 440 Mass. 309 [2003]), the state senate subsequently asked the state supreme court for an advisory opinion on a proposed bill substituting the parallel institution of civil unions for these couples. The court responded that the proposed bill continued the inequality of status of the original matrimonial law that had confined marriage to traditional couples. "The dissimilitude between the terms 'civil marriage' and 'civil union' is not innocuous; it is a considered choice of language that reflects a demonstrable assigning of same-sex, largely homosexual, couples to a second-class status" (*In re* Opinions of the Justices to the Senate, 440 Mass. 1201 [2004], at 1207; see also 1210).

In another example, the state of California argued in 2008 that because its domestic partnership legislation afforded same-sex couples nearly all of the rights and obligations enjoyed by married couples under state law, the California Constitution's guarantee of the fundamental right to marry was not infringed. The California Supreme Court responded, however, that the substantive protection implied in the right to marry includes not only a negative right against undue governmental interference, but also a positive right to affirmative state support for families. "Under these circumstances," the court stated, "we conclude that the distinction drawn by the current California statutes between the designation of the family relationships available to opposite-sex couples and the designation available to same-sex couples impinges upon the fundamental interest of same-sex couples in having their official family relationship accorded dignity and respect equal to that conferred upon the family relationships of opposite-sex couples" (*In re* Marriage Cases, 43 Cal. 4th 757 [2008], at 846–47; see also 819, 855; Ball 2003, 8–17, 75–76; Pierceson 2005, 29–30, 33–35, 45–48, 50–51). Also in 2008 the Connecticut Supreme Court, relying on the California decision, ruled that although Connecticut had civil unions, the lower court was wrong to hold that the dispute over the title of "marriage" was simply one of nomenclature. Because marriage had long been a basic civil right in the state, "our conventional understanding of marriage must yield to a more contemporary appreciation of the rights entitled to constitutional protection" (Kerrigan v. Commissioner of Public Health, 289 Conn. 135 [2008], at 262).

In 2009 the Iowa Supreme Court ruled that because Polk County had not made a convincing case that traditional couples offered the optimal environment for rearing children, its defense of the law confining marriage to traditional couples must be based on "stereotype and prejudice, or some other unarticulated reason" (Varnum v. Brien, 763 N.W.2d 862 [2009], at 901; see 899–901). Reminding the state that marriage is a civil contract, the court found this reason to constitute religious opposition (904). The state, however, most respects "the views of all Iowans on the issue of same-sex marriage—religious or otherwise—by giving respect to our constitutional principles. These principles require that the state recognize both opposite-sex and same-sex civil marriage" (905–6). Finally in 2010, a federal trial court in California struck down Proposition 8, a voter-approved initiative banning same-sex marriage just months after the state supreme court had approved same-sex marriages there. The judge ruled that because the ban did not advance any rational basis for prohibiting same-sex marriages, "Proposition 8 was premised on the belief that same-sex couples simply are not as good as opposite-sex couples. . . . Moral disapproval alone is an improper basis on which to deny rights to gay men and lesbians" (Perry v. Schwarzenegger, 704 F.Supp.2d 921 [Cal. 2010], at 1002, 1003).

Considered together, these recent state cases suggest that traditionalists, like the supporters of Amendment 2 in Colorado, seek to characterize themselves as the endangered group in need of protection. Defense of the status quo, however, is an insufficient reason for public expressions of civic inequality.

Marriage as the Free Exercise of Conscientious Belief

Although the debate surrounding same-sex marriage is often portrayed as one between secular opinions and religious ones, this picture oversimplifies the nature of the discussion. Proceeding from individual to collective expressions of conscience, Mark Strasser observes that "*some* rather than all religions refuse to recognize same-sex unions, and Quakers, Unitarians, Buddhists, Reconstructionist Jews, and Reform Jews might all celebrate same-sex unions" (Strasser 2002, 118). Strasser's careful wording suggests that some religious leaders or congregations may in fact celebrate these unions—a suggestion that expands the diverse perspectives represented in the debate. The United Church of Christ, for instance, has endorsed marriage for same-sex couples, and debate continues in the Evangelical Lutheran, Methodist, and Presbyterian churches (DeLaet and Caufield 2006). Conservative Jews and some Episcopal congregations now also support same-sex religious unions (Nussbaum 2010, 131). Divisions over same-sex marriage have appeared even among evangelical Christian churches (Kirkpatrick 2004) and among African Americans (Clemetson 2004).

Therefore, as Strasser notes, opposition to same-sex marriage is not the sole religious viewpoint that must be upheld to protect the sanctity of marriage. "Rather, the most that can be claimed is that the state position supports the religious dictates of *some* but not all religions" (Strasser 2002, 119), not to mention religious believers who exhibit diversity even within religious organizations they support. For Strasser the point is neither that laws coinciding with religious tenets violate the establishment clause, nor that such laws must be justifiable independent of religion to be constitutionally legitimate. Even if all religious traditions were unanimously opposed to same-sex marriage, such opposition would not dictate any particular course of action, in Strasser's opinion. If the state were to require at least one religious tradition to sanction a civil marriage, atheists would have trouble marrying civilly if they could not find a religious tradition to sanction their marriages. Furthermore, if the state were to recognize any union that is sanctioned by at least one religious tradition, polygamous unions could be freely entered. Strasser concludes, "Even were all the religions to agree that same-sex marriages should not be recognized, that alone would not justify the state's refusal to do so" (121). In David Richards's terms, opposition to same-sex marriage is still a sectarian viewpoint, especially given disagreement both among and within religious traditions.

Some commentators go further than Strasser. Debra DeLaet and Rachel Paine Caufield point out that although proponents of traditional marriage believe "they are defending the essential meaning of marriage as commonly understood throughout history" (DeLaet and Caufield 2006), this institution's form and content have varied greatly over time. In fact, defenders "are putting forward a *sectarian* definition of marriage and claiming to be the authentic voice of the common Christian tradition and, even more to the point, of a cross-cultural, universal tradition. To the extent that the state endorses a sectarian definition of marriage that privileges some religious views over others, it violates First Amendment religious rights." Specifically, they explain, the state is endorsing "the practices and beliefs of some religious traditions over all others (and religion over nonreligion), conditioning the receipt of benefits based upon the practices and beliefs of one particular religious doctrine, and violating the Establishment Clause." More generally, by defining marriage exclusively and traditionally, state policy violates separationist doctrine by privileging one type of religious perspective; it violates accommodationist doctrine by denying recognition to marriage as defined by other religious perspectives; and it violates the neutrality standard by failing to maintain neutrality either among religions or between religion and nonreligion. In chapter 4 I discuss the exclusion of same-sex couples from civil marriage as a kind of establishment of religion. In the remainder of this chapter I address this exclusion as a violation of the First Amendment's free exercise clause.

Because the government does not interfere with the activity of religious communities that endorse and are willing to celebrate same-sex unions, De-Laet and Caufield hold that these unions do not directly implicate the free exercise clause (DeLaet and Caufield 2006). Michael McConnell similarly distinguishes between the privatization approach to the religion clauses, which consigns religion-sensitive issues to the private sphere, and the equal access approach, often associated with neutrality between religion and non-religion because it allows "competing groups to participate in the public sphere on equal terms" (McConnell 1998, 237; see also Everson v. Board of Education, 330 U.S. 1 [1947], at 15; Zorach v. Clauson, 343 U.S. 306 [1952], at 313). These approaches correspond roughly to the familiar categories of separation and accommodation.

As a separationist or disestablishment claim, McConnell argues, the recognition of same-sex marriage "would not solve the 'establishment' problem, but only broaden the 'establishment' to give favored status to two 'churches'" (McConnell 1998, 250; see 249–50). That is, marriage in this scenario would still be a legally defined status, in which participation depends on adherence to its terms—a point that undoubtedly resonates with queer, feminist, and libertarian skeptics about marriage as a public institution. True disestablishment of marriage instead requires eliminating marriage as a public institution; couples would privately form and celebrate their unions, just as like-minded individuals exercise freedom of association by forming and institutionalizing religious groups. Babst similarly explains that the privatization alternative is "to let individual couples decide for themselves within their communities of faith, or otherwise, what marriage signifies for them and their communities, rather than have a definition imposed on them by the State" (Babst 2002, 83). This move does not preclude the expression of a secular public interest through law concerning divorce, adoption, inheritance, and other material interests (84). I do not necessarily endorse disestablishment along these lines. I simply observe that logically speaking it embodies separation more surely than the simple inclusion of same-sex couples in the institution of marriage as it is currently defined.

Where the privatization approach disestablishes marriage as a public institution, the equal access approach retains it as a public institution but presumably opens it to nontraditional individuals, such as those forming same-sex unions. But McConnell argues that because "most combinations of human beings are ineligible for matrimony," the case for same-sex marriage as a free exercise or equal access claim is weak (McConnell 1998, 249). Like DeLaet and Caufield, he notes that free exercise already protects the right of religious communities to celebrate same-sex unions. Moreover, he points out, when the Supreme Court banned polygamy as a civil institution (Reynolds v. United States, 98 U.S. 145 [1879]), George Reynolds was seeking neither benefits nor the recognition of polygamous marriage, but only the right to be left alone. "In other words," McConnell summarizes, "Reynolds unsuccessfully sought what homosexuals already have: the right to live with the person(s) of their choice, as if married, without hindrance from the state. . . . It is one thing to say that the government may not interfere with a religious (or sexual) practice in the privacy of the home, and quite a different thing to say that the government must adjust the definition of a public institution to conform to the doctrines or desires of a minority" (McConnell 1998, 249; see also DeLaet and Caufield 2006). Although claims that tell the government what it must do may rarely succeed, one should not conclude that such claims should not be made at all. The rights of equal citizenship have often required Americans to consider the "doctrines or desires" of minority groups in nontraditional ways if minority groups are to be fully included. Moreover, a majority of Americans, straight or gay, desire that Americans in general have the ability formally to celebrate intimate long-term commitments, even if they personally choose to eschew them.

For Nussbaum as for McConnell, "it seems difficult to imagine any Free Exercise claim in this area." Because the Church of Jesus Christ of Latter-day Saints, or Mormon church, at least strongly urged polygamy on its members, Reynolds could be regarded as having a free exercise claim to be allowed to live free of prosecution. Yet even if one is sympathetic to Reynolds, as

Nussbaum is, this claim "does not establish a right, on religious grounds, to the state's *recognition* of one's religious marriage. No denomination I know of, moreover, requires same-sex marriage or holds it to be a necessary part of a good religious life" (Nussbaum 2008, 338; see 334–46). The fact that same-sex intimacy is no longer an object of prosecution, Nussbaum explains, renders same-sex couples more dissimilar to Reynolds than they once were.

However, the position of same-sex couples differs from that of Reynolds in other ways that give greater credibility to potential free exercise claims than Nussbaum realizes. First, they are not necessarily basing their desire to marry on religious beliefs they seek to honor through practice. Whether their desire to marry is religiously or secularly based, they are seeking civil marriage with or without religious marriage. In *Turner v. Safley* (482 U.S. 78 [1987]) in 1987, the Supreme Court noted that "the commitment of marriage may be an exercise of religious faith as well as an expression of personal dedication" (96). Strasser points out, however, that the court "did not suggest that marriage would have religious significance only if a duty to marry had been imposed by that religion, and *Turner* makes it clear that the state would be remiss for imposing unnecessary burdens on marriage even without, for example, an explicit religious duty to tie the marital knot" (Strasser 2002, 122). Because religious organizations may marry some couples and refuse religious marriage to others, some same-sex couples have only civil marriage as an option. A second difference between Reynolds and same-sex couples is that same-sex couples make their claims as individuals or as individual couples on the basis of their own conscientious beliefs. Members of recognized religious organizations are not the only individuals whose free exercise claims deserve consideration. Free exercise cases have encompassed both the conscientious claims of those whose beliefs do not stem from recognized religious traditions and also the claims of those whose personal beliefs differ from those of others within their own religious traditions.

If McConnell's point is that same-sex couples lack a persuasive free exercise claim because most combinations of individuals cannot marry, traditionalists make the converse argument. That is, if same-sex couples are deemed eligible to marry in accordance with the free exercise of their conscientious beliefs, then any combination of individuals may make this claim. Traditionalists fear, of course, that recognizing same-sex marriage will open the floodgates to claims that the state should recognize any and every type of union. Richard Wilkins summarizes this fear: "Should the courts depart from the established heterosexual definition of marriage, there will be little (if any) principled ground upon which to deny marital status to any and all consensual sexual groups. Bigamy, group marriage, and—yes—even consensual incestuous coupling could all (and probably would all) lay claim to the same legal entitlements" (Wilkins 2003, 233). In short, if same-sex couples assert the right to marry as an instantiation of the free exercise of conscience, so can everyone else. This slippery slope argument assumes, however, that each set of claims cannot be considered on its own merits. Although a cogent case may be made for same-sex marriage, this cogent case does not automatically apply to other nontraditional alternatives.

Polygamy serves as an example, one that is often cited by those who fear that legalizing same-sex marriage will open the door to other kinds of nontraditional marriage. Yet closer examination reveals key differences between arguments in favor of polygamy and same-sex marriage. Richards notes that because polygamy has traditionally reinforced unjust or unequal gender roles, it "thus cannot be regarded as a constitutionally reasonable form of intimate life consistent with these principles" of equal rights (Richards 1999, 166; see also Richards 2005, 139–40). Richards acknowledges that rights of conscience may be abridged if justified by compelling secular grounds or a compelling public reason. Eskridge explains, "The adult man's right to have two wives can . . . be limited if the state can show . . . that polygamy would undermine the status of women in the family and in society. There is no similarly persuasive justification for denying a lesbian the right to marry the partner of her choice" (Eskridge 2003, 182). In addition, Jonathan Rauch argues that polygamy—the dominant form of marriage across cultures through history, in his view—disadvantages men as well as women. "Polygamy was largely about hierarchy: it helped men to dominate women, and it helped high-status men, with their multiplicity of highly desirable wives, dominate low-status men" (Rauch 2005, 15–16). Because marriage stabilizes men, Rauch says, reducing the chances of marriage for low-status men is a recipe for creating an underclass of unmarriageable men, "peering up resentfully at elite men with one or more wives on each arm" (129; see 128–31, 18–21).

Richard Posner provides potential ammunition against those who seek to link the legal recognition of same-sex relationships with the legalization of polygamy. The scarcity of women that results from polygamy, Posner argues, should increase the incidence of "opportunistic homosexuality." As the exponent of a controversial economic theory of homosexuality, Posner infers sexual orientation or preference from sexual behavior when the costs are equal for both opposite-sex and same-sex relations. Those of "predominantly heterosexual preference" may "engage in homosexual behavior when the cost of heterosexual behavior is prohibitive" (Posner 1997, 179; see also 174, 179–80). In other words, Posner sees an increase in same-sex relationships as a consequence of legal polygamy, not as a causal factor. The difficulty for those who liken the legalization of same-sex marriage to the legalization of polygamy is that the potential link goes in the opposite direction from what they envision.

These arguments carry weight, but they are not in themselves dispositive. Queer, feminist, and libertarian skeptics, among others, can cite ways that traditional, monogamous, religious or civil marriage has reinforced unjust gender roles, as least historically. For example, Mill declared in 1869 that "marriage is the only actual bondage known in our law. There remain no legal slaves, except the mistress of every house" (196). In addition to women's legal subordination concerning free movement, property, and offspring, women were also subordinate, Mill observed, in a way that even slaves were not. "Above all, a female slave has (in Christian countries) an admitted right, and is considered under a moral obligation, to refuse to her master the last familiarity" (148). Although Mill did not suggest that their masters never forced slaves into sexual relationships, his point was that wives had no legal right whatsoever to object.

Regarding the 1879 decision in *Reynolds v. United States*, Rosenblum observes, "Official indifference toward the civil standing of women under the terms of conventional marriage proves the disingenuousness of the *Reynolds* court's avowed intention to protect Mormon wives from patriarchal authority" (Rosenblum 1997, 77; see also Eskridge 1999, 299–302). Nussbaum adds that "despite mainstream Christianity's proud pretense that monogamy is the true and only virtuous way, this same people accepts a sacred text in which polygamy is ubiquitous, and is nowhere divinely condemned" (Nussbaum 2008, 184; see also 195, 179–98). Reviewing the comparative social and political standing of Mormon and traditional wives, she concludes that "it is not so easy to find compelling arguments against polygamy that are not also arguments against key elements of the [then] dominant form of monogamous marriage" (188; see also 195). If equality of the sexes had grounded a compelling state interest in prohibiting polygamy in 1879, courts would also have had to address divorce law, the franchise, marital rape, and the exclusion of women from the professions at the time—"all of these being the trappings of conventional monogamy" (197; see also Mill 1869, 146–49).

Questions pertaining to consent can apply to both monogamous and polygamous marriage. Speaking specifically of Mormons in the United

States, Mill observed that both monogamous and polygamous marriages are voluntary, at least insofar as any marital choice is voluntary when customs that teach "women to think marriage the one thing needful, make it intelligible that many a woman should prefer being one of several wives, to not being a wife at all." Although polygamy does not occasion much comment when observed in other parts of the world, he noted, it "seems to excite unquenchable animosity when practiced by persons who speak English and profess to be a kind of Christian." Nonetheless, although he himself deeply disapproved of polygamy, he concluded that when Mormons have fled persecution "and established themselves in a remote corner of the earth, which they have been the first to render habitable to human beings, it is difficult to see on what principles but those of tyranny they can be prevented from living there under what laws they please, provided they commit no aggression on other nations, and allow perfect freedom of departure to those who are dissatisfied with their ways" (Mill 1859, 91–92).

Nussbaum observes that ascertaining consent can be difficult when marriage is presented as a spiritual requirement (Nussbaum 2008, 186). We should try, she suggests, to ensure that women are not pressured into any sort of marriage, polygamous or monogamous, and instead seek to expand "education and employment opportunities for women, since a woman can hardly consent freely when the alternative is destitution" (195–96; see also Mill 1869, 143–45). Rather than addressing this kind of issue, however, *Reynolds* and subsequent decisions regarding Mormons instead focused on the First Amendment's lack of protection for religiously motivated actions, the threat of uncivilized customs such as polygamy to domestic peace and safety, and the threat to democratic self-government posed by patriarchal and authoritarian family life (Nussbaum 2008, 193–97; see also Feldman 2006, 101–10).

Contemporary Mormon women in fundamentalist, breakaway Mormon communities have defended plural or polygamous marriage. Elizabeth Joseph, a lawyer in a polygamous marriage involving nine wives, argues that, the Old Testament aside, "compelling social reasons make the life style attractive to the modern career woman." Women can trade off household and child rearing tasks with each other and "fully meet their career, mothering, and marriage obligations." Although she concedes that it is not for everyone, "polygamy provides a whole solution. I believe American women would have invented it if it didn't already exist" (Joseph 1991; see also Rosenblum 1997, 78–79). Thus one cannot automatically write off plural marriage as an instance of false consciousness. Evan Gerstmann points out this parallel between polygamy and same-sex marriage, noting that vague speculation "about the potential evils of nontraditional families is exactly the sort of attack that has so often been used against same-sex couples" (Gerstmann 2008, 106). Moreover, when a lifestyle is driven underground, its closeted nature may be what feeds abuses such as the forced marriage, sexual exploitation of minors, and welfare dependency often associated with polygamy. "We should not blithely conclude that such antisocial behavior is inherent in the lifestyle itself," Gerstmann points out, echoing Sullivan's assertion (discussed in chapter 3) that the seeming dysfunctionality of same-sex relationships is a consequence of the way they have been ostracized, not of their intrinsic nature. "Indeed, it is surprisingly difficult to articulate why it is perfectly legal for a man to sleep with many women and have children by all of them, even though it is illegal for that man to marry those women" (Gerstmann 2008, 108; see also Eskridge 1999, 289–91).

DeLaet and Caufield make the related point that if existing Mormon fundamentalist polygamists could live openly, "the government might find it easier to enforce existing laws against statutory rape, incest, and domestic violence" (DeLaet and Caufield 2006). Gerstmann does acknowledge that issues like insurance benefits, custody, and the setting of a logical stopping point to marrying multiple spouses all militate against polygamy, whereas Nussbaum alludes to general administrative complexity (Gerstmann 2008, 110; Nussbaum 2008, 197). Rauch notes, however, that persons experiencing same-sex attraction, unlike individuals in any other group, are currently barred in most jurisdictions from marrying even one person they love (Rauch 2005, 127; see also Gill 2001, 210–11). As Gerstmann explains, there is "a difference between a right to marry whomever you want and marrying however many people you want." Unlike legalizing same-sex marriage, legalizing polygamy potentially affects every traditional couple's marriage, because married persons would be able to marry other partners while remaining married to their original spouses (Gerstmann 2008, 110; see 110–11). For Babst, Mormon plural marriage is based on a community ethos that takes precedence over individual choice, whereas same-sex marriage, like opposite-sex marriage, focuses on personal choice that encompasses a liberty interest in marrying whom one chooses (Babst 2002, 98; see 94–99).

My overall point is not that polygamy is an admirable institution. Rather, its legitimacy, like that of same-sex marriage, should be determined on its own merits or demerits. Gerstmann argues, "In evaluating ways of living, we must not rely upon mere speculation or intuitions that support our prejudices; we should hold ourselves to stringent standards of evidence" (Gerstmann 2008, 109–10). A rush to judgment played out on a national stage in spring 2008, when the Texas Supreme Court upheld an appellate court ruling that the state's Department of Family and Protective Services had acted illegally in taking 468 children from a fundamentalist Mormon ranch on unproven grounds of physical and sexual abuse. Although the state could prosecute individual cases where abuse might be demonstrated, the court ruled it had acted too sweepingly in separating all the children from their parents without proof of harm (Blumenthal 2008). In other words, the court implied that the polygamous living arrangements of these families led to a judgment grounded on stereotypes and unsupported generalizations.

In the context of same-sex marriage as a religious right or right of con-science, then, recognizing some claims to religious rights as legitimate need not mean recognizing all claims. The overall point is well put by Philip Selz-nick. Commenting on Justice Blackmun's dissent in *Bowers v. Hardwick*, Selznick observed that "to say that there are many 'right' ways [of conduct-ing intimate relationships] is not to say that any way is right. . . . Not every intimate association is defensible, nor is every one so fundamental as to merit constitutional protection" (Selznick 1989, 511–12). As citizens in a liberal democratic society, we and those who represent us ought to be able to judge with discernment in determining which sorts of unions are expres-sions of legitimate liberty interests and central constituents of our identities and weeding out those likely to harm the interests of some participants in these unions. Traditionalist opponents of same-sex marriage believe that the institution should not be opened to new kinds of couples lest the floodgates give way completely, but the institution of marriage is sufficiently capacious to admit same-sex couples, whether as a fundamental secular right or as a religious right, while providing the basis for stability that it always has.

In considering same-sex marriage as a broadly defined right of conscience that should be allowed free exercise, then, one should start "from the prem-ise that religion, in the sense of the search for fundamental or transcendent truths, is an integral part of human freedom and human experience, and that it is for this reason that we persistently seek its protection" (Underkuf-fler-Freund 1995, 847). Moreover, in defending the liberty of religious belief and practice as a central human capability, Nussbaum argues that "to be able to search for an understanding of the ultimate meaning of life in one's own way is among the most important aspects of a life that is truly human." Because this search may involve religious belief and practice, "to burden these practices is thus to inhibit many people's search for the ultimate good"

(Nussbaum 2000, 342). These fundamental or transcendent truths or understandings of life's ultimate meaning do not need to be conventionally religious. For example, the cumulative weight of court cases recognizing the rights of conscientious objectors to exemptions from military service or from the manufacture of weapons of war counts nonreligious ethical and moral beliefs as equivalent to religious ones in their eligibility as conscientious beliefs. Conscientious objection cases therefore provide a useful referent.

In 1965 in *United States v. Seeger* (380 U.S. 163 [1965]), the Supreme Court interpreted broadly Congress's provision that belief in a relationship with a supreme being—but not political, sociological, or economic considerations or a purely personal moral code—can ground conscientious exemption from military service. Justice Thomas Clark suggested that "a sincere and meaningful belief which occupies in the life of its possessor a place parallel to that filled by God of those admittedly qualifying for the exemption comes within the statutory definition," which makes clear that Congress did not intend to classify some religious beliefs as more relevant than others for purposes of claiming exemption from military service (176). To the court the objective test was "namely, does the claimed belief occupy the same place in the life of an objector as an orthodox belief in God holds in the life of one clearly qualified for the exemption?" (184). Five years later in *Welsh v. United States* (398 U.S. 333 [1970]), Justice Hugo Black, writing for the court, found that Elliot Welsh's convictions as a conscientious objector were religious in a broad, ethical sense, even if not in a conventional sense, and that Welsh's inclusion of political and economic objections to war did not thereby render inoperative his moral and ethical ones (340–43).

Most interesting for present purposes is a concurring opinion in *Welsh* by Justice John Marshall Harlan. Initially he appeared to oppose the decision (Welsh v. United States, 398 U.S. 333 [1970], at 351), maintaining that Congress surely proceeded from the conventional understanding of religion, which is to "associate religion with formal, organized worship or shared beliefs by a recognizable and cohesive group" (353). Rather than dissenting, however, Harlan concluded that once Congress chose to offer exemptions from military service to conscientious objectors, "it cannot draw the line between theistic or nontheistic religious beliefs, on the one hand, and secular beliefs on the other" (356). An exemption policy that merely eliminates the theistic requirement in favor of a broader distinction between religious views (theistic or nontheistic) and nonreligious views is not constitutionally viable. That is, to be neutral the policy must be broadened still further to allow exemptions for all conscientious objections, including those emanating from purely moral, ethical, and philosophical sources (357–58).

However, in his dissent in *Welsh*, Justice Byron White argued that a free exercise exemption for conscientious objectors, not required by the First Amendment, does not constitute an establishment of religion just because it fails to include nonreligious objectors, any more than *Sherbert v. Verner* constituted an establishment of religion by ruling that observant Seventh-Day Adventists should be eligible for unemployment compensation despite their unavailability for work on Saturdays. The very meaning of the free exercise clause is that "there is an area of conduct that cannot be forbidden to religious practitioners but that may be forbidden to others" (372). Justices Harlan and White thus represent opposite ends of a spectrum. Where White suggested that conscientious exemptions are a matter of grace and thus need only be offered to the conventionally religious, Harlan argued that once grace is offered, it must be offered to all who appear similarly situated in broad terms of conscientious belief.

If these cases are applied to the issue of same-sex marriage, *Seeger* suggests that the desire to marry occupies the same place for same-sex couples that it occupies for traditional couples. Same-sex couples who desire to marry are not following a merely personal moral code; rather they wish as citizens to participate in a universally recognized institution for the same reasons that traditional couples do, to publicly and privately affirm their personal long-term commitments. And like Harlan in *Welsh*, along with David Richards, one can argue that morally and ethically based desires to marry are on an equal footing with religiously based ones. One may also argue that opposite-sex and same-sex couples are similarly situated. That is, insofar as marriage exists as a civil institution, all couples who wish to participate according to the terms on which it is offered should be potential recipients of grace, so to speak, and should be eligible to do so.

Equating moral and ethical beliefs with religious ones does not begin or end with these cases. For example, in 1968 in *Epperson v. Arkansas* (393 U.S. 97 [1968]), the Supreme Court struck down the Arkansas law against teaching evolution in public schools because the law was based on a sectarian interpretation of the Bible: "The First Amendment mandates governmental neutrality between religion and religion, and between religion and nonreligion" (104). In 1992 in *Lee v. Weisman* (505 U.S. 577 [1992]), as we have seen, the court affirmed its ban on public school prayers by striking down student-led prayer at graduation ceremonies. In his concurring opinion Justice David Souter stated that the establishment clause applies "no less to governmental acts favoring religion generally than to acts favoring one religion over others" (610).

These comparisons can extend to the two 2005 cases addressing the public placement of the Ten Commandments, discussed in chapter 4. In *Van Orden v. Perry* (125 S. Ct. 2854 [2005]) Justice John Paul Stevens observed in his dissent that although a number of religious traditions may subscribe to these injunctions, past cases have "reaffirmed the principle that the Establishment clause requires the same respect for the atheist as it does for the adherent of a Christian faith" (2876). The Constitution's framers and various state constitutions interpreted religious freedom as referring only to various Christian denominations (2885–86); but "as religious pluralism has expanded, so has our acceptance of what constitutes valid belief systems" (2890). The court went the other way in the companion case to *Van Orden*, *McCreary County v. ACLU of Kentucky* (125 S. Ct. 2722 [2005]). Justice Scalia adhered in his dissent to a more traditional interpretation of conscience. Arguing that the United States, unlike many European countries, has never pretended to be a secular nation, Scalia asked how the court could "*possibly* assert" that the First Amendment requires neutrality between religion and nonreligion and forbids any purpose that favors a general adherence to religion (2750). Accommodating religious organizations by exempting them from various burdens and prohibitions "surely means to bestow a benefit on religious practice" (2751). Although these cases, like *Epperson* and *Lee*, are generally considered establishment cases, they directly compare nonreligious beliefs with conventionally religious ones, and they indirectly carry implications for the free exercise of the former.

One may infer a dialogue in comparing Stevens's dissent in *Van Orden* with Scalia's dissent in *McCreary*. Stevens asserted that governmental neutrality requires that religion in general not be favored over nonreligion, and Scalia responded that neutrality requires only that some religious traditions not be favored over others. If religion is broadly defined to involve the search for fundamental and transcendent truths, however, Scalia's dissent can be interpreted to suggest that all couples whose religious or nonreligious ethical, conscientious convictions impel them to seek civil marriage should be allowed to participate in this institution, although in reality Scalia limits his advocacy of free exercise to religions that have been traditional in the United States. Under the broader interpretation, however, marriage is the public expression, in David Richards's terms, of the fundamental right to an intimate life that, like the right to conscience, "protects intimately personal moral resources . . . and the way of life that expresses and sustains them in facing and meeting rationally and reasonably the challenge of a life worth living, one touched by enduring personal and ethical value" (Richards 1999, 74). For Scalia, just as religion in general may be favored over nonreligion, marriage in general can still be favored over intimate relationships outside of marriage.

Stevens's dissent in *Van Orden* can also be interpreted to favor the recognition of same-sex marriage. If one views his opinion from the perspective of an entire universe of types of intimate relationships, he could be read as suggesting that government must be neutral between marriage and other types of relationships, as it must be between religion and nonreligion. This interpretation suggests the disestablishment of marriage as a public institution as described by McConnell and Babst. If, however, one considers his point about increasing religious pluralism, the thrust of his argument opens the institution of marriage beyond that which conforms to earlier expectations. If "our acceptance of what constitutes valid belief systems" has expanded in the area of religion (Van Orden v. Perry, 125 S. Ct. 2854 [2005], at 2890), so also has our notion of what conscientious convictions deserve to be included alongside conventional ones.

The case most pertinent to the free exercise of conscientious belief is *Thomas v. Review Board* (450 U.S. 707 [1981]), in which the Supreme Court ruled in 1981 that a Jehovah's Witness refusing to work in a factory department making turrets for military tanks instead of the steel he had previously been fabricating should not be denied unemployment compensation by the state of Indiana. Although a fellow Jehovah's Witness with a laxer interpretation had advised Eddie Thomas that making weapons parts was not unacceptable, and although the Indiana Supreme Court had found that Thomas's claim was a personal philosophical choice rather than a religious one that would itself still not constitute good cause under Indiana law, Chief Justice Burger stated for the court that when Thomas drew a line between making sheet steel and tank turrets, "it is not for us to say that the line he drew was an unreasonable one." The free exercise guarantee is not limited to beliefs on which all members of a religious tradition agree (715–16). Overall, "Where the state conditions receipt of an important benefit upon conduct proscribed by a religious faith, or where it denies such a benefit because of conduct mandated by religious belief, . . . a burden upon religion exists. While the compulsion may be indirect, the infringement upon free exercise is nevertheless substantial" (717–18).

As the sole dissenter in *Thomas*, then Justice William Rehnquist contended that a religious exemption from the ordinary requirements of government unemployment compensation violates the establishment clause in purpose, in the advancement of religious belief, and in the resulting entanglement of the state by causing it to inquire into the religiosity and sincerity of individuals' beliefs. By reading the free exercise clause too expansively here, Rehnquist countered, the court has held that "a State is constitutionally required to provide direct financial assistance to persons solely on the basis of their religious beliefs." In his view the reach of the free exercise clause should be limited to its application to laws prohibiting religious practices altogether. However, here Indiana law did not deny unemployment benefits on the basis of religious belief but "simply made the practice of . . . religious beliefs more expensive" (Thomas v. Review Board, 450 U.S. 707 [1981], at 722). Whether the subject is Sunday closing laws or unemployment benefits, Rehnquist explained, "where a State has enacted a general statute, the purpose and effect of which is to advance the State's secular goals, the Free Exercise Clause does not in my view require the State to conform that statute to the dictates of religious conscience of any group" (723). That is, states are not mandated but are permitted voluntarily to grant exemptions from general unemployment regulations, because "such aid redounds directly to the benefit of the individual" (727).

A comparison of Burger's and Rehnquist's opinions in *Thomas* finds that Burger saw a substantial impairment of the free exercise of religion when the receipt of a benefit—in this case unemployment compensation—is predicated on the seemingly forbidden conduct of making tank turrets and is denied because of the conduct involved in voluntarily leaving one's employment. In contrast, Rehnquist saw little impairment. Thomas was not being coerced to remain in objectionable employment, in his view, but was simply being asked by the state of Indiana to bear the same burden borne by anyone else who, for whatever reason, deemed the benefits of his or her current employment to be outweighed by its costs. In this respect Rehnquist's view is similar to that of the court in *Thornton v. Calder*, in which the Supreme Court ruled that the Connecticut sabbath protection law unfairly advantaged sabbath observers over nonobservers, because only the former could freely select a weekend day off. Similarly for Rehnquist in *Thomas*, religious adherents and the nonreligious are on an equal footing because neither can enjoy exemptions on the basis of belief. Burger's opinion, in contrast, resembles that of the court in *Sherbert v. Verner*, in finding that religious practice burdened by generally applicable laws may require accommodation that need not be proffered to practices that do not flow from religious belief.

Despite Rehnquist's objections, if religion is broadly defined as constituting a conscientious individual search for fundamental and transcendent
truths, the Supreme Court's decision in *Thomas* cannot be viewed either as
favoring one sort of religious belief over others or as favoring religion in
its narrower definition over nonreligion. Applying this point to same-sex
marriage, one can argue that matters of conscience should be reserved for
individual determination absent evidence of harm, defined as civil injury
to others. If same-sex couples wish to marry civilly—whether for spiritual
reasons that do or do not accord with the mainstream positions of their
religious traditions, or for moral and ethical reasons that are not conventionally religious but occupy the place of religion in their belief systems—they
should be able to do so. Otherwise, in Burger's terms, the state conditions
receipt of the important benefit of civil marriage on heterosexual commitments conscientiously unavailable to same-sex couples, and it denies them
this benefit because of the same-sex commitments that do flow from their
conscientious convictions. *Thomas v. Review Board* can help make clear why
people who experience same-sex attraction should be accorded not only
negative freedom from interference in their private intimate relationships,
but also positive empowerment to participate civilly in a public institution.

Undue entanglement of the state with religion, which Rehnquist feared
would accompany religious accommodation in *Thomas*, only occurs if the
government deems it necessary to determine the nature and sincerity of
every couple's religious, moral, and ethical beliefs when they apply to marry.
The state conditions the marriage of traditional couples on legal and secular
requirements, however, not on ethical or religious ones. All the state must
do is open marriage to same-sex couples on the same terms as traditional
couples. Those whose religious, moral, and ethical beliefs impel them to
marry can avail themselves of the opportunity, and others can eschew it.
On a related note, Douglas Laycock suggests that conflict over same-sex
marriage would be reduced if civil and religious marriage were separated in
the law. When conservatives argue that marriage is sacred and that same-sex
marriage threatens its sanctity, they are using religious terms to defend a civil
institution that no longer enforces the sexual morality central to religious
understandings of marriage. Ideally, Laycock argues, the term "marriage"
should apply only to religious unions performed by clergy, whereas "civil
unions," performed by civil servants, might better describe the legal unions
contracted by both same-sex and opposite-sex couples. Couples can enter
either or both of these statuses. Overall, he concludes, it would be a step
forward to disabuse people of the idea that "the 'sanctity' of marriage de-

pends on law, not faith" (Laycock 2008, 207; see also 201–7; Babst 2002, 14, 17–18; Metz 2004, 100; Metz 2010, 114–19; Shanley 2004a, 112–13).

Including same-sex couples in the civil institution of marriage when this institution is stripped of religious meaning does not constitute a total disestablishment, however, as long as the civil institution exists. Skeptics and libertarians object to the rigidity of marriage as a civil institution irrespective of any connection to religion. Laycock's suggestion disestablishes marriage, or the institution that is known by that name. But whether an institution through which the state confers rights and responsibilities on couples who wish to enter it is called "marriage" or "civil union," it still exists as an available status. True disestablishment of marriage or marriage-like institutions would mean that no such encompassing civil status would exist at all, and individuals would negotiate their own relationships through private and voluntary contracts governing interests in property, the protection of offspring, and so forth. Neither this kind of disestablishment nor the replacement of civil marriage with civil unions are politically realistic options. I do agree with Laycock, however, that failure to separate the civil from the religious elements of marriage, at least in our thinking, obfuscates the importance of extending marriage to same-sex couples as a free exercise of conscientious belief for those who want to take advantage of this status.

Finally, although the state supports conscientious objection to military service and to employment that supports military endeavors by affording accommodation to conscientious beliefs in specific circumstances, it would be a stretch to conclude that the state welcomes such objections. In contrast, because the state obviously encourages and supports the institution of marriage, it should welcome subscribers who have previously been excluded. This does not mean that it must welcome every aspiring participant. The suitability of applicants from one group may arguably satisfy the objectives sought by maintaining marriage as a public institution, whereas applicants from another group may not be suitable in this way. The case for each group must be considered on the merits.

Possible Objections to the Free Exercise Analogy

Under a broad definition of "religion," one may pose objections to treating same-sex marriage as a right of conscience. In the military service cases, those aspiring to conscientious objector status have petitioned the government to refrain from placing them within a particular classification: people of whom military service would otherwise be expected. Same-sex couples aspiring to marry, in contrast, are asking the state to take positive action to place them within a particular classification: couples permitted to marry. McConnell and Nussbaum argue that the right to free exercise of religion should not dictate the civil definition of marriage. McConnell suggests that there is a difference between requiring the government not to interfere with private religious or sexual practices and requiring it to adjust its own definition of a public institution. "Free exercise protects the right of religious communities and their members to perform marriage ceremonies as they wish. . . . But free exercise does not dictate how the state should define 'marriage' in its public aspect" (McConnell 1998, 249). Rehnquist similarly asserted, "The Free Exercise Clause does not in my view require the state to conform that statute to the dictates of religious conscience of any group" (Thomas v. Review Board, 450 U.S. 707 [1981], at 723).

The difficulty with these objections is that both McConnell and Rehnquist focus on religious communities or on the communal nature of religious belief. The *Thomas* court found for Thomas as an individual, not for Jehovah's Witnesses as a group. It did not matter that he was not necessarily in accord with others of his own religious tradition. Likewise with regard to same-sex marriage, no one should interfere with the right of religious communities to solemnize whatever unions they choose; I focus instead on the individual or on same-sex couples who, as two individuals, wish to participate in the civil institution of marriage. No one is suggesting that religious communities be compelled to solemnize unions they oppose, and those denied religious solemnization of their unions in one religious community may seek other religious communities that will accede to their wishes. What same-sex couples want, however, is the civil solemnization of their unions in the eyes of the state. Their religious or nonreligious moral and ethical beliefs may impel them to participate in the institution of marriage not—or not only—to attain conventionally religious legitimacy, but rather to attain civil legitimacy.

Although it may appear paradoxical to suggest that the desire for civil recognition emanates from religious or conscientious moral belief, admission to a key social institution on the same terms as others can be an important focus. As Jyl Josephson notes, "Marriage posits a specific desirable form of intimacy and family life—despite contemporary reality—and reinforces that form through legal, economic, political, and social privileges" (Josephson 2005, 271). In other words, civil marriage is held out as a goal to which one should aspire. The inability to make this commitment publicly—not only "in the eyes of God and this congregation" but also in the eyes of the state and the hypothetical assemblage of one's fellow citizens—can thwart individuals, in David Richards's terms, in "the free exercise of the moral powers of rationality and reasonableness in terms of which persons define personal and ethical meaning in living" (Richards 1999, 18). If the ability to live out the implications of one's deepest commitments is a form of conscience, Richards argues that this ability should be protected, just as our tradition of religious liberty has typically protected, or at least aspired to protect, all forms of conscience, both theistic and nontheistic (88, 94).

Therefore, although the free exercise of religious communities as such is not impeded, the free exercise of some individuals is blocked. The *Thomas* court found that "where the state conditions receipt of an important benefit upon conduct proscribed by a religious faith, or where it denies such a benefit because of conduct mandated by religious belief, . . . a burden on religion exists. While the compulsion may be indirect, the infringement upon free exercise is nonetheless substantial" (Thomas v. Review Board, 450 U.S. 707 [1981], at 717–18). Although Rehnquist contended that the exercise of Thomas's religious beliefs was not prohibited but was simply made more expensive, excluding same-sex couples from the institution of marriage denies civil marriage altogether to these couples. If one views the desire to marry as an instance of conscientious belief based upon deeply held religious, moral, or ethical convictions, the state, in the court's terms, is conditioning an important benefit upon conduct—commitment to someone of the *opposite* sex—and proscribing that benefit, making it unavailable, to individuals with a same-sex orientation on the basis of their conscientious moral and ethical beliefs. Correspondingly and simultaneously, the state denies the benefits of marriage to same-sex couples "because of conduct mandated by religious belief," that is, because of the same-sex commitments impelled by these couples' deeply held convictions.

Although the state is not targeting specific conduct flowing from conscientious beliefs, excluding same-sex couples from marriage has the same effect as targeting the conduct does. This trajectory results in a substantial infringement on the free exercise of these beliefs. From this perspective, then, it should not matter that same-sex couples' desire to be included in the civil institution of marriage requires a positive action rather than a refraining action. The free exercise of conscientious beliefs can be thwarted as effectively by one dynamic as by the other. Moreover, because *Thomas* and *Sherbert* involved unemployment compensation, both cases were also requests for the positive awarding of material benefits. Therefore, an interpretation of the free exercise clause that mandates positive state action, not simply a withholding of interference, has precedent.

A second objection to treating the desire for same-sex marriage as a right of conscience focuses more directly on the benefits, civil and otherwise, that accompany civil marriage. Consider again the components of what we call "marriage," as discussed in chapter 1. First, a personal bond and a desire for a long-term commitment obviously must exist between any two people who wish to marry. Second, the longer two people are together by whatever definition, they come to be treated and referred to as a couple by their friends, associates, and others in their community, thus forming a relationship that is publicly recognized, with or without some ceremony of affirmation. If same-sex couples desire the third component, a religious union, they can generally find some religious leader to perform a rite to bless the union, or they may seek a religious community within which their commitments may be solemnized. Why then should civil marriage matter?

It certainly matters to those with unconventional conscientious beliefs, such as agnostics or atheists, who may desire some sort of formal rite but for whom there is really no organized community of conscience. Additionally, as noted throughout this book, there is the perceived desirability of participating in a historically and highly esteemed social institution. Maggie Gallagher, a traditionalist opponent of same-sex marriage, argues that material benefits are unimportant to same-sex couples. Canvassing the ten largest cities with domestic partner registries and the ten largest corporations with domestic partner benefits, she found that in both contexts same-sex partners were registered or utilized their partners' health insurance in numbers equal to about 0.1 percent of the eligible population. She concludes that most same-sex partners, like opposite-sex cohabitants, are likely not interested in marriage anyway. "Instead, the drive for same-sex marriage appears to be a largely symbolic cultural issue; the goal (or at any rate the main effect) is not filling a need for health insurance or other practical benefits, but making a powerful social statement" (Gallagher 2003, 20).

Gallagher implies that the "largely symbolic cultural issue" involves altering our society in a direction with which she does not agree, but I believe that the issue involves treating all committed couples as possessing equal worth. The social statement made by including same-sex couples in civil marriage replaces a public expression of civic inequality with a public expression of civic equality: an acknowledgment that same-sex couples' relationships carry worth and value equal to those of opposite-sex couples. Gallagher also contradicts herself when she assumes that few such couples really want to marry. If same-sex couples who wish to marry are really as few as she surmises, including them is unlikely to do the damage that she predicts. If, however, there are enough marriage-seeking same-sex couples to change the institution in ways that she deplores, she cannot argue against their inclusion on the basis of the low numbers of couples who might avail themselves of that opportunity. In other words, she cannot have it both ways.

The frequency with which individuals may freely exercise their conscientious beliefs should not in any case bear on whether they are afforded the opportunity to do so. In *Thomas v. Review Board*, the fact that not all Jehovah's Witnesses view working to make tank turrets as strictly as Thomas viewed such work did not deter the Supreme Court from finding in his favor. As a similar example of the unimportance of numbers when basic liberties and rights are at stake, consider *United States v. Virginia* (518 U.S. 515 [1996]), in which the Supreme Court in 1996 struck down the single-sex status of publicly funded Virginia Military Institute (VMI) despite the inception of a parallel program for women elsewhere. Strasser explains that the court's "focus was not on whether the classes were being treated differently, but on the particular women who had the will and capacity to succeed at VMI and on the loss of VMI's unique training and opportunities that these women would have suffered had VMI's exclusion of women not been struck down" (Strasser 2002, 18; see 18–19, 33–35).

In *United States v. Virginia* the court found that, first, it did not matter how many women were interested in or qualified for VMI's rigorous program; the fact that some who might qualify were excluded from a public institution was enough. Similarly, the fact that marriage is not for everyone, whatever his or her sexual orientation, does not matter; the fact that some same-sex couples wish to undertake this commitment should be enough. Second, the court found that opening VMI to women did not mean endorsing the enrollment of women as a kind of special right. Rather, it simply extended an opportunity to them that was already afforded to men. In the same way, recognizing same-sex marriage simply extends to same-sex couples the opportunity to participate in an institution that has long been afforded to opposite-sex couples.

During hearings in *United States v. Virginia*, experts for the state of Virginia and VMI testified as to the unsuitability of VMI's adversarial system of education for women. Justice Ruth Bader Ginsburg, writing for the majority, likened their testimony to that of nineteenth-century experts like Dr. Edward H. Clarke of Harvard Medical School, who had argued that rigorous academic competition would damage young women's reproductive development. Clarke wrote, "Identical education of the two sexes is a crime before God and humanity that physiology protests against, that experience weeps over" (quoted in Strum 2002, 298; see also Richards 1999, 40, 138–40, 150). Clarke's statement illustrates the barriers posed by gender stereotypes that themselves reflect a context of past gender-based discrimination. The analogy to stereotypes regarding same-sex relationships and their recognition could hardly be more obvious.

With reference to stereotypes, Samuel Marcosson illuminates a common theme that can be found in the context of racial exclusion in suburbs; Colorado's Amendment 2, overturned in 1996 in *Romer v. Evans*; VMI's exclusion of women, which was ended the same year by *United States v. Virginia*; and the exclusion of same-sex couples from marriage. Marcosson observes, "Like Amendment 2, refusing to recognize same-sex marriage uniquely disadvantages gay Americans in a way that is intrinsic to the maintenance of heterosexual privilege. Exclusively heterosexual marriage is for straight citizens precisely what VMI was for men and suburbs have been for whites: an enclave that preserves the separateness and presumptive superiority of the group that has shut the door behind it" (Marcosson 1998, 244). The exclusivity of traditional marriage has a historical basis and therefore is not immediately analogous to the courts' deliberate protection of suburban schools' insularity. However, maintaining marital discrimination now in the face of the campaign to eliminate it represents a device "by which the powerful majority idealizes its own self-image, and defines the 'other' by virtue of its being unable to live up to that standard" (245).

More specifically, Marcosson argues, "By reserving the ideal represented by marriage for itself, the heterosexual majority is attempting to define itself by reference to this lodestar: to be married is to be an adult, to accept commitment, to pledge oneself to fidelity and loyalty and devotion. It is to be part of society's most sacred institution and its traditional unit of procreation," while excluding "the hedonistic, present-oriented, promiscuous, and selfish homosexual" (Marcosson 1998, 246). Similarly, VMI posed the stereotypically heterosexual male ideals of male bonding, strength, and discipline against the threat to male status, identity, and privilege represented by the inclusion of women. "The message of disapproval of homosexual relationships sent by denying them the legal status of 'marriage' is meant to reinforce and idealize heterosexuality; this, in turn, is inextricably connected to the same project of reinforcing gender norms that was at the core of the exclusion of women from VMI" (248; see 246–50). Marcosson's analysis resonates with the opinion in *Perry v. Schwarzenegger* (704 F.Supp.2d 921 [Cal. 2010]), which struck down California's Proposition 8. That is, for voters the appeal of that proposition lay in its implication that opposite-sex couples are morally superior to same-sex couples.

Although maintaining the privileged enclaves of white suburbia, discriminatory political entities in Colorado, and an all-male VMI certainly
constitutes establishments that disadvantage those who are excluded, these
exclusions also carry free exercise implications. If the adherents of a majority
religion pass or maintain laws that impinge upon the ability of unpopular
minority religions to practice their faiths freely when these practices are not
in themselves illegal, most observers might say that these laws interfere with
the free exercise of religion. Depending upon the context, they might also
conclude that the effect, and in some cases the purpose, of these laws is to
maintain the majority's privileged status by reinforcing its own self-image as
the ideal embodiment of the practice of religious faith. On a related note,
Babst argues that heteronormativity, or the idea that heterosexuality is the
norm, is grounded on monism, or the idea that only one way of being is
normal and that alternatives are deviations from that norm (Babst 2009,
187–88). The norm of heterosexuality in the West springs from the Hebrew Bible, he explains. "The identity formed by heteronormativity, to the
extent that it is moored in religion, is forged antithetically to any rival, with
just the same consequences for pluralism in thinking about sexuality as the
Hebrew Bible allowed for any rival religious identity." Nevertheless, "humanity turns out always to have been all along more pluralist in its religious
understandings, as well as in its actual sexual practices, whether sanctioned
or not" (Babst 2009, 188; see 187–90). Put differently, heteronormativity
establishes a particular kind of sexuality as the norm, superior to all others,
just as surely as an establishment of religion posits a particular kind of belief
system as the norm, superior to all others. The consequences of this parallel
have hindered the recognition of human pluralism, with often predictable
consequences for the free exercise either of sexuality or of religion.

Finally, there are of course those legal and economic advantages that
accompany civil marriage alone. This point might lead those with a cyni-
cal turn of mind to suggest the opposite of Gallagher's point: that same-sex
couples actually are in it only for the material benefits. If true, however, this
alone still poses difficulties for opponents of same-sex marriage. Even classic
arguments for religious toleration, such as those made by Locke, have recognized that civil authority must establish civil criteria of material or worldly
injury to life, liberty, and property that may then determine the appropriate
scope and limits of the free practice of religion. That is, to avoid harm to
the worldly rights or interests of citizens, the line between what is civil or
secular and what is religious must be determined by civil government, not
by advocates of religion, and this line may change with the demands of the

public interest, which is itself civilly determined (Creppell 1996, 224; see also McClure 1990, 373–81; Locke 1689, 48–50).

Receipt of the legal and economic benefits that only civil marriage confers is certainly a vital secular good and an individual interest that should not be conditioned on adherence to a sectarian definition of marriage, even if— or especially if—the sectarian aspects result from merely a "shadow establishment," in Babst's terms. The traditional definition of marriage is one that prohibits some couples from making commitments that may be expressions of deeply held conscientious beliefs. If same-sex couples seek civil marriage for its public statement of their conscientious religious, moral, and ethical commitments, then free exercise considerations take on added importance.

CHAPTER 6

Establishment and Free Exercise

Who Should Be Outsiders?

Chapter 1 compares national citizenship and civil marriage as institutions that have lessened in importance as sources of rights and benefits. Participation in each case is consensual; both noncitizens and unmarried persons must consent if they are to attain these statuses. In the consensual model, however, both citizenship and marriage rest not only on the consent of the individuals seeking them but also on the consent of the state in whose eyes individuals want to be treated as citizens or as married persons. Those who wish to become citizens may not primarily desire the accompanying material benefits. Instead they may value first and foremost the ethical worth that their relationships embody (Smith 2009, 932). The same is true of civil marriage. Whether or not national citizenship and civil marriage are the most appropriate bases for forming and maintaining community memberships and families in the twenty-first century, they are institutions in which many individuals want to participate. Some believe that the existence of sufficiently personal ties with or within a society entitles those holding such ties to citizenship, an ascriptive definition seemingly at odds with the consensual model of citizenship. Regarding civil marriage, however, the de facto ties that same-sex couples form entitle them to participate in this institution on an ascriptive as well as consensual basis. Because same-sex relationships afford as much value to same-sex couples as opposite-sex relationships afford to traditional couples, the state should legitimate and affirm them through the status of civil marriage. Because civil marriage is a public institution, to do less embodies a public expression of civic inequality.

People's ruminations about diversity in both national citizenship and civil marriage founder upon fears of change in institutions that people view as right because they are traditional, to the exclusion of all novel configurations. For example, in 2009 Marcus Epstein, author of a report for American Cause, an anti-immigration group, said, "Diversity can be good in moderation—if what is being brought in is desirable. Most Americans don't mind a little ethnic food, some Asian math whizzes, or a few Mariachi dancers—as long as these trends do not overwhelm the dominant culture" (quoted in *New York Times* 2009b). Many traditionalists, I surmise, react the same way to same-sex marriage. To trade in popular stereotypes, they do not mind a little high fashion, some unconventional interior decorators, or a few gay pride parades. If same-sex couples demand to be treated like normal couples when "everyone knows" they are not, however, traditionalists begin to believe that LGBT persons threaten to overwhelm the dominant but apparently vulnerable heteronormative culture. In fact, some may see the desire to marry as more threatening than overtly different behavior, because the desire to marry may appear normal and harmless and may thereby catch people off guard. The traditionalists fear that people then will be less prepared to defend the dominant culture against threatening but unrecognized incursions.

The work of John Stuart Mill is instructive regarding people's attachments to the institutionalized customs of the dominant culture. In his 1869 work *The Subjection of Women*, he lamented the fact that those who advocate equal legal rights for women are forced to argue for equality, when in his opinion equal legal rights should be the initial assumption. Those who do not want to treat women equally should instead bear the burden of proving that women are not fit for legal equality. The difficulty, however, is that entrenched convictions are often based on feelings, not on reasoned arguments. Mill explains, "So long as an opinion is strongly rooted in feelings, it gains rather than loses in stability by having a preponderating weight of argument against it. For if it were accepted as a result of argument, the refutation of the argument might shake the solidity of the conviction; but when it rests solely on feeling, the worse it fares in argumentative contest, the more persuaded its adherents are that their feeling must have some deeper ground, which the arguments do not reach" (Mill 1869, 119). Some of the traditionalist arguments against same-sex marriage fit this description. The new natural lawyers, for example, single out the lack of complementarity of same-sex couples' sexual organs as a kind of deeper ground for their conclusion that although these couples may participate in the ritual forms of marriage, civil or religious, the substance of true marriage is lacking. Yet in *Perry v. Schwarzenegger* (704 F.Supp.2d 921 [Cal. 2010]), the federal lawsuit against the constitutionality of California's Proposition 8, Judge Vaughn Walker asked how opposite-sex marriages might be harmed by same-sex marriage. Defending lawyer Charles Cooper replied, "Your Honor, my answer is: I don't know. I don't know" (quoted in Talbot 2010, 51).

When an opinion rooted in feeling is entrenched, Mill went on to explain, a proponent of change "should be expected not only to answer all that has ever been said by those who take the other side of the question, but to imagine all that could be said by them." After refuting all existing and anticipated arguments against change, "I should be thought to have done little; for a cause supported on the one hand by universal usage, and on the other by so great a preponderance of popular sentiment, is supposed to have a presumption in its favour, superior to any conviction which an appeal to reason has power to produce" (Mill 1869, 121). This resonates with a point made by Jonathan Chait: "If you place zero weight upon the preferences of gays, then all you have to do is suggest a *possible* harm, however remote, associated with gay marriage" to discredit the idea entirely. As proof, Chait cites a traditionalist opponent who admits that however unlikely a particular scenario may be, she is reluctant to risk allowing same-sex marriage if the chances are "anything more than zero" (Chait 2009, 2). Mill noted, "Laws and systems of polity always begin by recognising the relations they find already existing between individuals" (Mill 1869, 122–23). This point is also true of civil marriage.

As chapter 1 describes, marriage became a civil institution when the state began to recognize existing unions, often the result of "self-marriage" and of informal public recognition that such unions are legal. In time, however, the state's sanction of personal commitments broadened into state definition and control of the rules by which couples might marry. Laws recognize existing relationships that are a matter of custom or choice. These legal systems congeal over time, though, in ways that are hostile to change even in the presence of reasoned argument for it. Mill cited chattel slavery and absolute monarchy as examples of the power of established systems that went long unquestioned in the same way male domination was unquestioned in his own time. "But was there ever any domination which did not appear natural to those who possessed it?" (Mill 1869, 129). Similarly, exclusively traditional marriage appears natural to those who do not question the heteronormativity of the dominant culture. Explaining this phenomenon further, Mill said, "So true is it that unnatural generally means only uncustomary, and that everything which is usual appears natural. The subjection of women to men being a universal custom, any departure from it quite naturally appears unnatural" (130; see 127–31). In the same way, because confining marriage to opposite-sex couples is viewed by its proponents as a universal custom, the idea of including same-sex couples "naturally appears unnatural."

Mill also has a response applicable to those who believe that same-sex couples are unsuited to the long-term committed relationship that marriage is meant to instantiate. Considering the seeming unsuitability of women's nature for legal emancipation, he wrote, "The anxiety of mankind to interfere in behalf of nature, for fear lest nature should not succeed in effecting its purpose, is an altogether unnecessary solicitude. What women by nature cannot do, it is quite superfluous to forbid them from doing" (Mill 1869, 143). Same-sex couples who do not at least aspire to the commitment that marriage represents are similarly unlikely to seek this status. Those who marry with good intentions and later find that they cannot live up to the ideals historically associated with marriage are certainly no different from traditional couples, whose high rates of infidelity and divorce are lamented by many of the same individuals and groups who seek to protect marriage by excluding same-sex couples from the institution. The exclusion of same-sex couples from marriage by reason of unsuitability is overinclusive, because many same-sex couples who want to marry already enjoy long-term committed relationships. Exclusion is also underinclusive, because many traditional couples who marry lack the ability or will to live out the terms that marriage is supposed to embody.

Absent the showing of a compelling state interest in prohibiting practices flowing from belief or orientation as a matter of conscience, I argue in this book that public policy should treat same-sex relationships as it treats opposite-sex relationships—just as it does between one religious belief and another. Current free exercise jurisprudence takes its cue from *Employment Division v. Smith* (404 U.S. 872 [1990]), in which the Supreme Court ruled that the state of Oregon could deny unemployment benefits to members of the Native American church for using peyote in religious ceremonies without demonstrating a compelling state interest, because the penalty for religious practice was only the incidental effect of a neutral and generally applicable law. Regarding marriage, however, there is no neutral and generally applicable law of which the exclusion of same-sex couples is merely the incidental effect—only the shadow establishment, in Gordon Babst's terms, of the heteronormative social order (Babst 2009, 183–85). As seen in recent state marriage cases (mentioned in chapter 5), existing law in many states can be and has been interpreted to include rather than to exclude same-sex couples. Here they seek not an exemption from existing law but simply inclusion in it. What harms the interests and rights of same-sex couples is not the application of neutral and generally applicable laws, but rather the failure to apply this law to them in the same way that it applies to traditional couples. Therefore, a compelling state interest must be shown if these couples are to be excluded from civil marriage.

In this concluding chapter I address the issue of same-sex marriage in the context of cultural conflict. First, no neutral compromise exists that simultaneously satisfies both opponents and proponents of same-sex marriage. What appears to be neutral is not so on a metatheoretical level. Second, just as the state not only allows the practice of religion within broad limits but also constitutionally protects its exercise, even when certain practices are distasteful to some observers, the state not only permits marriage by adult couples but also encourages it. As Carlos Ball argues, marriage provides a framework for expressing the human capabilities of both physical and emotional intimacy in a context of love and care. The state cannot legitimately extend participation in this institution to some couples but withhold it from others, especially when the reason for withholding it primarily centers on some people's distaste for some kinds of couples. Exclusion is clearly a public expression of civic inequality.

Context and the Culture Wars

In the context of the First Amendment religion clauses, Michael McConnell argues that no one can expect agreement on the meaning of endorsement. "Whether a particular governmental action appears to endorse or disapprove religion depends on the presupposition of the observer, and there is no 'neutral' position, outside the culture, from which to make this assessment. . . . It is nothing more than an application of the religion clauses to the principle: 'I know it when I see it'" (McConnell 1992, 148). Chapter 2 discusses the difficulty of agreeing even on what is meant by "neutrality" and hence by "endorsement"; chapter 4 addresses the difficulty of applying these concepts in the establishment context concerning both religion and sexuality. I agree with McConnell then that no Archimedean point exists from which one can make these kinds of judgments.

The problem to which McConnell alludes may be illustrated by Justice Antonin Scalia's dissent in *Romer v. Evans* (517 U.S. 620 [1996]). Where Justice Anthony Kennedy argued in his opinion for the court that the disadvantages imposed by Colorado's Amendment 2, forbidding antidiscrimination protections, appeared to be "born of animosity toward the class of persons affected" (634), Scalia replied that Colorado was entitled to disfavor, to exhibit moral disapproval of, or even to exhibit an "animus" toward conduct its citizens considered reprehensible (644–45). For Kennedy, Amendment 2 removed the possibility of seeking or keeping protections against discrimination based on sexual orientation, thereby endorsing a diminution of this class's status compared to its baseline situation before the amendment passed. *Romer* was simply restoring a level playing field. To Scalia, however, Amendment 2 was enacted by a democratic majority to reflect its moral sentiments. The court in *Romer* was rendering illegitimate Colorado's desire to uphold the sort of morality its citizens preferred, endorsing instead its own moral preferences. Therefore, *Romer* was upsetting the playing field, rather than leveling it.

If judgments about what policies are neutral and what constitutes endorsement depend on the framework within which issues are presented and viewed, no solution to controversies such as that over same-sex marriage appears uniformly neutral from every perspective. Even when we earnestly apply ourselves to refine policies to instantiate neutrality, we only succeed in terms of particular interpretations of neutrality that necessarily favor some definitions of neutrality over others. Therefore, I do not hesitate to espouse and argue for definitions that within broad limits allow all citizens to exercise personal autonomy in living their intimate lives despite other citizens' disapproval. As David A. J. Richards explains, in the American constitutional tradition "the right to intimate life is as much a basic human right as the right to conscience; conscience is so personally engaged with the issues of intimate sexual life because both involve the resources of thought, conviction, feeling, and emotion at the heart of the ultimate concerns of moral personality" (Richards 2005, 110; see also 74, 103–4). The right to intimate life does not need to include marriage, just as the right to follow one's conscientious beliefs concerning religion, or for that matter nonreligion, does not need to include any particular set of specific practices. Nevertheless, for the state to deny to some individuals a set of practices that other individuals are allowed and encouraged to pursue publicly expresses the civic inequality of those who are denied.

Despite McConnell's conviction that no truly neutral position exists on many divisive issues, he does consider the hypothetical possibility of a neutralist or compromise position regarding sexuality. His thought experiment is particularly interesting because he specifically takes his cue from religious neutrality and extends it to neutrality concerning sexual orientation. Religion and sexuality alike, McConnell suggests, involve choice but also go beyond it, encompass both opinion and conduct, possess both public and private aspects, and in short "are central aspects of personal identity" (McConnell 1998, 234). The pluralist solution to religious difference has been to avoid taking a public position on the merits of contending religious views. Might then the solution to deep divisions about the morality of same-sex relationships be a refusal to take a public position on this topic as well? A "First Amendment" position treats both conflicting views "as conscientious positions, worthy of respect, much as we treat both atheism and faith as worthy of respect" (235). McConnell's suggestion instantiates neither neutrality nor civic equality. It is worth considering, however, because the reasons for its failure teach something about both neutrality and civic equality.

Sketching the jurisprudence of the religion clauses, McConnell distinguishes between the privatization approach that consigns religion-sensitive issues to the private sphere, and the equal access approach that allows "competing groups to participate in the public sphere on equal terms." In the context of sexuality, privatization "would insist that all activities directly related to the formation of opinion about homosexuality be confined to private institutions, where there should be no interference with either beliefs (orientation) or conduct." Equal access would call for equal treatment in the public domain of all private views, but "would be careful not to convey the impression that the government is expressing a view" (McConnell 1998, 237). If these jurisprudential categories are applied to sexual orientation and practice, McConnell's test is whether governmental stances in various areas convey moral approval or disapproval, or whether they merely allow those who endorse or disapprove of various types of sexual expression to participate on equal terms in the public sphere, just as those of diverse religious beliefs do.

In application, although a "disestablishment approach" might guarantee equal protection of the laws from private violence for the free exercise of sexual orientation (McConnell 1998, 240–41), McConnell suggests that this approach might well uphold the now repealed ban on military service by openly gay or lesbian personnel. Apart from an arguably legitimate need for conformity, the massive educational effort to discipline "aggressive, undercivilized" troops, in McConnell's words, and educate them to accept openly gay comrades would have to inculcate full acceptance of their moral legitimacy, rather than mere civil toleration. This effort in turn belies efforts at neutrality because the government endorses a moral position in the process. Although gay pride celebrations are protected like private religious speech even on public property, "the government must scrupulously refrain from even the appearance of endorsement" (243), meaning no more mayors marching in gay pride parades. For public schools, a "disestablishment approach" leads to difficulties in making effective distinctions between teaching about religion and teaching religion itself similarly problematize sex education, because even moral neutrality among types of sexual expression is itself a moral attitude (244–47). Although student-run gay clubs in public schools, like religious clubs, would be protected as instances of equal access in this approach, their supporters would have to refrain from accusing opponents of prejudice or bigotry. Instead, each school would have "to declare that the school board is not a competent judge of the truth of these matters, and to leave the citizens (including students) free to take positions on their own" (248). Finally, antidiscrimination laws would be allowable in a "disestablishment approach," with exemptions for conscientious belief, so long as they convey the secular and institutional message that "disapprobation of aberrant sexual practices ought to be expressed by means other than the economic power of employers over workers" (254). Such laws would not be permissible if they intend to effect a cultural education and transformation of attitudes toward same-sex relationships (252–55). In all examples given here, the context is crucial in ensuring that the government is not perceived to be endorsing a message.

McConnell believes that same-sex marriage can be justified under neither a separationist nor an equal access approach. A truly separationist arrangement requires the abolition of marriage as a public institution, leaving marriage to religious organizations that may at their own discretion unite couples seeking religious solemnization of their bonds. This disposition resembles Douglas Laycock's argument that ideally the designation of "marriage" should apply only to religious unions performed by clergy, whereas the term "civil unions" can describe the legal unions contracted by both same-sex and opposite-sex couples through civil servants such as county clerks or judges. In this arrangement couples can enter into either or both of these statuses, depending on their personal desires or the willingness of religious organizations to unite them in marriage (Laycock 2008, 201–7). Charles Reid, in contrast, argues that a separation of religion and law is unworkable because even civil marriage, as it developed in the West, has taken its bearings from the religious values of procreation, permanence, and fidelity. In the nineteenth-century United States, "Christianity was accepted as a source of the common law and judges and jurists were not shy about drawing from conventional Christian sources to explain whole areas of law" (Reid 2008, 181–82; see also Shanley 2004c, 7). Marriage involves a commitment to transcendent values, Reid argues, from which it cannot be detached without becoming mundane as an institution.

In large part this conflation of civil and sacred derives from the fact that clergy in the United States are deputized as agents of the state for the purpose of celebrating marriages, which are therefore simultaneously religious solemnizations and the execution of civil contracts. I emphasize, however, that couples want to enter into unions called "marriage" not only or even primarily for its material benefits; rather they do so because marriage as such has historically been the gold standard for the public recognition of long-term committed relationships. I believe that the civil institution of marriage is capacious enough to admit same-sex couples without losing its association with the transcendent values that Reid is so anxious to preserve—even if individual couples, whether traditional or same-sex, define them in varying ways. The plaintiffs in the recent state marriage cases mentioned in chapter 5 have sought the title of "marriage" for their civilly contracted unions, arguing that although relegating the formal recognition of same-sex relationships to the status of civil unions attempts to establish a separate but equal institution, in truth it confers a badge of inferiority on same-sex relationships. As McConnell suggests, the context is all-important when we are inferring what message a particular institutional arrangement conveys. Therefore, as long as marriage exists as a public, civil institution, its establishment as an institution only for traditional couples is analogous to an establishment of religion that confers status and benefits only on its own adherents. Moreover, same-sex couples do not have the option of "converting" to the established "religion" to participate in civil marriage. Those experiencing same-sex attraction do have the formal option of marrying individuals of the opposite sex. They may do so, however, only at the price of relinquishing the authenticity of their own identities and intimate relationships, just as individuals whose consciences draw them to one religion would pay a similar price if they felt compelled to convert to a different religion to avoid civic inequality.

Although McConnell's attempt to compromise by providing a First Amendment solution to moral disagreements on the value of same-sex relationships is ingenious in its conceptualization, I do not believe that it works. Although he does not say so explicitly, McConnell implies that positive action on behalf of same-sex couples by allowing them to marry falls into the same category as antidiscrimination laws in general. According to his First Amendment approach to sexuality, these laws are permissible only if they are not meant to educate and transform attitudes toward same-sex relationships. The admission of same-sex couples does, however, affect attitudes when these couples are treated with the same respect accorded to traditional couples—a major reason why same-sex couples seeking to marry want to be included in the institution called "marriage" in the first place. Overall, McConnell suggests that if same-sex rights supporters' concern is with the real effects of discrimination rather than with ideological victories, they should not attempt to make antidiscrimination laws into moral statements. Otherwise "it will be apparent that their real purpose is . . . to impose their beliefs through the power of the state" (McConnell 1998, 255). However, admitting same-sex couples to civil marriage is a moral statement of sorts, whether or not it is so intended. Is it therefore an attempt to combat discrimination, or is it sought as an ideological victory? Both the presence and absence of antidiscrimination laws, and both the inclusion and exclusion of same-sex couples from the institution of marriage, constitute moral statements and are thus nonneutral.

Even when the government's actual and stated purpose is not to endorse a particular moral viewpoint, parties to a controversy view either action or inaction as a de facto endorsement of one side or the other. As chapters 2 and 3 make clear, conflicting sets of social facts ensure that what one side views as civilly benign appears civilly injurious to the other side. According legitimacy to same-sex relationships by recognizing same-sex marriage appears benign to advocates, because it simply gives the same recognition and respect to the intimate, lasting commitments of same-sex couples that traditional couples have always received. This move appears injurious to opponents, however, because it elevates couples in relationships they find immoral, offering them the same status that these opponents themselves have uniquely enjoyed. Even the disestablishment of marriage as a public institution, relegating its spiritual and ethical meaning to the private sphere, is nonneutral. Although traditionalists and same-sex marriage proponents disagree about the legitimacy of same-sex marriage, partisans on each side ironically entertain, as Patrick Neal puts it, the same conceptualization of their conceptions of the good (Neal 1997, 37–38). That is, neither side wishes to engage in the merely private pursuit of what it understands to be the value of marriage. Both want the endorsement that accompanies only a public institution.

The nonneutrality of McConnell's First Amendment solution is made clearer by referring briefly back to Chai Feldblum's discussion of neutrality, addressed in chapter 2. When the government decides through the law that a particular way of life is harmful neither to those who live it nor to others exposed to it, Feldblum suggests, this decision is a position of moral neutrality. The government is not saying that same-sex relationships, for example, are either bad or good, so the government on this issue can be said to be morally agnostic about the good. This position corresponds to McConnell's hypothetical solution, in which school boards could not take a position on either the acceptability or unacceptability of same-sex relationships, because they are not competent judges of truth in this area. Feldblum also suggests, however, that when the government enacts civil rights laws that prohibit discrimination in housing, employment, and places of public accommodation on the basis of sexual orientation, the state has "made the prior moral assessment that acting on one's homosexual orientation is not so morally problematic as to justify private parties discriminating against such individuals in the public domain" (Feldblum 2008, 131). Although same-sex activity is deemed neither bad nor good then, at least it is deemed not harmful, unlike domestic violence or rape. Therefore, those who engage in it warrant protection from discrimination, and such discrimination is wrong.

From one perspective Feldblum is correct. When the government within broad limits protects against discrimination against those who engage in particular practices, whether religious or sexual, it takes a morally neutral stance. It neither prefers Presbyterians to Episcopalians nor prefers religious adherents to atheists. It favors neither traditional couples over same-sex couples, nor those who desire intimate relationships over those who express no interest in them. The law states that discrimination against any of these categories of individuals is wrong. From a metatheoretical perspective, however, Feldblum's definition of neutrality is not neutral. By indicating that discrimination is wrong, the law cannot simultaneously encompass the view that one religion or sexual orientation is superior and also the view that all share an equal plane and must therefore be equally protected. The absence of antidiscrimination laws also sends a message about morality. Feldblum explains, "When the government *fails* to pass a law" to prohibit discrimination "on the basis of sexual orientation . . . or *fails* to allow same-sex couples access to marriage . . . the government has similarly taken a position on a moral question. The state has decided that a homosexual or bisexual orientation is not morally neutral, but rather may legitimately be viewed by some as morally problematic" (Feldblum 2008, 132; see 132–33).

The same logic applies to religion. If the record demonstrates that some religions are traditionally despised or even merely disfavored and that their members suffer discrimination, and if the government allows majority sentiment to prevail by doing nothing, it takes a moral position by default. Although some people will always view certain sexual orientations or religions as morally problematic and are entitled to do so, the government's failure to act means that public authority itself signals that these orientations or religions are problematic. Within a broad range the liberal state purports to be hospitable to diversity, and it must step up to protect ways of life within that range that according to their own prior moral assessment, in Feldblum's terms, are not harmful and therefore are not morally problematic. As Anna Elisabetta Galeotti explains, if some individuals are marginalized and excluded on the basis of their group membership, "then the normative response cannot be toleration as non-interference, but toleration as the symbolic recognition of differences as legitimate options in pluralist democracy" (Galeotti 2002, 67). From a metatheoretical perspective, then, neither action nor inaction is neutral. Therefore, seeking it is misguided.

McConnell is correct to suggest that inculcating the acceptance of openly gay troops by military personnel is not neutral but is itself a moral position. The now repealed policy of "don't ask, don't tell," however, was also nonneutral. No policy can be neutral between the acceptance and rejection of certain categories of individuals. Both kinds of policies are also metatheoretically nonneutral. They cannot encompass both the view that troops of some sexual orientations must remain closeted and also the view that troops of all sexual orientations must be free to serve without hiding their true identities. Alternatively, if school boards protect student-run gay clubs under equal access principles but simultaneously discipline their supporters if they accuse opponents of prejudice or bigotry, the two facets of this policy do not balance to render it neutral. Apart from free speech issues, a school board in this scenario would be holding that protecting interests of those experiencing same-sex attraction is a legitimate option, at the same time decreeing that those who defend this option by questioning their critics' motives are pursuing an illegitimate option. Those who oppose gay clubs can criticize their existence as much as they like on any grounds, presumably, whereas those who support them cannot criticize their opponents in the same way. As an incidental matter, if these clubs are student-run, the speech of their proponents is also a student matter, and no message can be imputed to the school board. If the board allows the existence of both gay clubs and clubs formed specifically to oppose "the gay lifestyle," and if it allows adherents of each freely to criticize the other, this policy *is* neutral on a first-order level. But it is still nonneutral on a second-order or metatheoretical level. That is, it cannot encompass both the view that one sexual orientation is superior and also the view that all orientations are legitimate options and that their supporters should therefore be free to organize, criticize their opponents, and so forth.

Thus, the first difficulty with McConnell's First Amendment solution to moral disagreements about the value of same-sex relationships is that no neutral position exists—something he himself recognizes concerning religion. The second difficulty lies in the asymmetry between the way we conceive of religious neutrality and the way he conceptualizes neutrality regarding sexual orientation. He correctly points out that the pluralist solution to religious difference has been to avoid a public position on the merits of contending religious views. When the government avoids taking a public position or endorsing one or some religious views over others, however, it is attempting to be neutral as to the substance of the competing views in question.

McConnell's solution is akin to an attempt at neutrality between the idea that a particular religion should be accorded recognition equal to that accorded to other religions, and the idea that a particular religion that may offend many people need not be recognized and respected. As chapters 3 and 5 discuss, Richards suggests that although same-sex attraction is a form of conscience central to ethical identity, it has traditionally been silenced "as a kind of ultimate heresy or treason against essential moral values" (Richards 1999, 90; see also 92, 70, 126–27; Richards 2005, 107–8). From this perspective opposition to identity claims as a form of conscience suggests that this identity "is as unworthy of respect as a traditionally despised religion like Judaism; the practice of that form of heresy may thus be abridged, and certainly persons may be encouraged to convert from its demands or, at least, be supinely and ashamedly silent" (Richards 1999, 93; see also Richards 2005, 108–9).

Applying McConnell's solution to this analogy, it is as if those on one side argue that Judaism should be recognized as equivalent to other religious beliefs, while those on the other side argue that Judaism is an offensive belief system that does not need to be respected. Moreover, the government can be neutral and avoid a moral position in this dispute. If it did so, Jews would be protected against private violence and possibly against employment discrimination, but there would be many conscience-based exemptions. The government would also have to ensure that its efforts are not intended to effect a cultural education and transformation of attitudes. It would not be surprising in this scenario to find that people become desensitized to instances of discrimination that would immediately be recognized as discrimination in an alternative context. Political correctness would impel a nominal respect for Judaism, but cultural reality would convey heavy-handed reminders that such respect emanates not from conviction but from grace.

A case in point happened in a suburban school district in Minnesota. In summer 2011, several gay students filed suit, claiming that a 2009 district policy of neutrality toward sexual orientation had not only failed to stop antigay bullying but actually had stigmatized gay and lesbian students by prohibiting teachers from responding aggressively to instances of bullying. School officials reported that they felt caught in the middle, whereas for gay rights advocates, "there is no middle ground on questions of basic human rights" (Eckholm 2011). The school district experienced eight student suicides between 2009 and 2011: two by students known to be gay and two more by students reported to be gay. Conservative Christian groups did not want the district to make any official endorsement of same-sex attraction, meaning any implication that same-sex attraction or marriage is normal. A position that supports gay students can be seen as endorsement, but this case illustrates the fact that a so-called neutral position appears to condone bullying.

The solution that McConnell suggests, then, creates neither neutrality nor equality among religious positions or sexual orientations, but rather creates neutrality among attitudes that citizens might take toward such positions or orientations. He implicitly admits this point when he mentions the massive educational effort that he thinks is needed to discipline military troops to accept openly gay comrades, concluding that the government will have to move beyond mere civil toleration to inculcate full acceptance of these comrades' moral legitimacy (McConnell 1998, 243). However, this point suggests that when a dominant consensus exists—whether represented by those offended by a religion or by same-sex relationships—governmental neutrality between that consensus and the minority position has the effect, regardless of intention, of endorsing the status quo. Commenting on McConnell, Feldblum notes that as with antidiscrimination laws, the government is taking a moral position by failing "to extend access to civil marriage to same-sex couples. . . . Government has not simply been sitting on the sidelines of these moral questions during all the time it has failed to pass laws protecting the liberty of LGBT people. Government has quite clearly been taking a side—and it has not been taking the side that helps gay people" (Feldblum 2008, 134). In other words, we need to admit forthrightly that, first, no neutral position or policy exists and that, second, some kinds of nonneutrality are preferable to others. A nonneutrality that expresses the civic equality of lesbian, gay, bisexual, and transgender persons is superior to a nonneutrality that not only pretends to be neutral but also constitutes a public expression of civic inequality.

In fairness McConnell recognizes that the two views he discusses regarding sexual orientation are bipolar in a way that religious diversity, with its multiplicity of religious organizations, is not. If a First Amendment–type solution is unfeasible, his alternative is government support for one side or the other but with plenty of room for the tolerance of dissenters. If traditionalism prevails, government will promote heterosexual monogamy but protect the "basic civil rights," left undefined, of all citizens, looking "the other way whenever it can" (McConnell 1998, 255, 257). If gay rights proponents prevail, public schools will teach that same-sex relationships are normal, and the government will extend antidiscrimination protections and same-sex marriage to those who experience same-sex attraction. In neither case will the government engage in propaganda and attempts at thought control.

McConnell views these alternatives as ways to avoid the culture war, with its focus on the perceived sins of the other side, whether these are sins of sexual immorality or intolerance (McConnell 1998, 256). The traditionalist alternative, however, carries many of the liabilities of our history until recently, conceivably extending a "don't ask, don't tell" attitude to society at large. Although it appears that he would not require antidiscrimination laws concerning sexual orientation, it is unclear whether he would even permit their adoption, in line with *Romer v. Evans*. The second alternative is clearly preferable, I believe, because although it is not neutral, it at least recognizes the civic equality of all citizens regarding their intimate lives, despite the objections of some.

Although his outline is less systematic than McConnell's, Andrew Koppelman also offers interesting observations about what he terms a "disestablishment" solution that is neutral concerning the moral status of same-sex intimacy. Religion holds a special place as a good in American culture, and it is not only protected but also favored by various exemptions. The definition of "religion," however, is sufficiently abstract that the objects of its protection can range from the sabbaths of recognized religious organizations to individual dissents about participation in the fabrication of weapons. Koppelman suggests the government might endorse the good of sexuality in a similarly abstract manner. Narrow definitions of the range of protection, he explains, have been superseded in "that many people now think that the good of religion is realized, albeit imperfectly, in denominations that are not their own. Many are also less sure than their ancestors were that their religion is the true and only way." Similarly, state policy can reflect the fact that "gay people have a respectable claim to moral parity" (Koppelman 1998, 223). The state does not need to be neutral toward all sexual practices, just as it is not neutral toward all religious practices; the adherents of unprotected practices can make the case for them on their own merits regarding both religion and sexuality.

Meanwhile, Koppelman hopes we can "agree that a lasting commitment with another person, which is somehow connected with the bodily intimacy that our sexual faculties make possible, is a good thing, perhaps even one of the best things in life" (Koppelman 1998, 223). If so, "perhaps we can agree that the claims gay people have made that their intimacy realizes something valuable is at least as colorable as the claims of members of unconventional religions that their religious activity realizes something valuable" (223–24). In the cases of both religion and sexuality then, "the state can recognize, promote, and protect the pursuit of the good in question, but should define that good at a sufficiently high level of abstraction as to be neutral between the competing factions." The state should end discrimination against same-sex couples, he argues, but it should also refrain from criticizing religious arguments that condemn same-sex intimacy (224; see also 225–26).

Koppelman's suggestion that the state endorse the goods of both religion and sexuality at a sufficiently abstract level of specificity is apt. Once again, however, a difference exists between theory and metatheory. A general endorsement of the good of sexuality is not neutral in its implications. That is, it implies that "gay people have a respectable claim to moral parity" (Koppelman 1998, 223). Similarly, antidiscrimination laws extending to sexual orientation suggest that those who experience same-sex attraction are as worthy of protection as the majority is. Moreover, these moves constitute the promotion, so to speak, of a sexual minority to a position of parity that it has not previously held. Although I believe that these moves are correct, they are not neutral and do not represent a compromise.

This point emerges particularly clearly in Koppelman's discussion of same-sex marriage, an area in which he admits the difficulty of achieving neutrality. McConnell explains his conviction that the push for same-sex marriage constitutes pressure to "adjust the definition of a public institution to conform with the doctrines or desires of a minority," for him meaning same-sex couples (McConnell 1998, 249). Koppelman counters that this conviction is misleading, saying, "The claim is rather that the present institution's contours can be defended only by relying on the forbidden view that heterosexual sex is morally superior to homosexual sex. . . . . In a sense, the Establishment Clause itself is a command that government adjust the definition of a public institution to conform with the doctrines or desires of a minority," or those disadvantaged by an establishment (Koppelman 1998, 226). That is, marriage that excludes same-sex couples is akin to an establishment that favors adherents of one religion over adherents of other faiths. It is less clear to Koppelman than it is to McConnell that true disestablishment concerning marriage requires the elimination of marriage as a public institution, relegating what it now encompasses to private civil contracts or to religious solemnizations that carry no civil authority. Koppelman explains,

"'Disestablishment' does not mean that the state must be neutral with respect to sexuality or household arrangements. It means only that the state must be neutral with respect to the moral status of homosexuality. If a preference for heterosexuality is the only reason for excluding homosexual couples from the existing institution of marriage, then that exclusion should end" (227). Various reasons may exist, of course, for a preference for traditional marriage. From McConnell's standpoint, how do we ascertain whether antidiscrimination laws are meant merely to guarantee equal access or are directed toward changing attitudes? No public policy is pure in reflecting only one type of motive. From Koppelman's viewpoint, how do we arrive at a neutral definition of neutrality itself?

Although Koppelman recognizes that admitting same-sex couples to civil marriage renders the two kinds of couples morally equivalent, he implies that he is pursuing neutrality as typically conceived, not metatheoretical neutrality. Both traditional couples and same-sex couples have equal moral claims to state formalization and recognition of their relationships. Admitting both couples to civil marriage is not, however, neutral on a metatheoretical level between those who want to retain marriage's traditional definition and those who want to expand it. Given the liberal commitment to civic equality, it cannot be metatheoretically neutral. Neither McConnell's First Amendment solution nor Koppelman's disestablishment approach to current controversies over same-sex intimate relationships can instantiate this kind of neutrality. Although McConnell's approach presents serious difficulties, even without them neither McConnell nor Koppelman can achieve neutral solutions despite potentially flawless reasoning. It cannot be done. As Feldblum shows, both action and inaction represent moral stances on some level. Therefore, I opt for the policy that constitutes a public expression of civic equality rather than inequality, nonneutral as it is.

Beyond the Culture War

Neither McConnell's First Amendment solution nor Koppelman's disestablishment suggestion can instantiate neutrality. Disagreement on the meaning of neutrality, as well as noncongruence between first-order neutrality and second-order (metatheoretical) neutrality, renders further attempts at refinement futile. Nevertheless, Koppelman's point that the state might endorse the goods of both religion and sexuality at a level of specificity sufficiently abstract to allow each good to be pursued differently by different individuals is worthy of further consideration. Rather than pursue neutral liberalism, for example, Ball develops a framework of ethical or moral liberalism that both addresses sexuality and also emphasizes the necessity of positive action to ensure that human beings can act to fulfill needs and capabilities that all share and that constitute our humanity. Threading his way between essentialism and strict social constructionism, Ball argues "that it is impossible for anyone, regardless of when and where he or she happens to live, to lead a fully human life in the absence of opportunities to meet basic needs and exercise basic capabilities associated with sexual intimacy" (Ball 2003, 9; see also 84). We can engage in moral evaluations about the nature of these needs and capabilities without making moral judgments aimed at pressuring "individuals [to] behave in certain ways, or to enter into certain relationships, because those are the ones considered morally acceptable by a majority of the society" (11).

Ball does not discount the importance of neutral, libertarian, or Millian liberalism as a defense against state interference in consensual sexual conduct within a broad range that does not cause harm to others. This negative liberty must be supplemented, however, by the realization "that the state has positive obligations to create the necessary structures and conditions for individuals to be able to exercise, in a meaningful way, their rights to freedom and autonomy associated with physical and emotional intimacy" (Ball 2003, 17; see 8–17). Rather than advocating the inculcation of particular notions of private virtue, Ball's moral liberalism "is grounded on individual autonomy and choice in the leading of lives that are fully human" (11). Same-sex couples, for example, may live their lives even without formal civil recognition of their relationships, a point that McConnell made against adjusting the civil institution of marriage to suit the desires of a minority. However, Ball notes that the refusal of most jurisdictions to recognize same-sex marriage still "entails withholding societal recognition of and support for their relationships," including but not limited to important material benefits. Although neutralist liberals such as Ronald Dworkin can argue that the morality of the majority should not be forced upon those who reject it, Ball points out that this does not explain "why the same principle should apply when the state sets policies that are neither coercive nor intrusive" (33). That is, the state neither coerces couples to marry nor intrudes into their relationships simply by making civil marriage available to them as an option. Therefore, a neutralist liberalism that focuses on noninterference cannot address the desires of same-sex couples or of others who cannot attain their goals simply by state noninterference, but who also require positive public action if they are to exercise their liberty in a meaningful way.

Ball follows Martha Nussbaum's approach in distinguishing between human capabilities, which society must provide individuals with opportunities to exercise, and human functionings, which may be accompanied by requirements or expectations that individuals function in some ways but not others. This distinction is important to maintaining choice and personal autonomy. Ball explains, "Our concern, therefore, should be with the societal conditions that promote or impede the exercise of basic human capabilities, not with whether individuals choose to exercise them or with how they do so, as long as others are not harmed" (Ball 2003, 84). Punishing individuals for engaging in consensual sexual intimacy impedes their exercise of human capabilities by interfering. Promoting opportunity requires refraining from interference. In contrast, prohibiting same-sex couples from marrying, though this opportunity is offered to traditional couples to support their capabilities for love and care, impedes the exercise of same-sex couples' capabilities by failing to provide opportunities for some that are accorded to others.

The remedy here is positive action to promote the same opportunity for same-sex couples to exercise the basic human capability of finding meaning in sexual intimacy that traditional couples enjoy. Otherwise, Ball concludes, the state fails "to meet its moral obligations to account for all the capabilities of all its citizens. . . . It is not for society to tell individuals how to live; it is for society to make sure that individuals have the *opportunity* to live full human lives" (Ball 2003, 84–85; see also 110–11). This point also applies to the arguments of traditionalists who think that a majority of LGBT persons are uninterested in marriage, as well as the arguments of skeptics about marriage who want to de-emphasize or abolish it in favor either of alternative caregiving institutions or of a complete privatization of personal relationships. What matters is the opportunity to choose the long-term formal commitment that civil marriage represents to many, irrespective of the numbers who avail themselves of it.

For Ball moral liberalism is moral because "there must be an ethical assessment of what is required for the leading of a full human life, even if that assessment is broad enough to aim for universal agreement. But moral liberalism is liberal because it values pluralism and diversity—it recognizes that different societies, as well as different individuals, have different ways of promoting and pursuing basic needs and capabilities" and because "it sees the capability to choose as playing a fundamental role in our lives" (Ball 2003, 87–88). Although some fear that allowing the state to determine the components of a fully human life may undermine rather than promote autonomy,

Ball emphasizes that the state's role is merely to provide a framework within which individuals may choose how to implement their capabilities; the state itself is not to dictate individuals' life plans or how they should pursue them. Ball's conception of moral liberalism here resonates with Justice Harry Blackmun's dissent in *Bowers v. Hardwick* (478 U.S. 186 [1986]). "The fact that individuals define themselves in a significant way through their intimate sexual relationships with others suggests, in a Nation as diverse as ours, that there may be many 'right' ways of conducting these relationships, and that much of the richness of a relationship will come from the freedom an individual has to *choose* the form and nature of these intensely personal bonds" (204–5).

If Blackmun highlights the importance of noninterference in individuals' private relationships, his point also encompasses, at least implicitly, the parallel need for a framework of opportunity if individuals are to exercise the basic capabilities associated with sexual intimacy. Ball's conception of moral liberalism clarifies this by recognizing not only the importance of choice that affects the individual alone, but also "autonomy as emanating largely from our relationships with and our dependencies on others" (Ball 2003, 92). Noninterference that insulates people's relationships in a private sphere can promote autonomy when it frees them from penalties for using birth control, obtaining abortions, or engaging in same-sex intimacy. This same noninterference in other contexts can "undermine rather than promote both well-being and autonomy," as in cases of marital rape and domestic violence, a point recognized by many feminists (93; see 93–98). Ball points out that many Supreme Court decisions that ostensibly have freed individuals from state interference—whether concerning birth control, marriage, the living arrangements of family members, or the rearing of children—have focused on the rights of individuals to define their relationships with others. "Moral liberalism recognizes that we both define ourselves and pursue our life goals largely through our affiliations with others. It is through these affiliations that we form a sense of identity and belonging that both nurtures and accounts for our well-being and autonomy" (98; see 98–99).

Key to Ball's analysis is his emphasis on the morality of sexual intimacy over the issue of immutability. The problem with the argument of immutability is that if society considers same-sex attraction to be a negative trait, the fact that it is immutable will not garner society's support for same-sex relationships. Individuals who may be deemed to possess an immutable tendency toward behavior that society has criminalized are not thereby excused for such behavior; criminal penalties may even be increased for those labeled as "incorrigible." Similarly, conduct that society merely frowns on may be allowed if a tendency toward this conduct is thought immutable, but society will not encourage or support this conduct—an attitude that "don't ask, don't tell" in the armed forces exemplified. However, if same-sex intimacy, like heterosexual intimacy, is regarded positively as a means by which people exercise their basic human capabilities, "then whether one 'chooses' to be a lesbian or a gay man would become as irrelevant a question as whether one chooses to be a heterosexual" (Ball 2003, 101). Furthermore, Ball explains, "Even if one's sexual orientation is given and not chosen, what one *does* with that status in terms of one's conduct and relations with others can always be characterized as an issue of choice, which takes us right back to the question of whether the exercise of the choice is good or bad" (101–2; see also Caramagno 2002, 107). Although society has a positive obligation to provide opportunities for the exercise of basic human capabilities that are integral to living a full human life, Ball maintains that conservatives are right to argue that the state should consider the moral value and impact of relationships in deciding whether to support them or simply tolerate them through noninterference. "Where conservative opponents of gay rights err . . . is in their moral assessments of the value and goodness of gay and lesbian relationships and families" (Ball 2003, 103; see 102–3).

Human beings possess a capability not only for physical but also for emotional intimacy. For Ball this combination is "one of the distinctive characteristics that make us human," and these capabilities "are constitutive elements in our personhood" (Ball 2003, 104). Characteristic of individuals of all sexual orientations, these capabilities flesh out Koppelman's idea of the good of sexuality, in whatever way particular persons in particular relationships may express it. When sexual intimacy "implicates not only the satisfaction of physical needs but also the need to be loved and cared for by another and the capability to love and care for another, then the societal obligations go from 'mere' noninterference to the creation of the necessary conditions that will promote and protect the ability of individuals to meet those additional needs and exercise those additional capabilities" (106). Depending on the society this social obligation may or may not mandate the recognition and support of specific kinds of relationships, such as marriage.

What is crucial is the provision of the opportunity for individuals to live full human lives in congruence with their needs and capabilities for intimate relationships. In the United States the availability of marriage has functioned as a principal, sought-after avenue for this provision. The public recognition, social support, and encouragement that this institution represents should in turn, at least aspirationally, reinforce and stabilize the expectations that typically accompany long-term commitments rooted in the capability for love and care. In sum, public policy should provide for individuals' choices as well as protect them from interference when these choices allow them to satisfy basic needs and exercise basic capabilities connected with physical and emotional intimacy. Because all humans possess the "distinctive human attributes and potentialities" for enduring commitments of love and care in the context of sexual intimacy, Ball says that all couples "should be granted access to the primary social institution that is meant to nurture and provide for those attributes and potentialities" (Ball 2003, 112; see 106–12).

Ball anticipates criticism from all sides for his conception of moral liberalism as it relates to sexuality. Leftist critics—or those whom I have termed queer, feminist, and libertarian skeptics about marriage—bristle at the idea that the state might value one kind of relationship, particularly a historically inegalitarian and patriarchal family form, over others. Ball responds that these qualities need not be endemic either to traditional or to same-sex marriage. More important, although more than one kind of relationship or family might be privileged, it is not unreasonable, Ball argues, for the state to prioritize relationships of love and care that promote the fulfillment of needs and the exercise of capabilities, possibly including civil unions and domestic partnerships as well as marriage, over those that do not (Ball 2003, 112–17). Moreover, insofar as the institution of marriage has contributed to the maintenance of male privilege and the persistence of gender roles, admitting same-sex couples will diminish these components, Ball suggests, just as extending marriage to interracial couples helped diminish the idealization of racial purity and white supremacy present in civil marriage. "The purported essentiality of gender reflects little more than the perceived essentiality of traditional gender roles and their accompanying male privilege" (128; see 126–29), just as the purported essentiality of racial purity in antimiscegenation efforts reflected little more than the perceived essentiality of traditional white supremacy. Instead of advocating for a state role of strict neutrality among types of relationships or for the withdrawal of support from any relationships, Ball suggests that leftist critics would do better to advocate for the reform of existing familial institutions and practices "in order to make them more humane and more inclusive" (115).

In addressing the arguments of conservative critics, Ball focuses on proponents of the new natural law. Although new natural lawyers view traditional marriage as an essential institution that is natural and prepolitical and is endowed with independent moral significance, Ball agrees with post-modernists that marriage is a socially constructed institution. Unlike post-modernists, however, he holds that such institutions promote the fulfillment of universal rather than socially constructed human needs and capabilities, with particulars subject to local variation. Human attributes, needs, and capabilities are prepolitical, not the institutions that provide, or should provide, opportunities for their exercise. In other words, marriage is a means that can provide the conditions for individual human flourishing, not an intrinsic end in whose service individuals should direct their lives. "As a social institution, marriage should be subject to criticism, revision, and, when appropriate, expansion as any other institution" (Ball 2003, 120; see 111–12, 118–20). Overall, Ball argues, proponents of the new natural law go awry by concluding that same-sex couples cannot attain the true mutuality through physical intimacy that is attainable by traditional couples. In reality "lesbians and gay men use their sexual capacities in the same ways as do heterosexuals, namely, in order to create, express, and experience mutuality," and/or in a context of affection and commitment that sexual intimacy may both express and engender (125; see 120–25). Like Andrew Sullivan and Jonathan Rauch, Ball argues that the availability of civil marriage promotes stability and continuity that benefit individuals, couples, any children whom a couple may be rearing, and society as a whole. Therefore, the state has a legitimate interest in supporting this kind of relationship (129; see also Hull 2006, 153), albeit for reasons that diverge sharply from those voiced by supporters of the new natural law.

To put this differently, the good of sexuality to which Koppelman alludes is the same for all, but varied individuals pursue it in varied forms. Within a broad range humans require noninterference with the exercise of their basic needs and capabilities for physical and emotional intimacy. Certain social institutions may be particularly well adapted to supporting this exercise within a context of committed relationships of love and care. Therefore, Ball argues, society should provide opportunities for individuals to exercise these capabilities by offering and supporting these institutions as options that individuals may choose. Although "the precise ways in which the state privileges and encourages some relationships over others should always be open to debate, . . . what should be recognized, however, is that the state has an interest in creating and an obligation to promote the necessary institutions and conditions that encourage long-term commitment and mutuality in intimate relationships" (Ball 2003, 115). Ball makes it clear that committed, sexually intimate relationships of love and care persist without society's recognition of and support for those of all sexual orientations. This fact, "however, does not exempt society from its obligations to promote and protect the basic human needs and capabilities of all its citizens" (111).

Ball's defense of moral liberalism may seem in ill accord with chapter 3's argument that the government should not try to shoehorn individuals into marriage. Why does the government's marriage initiative, which encourages marriage as a matter of public policy, fail to qualify as provision, support, and encouragement of individual choice in a relationship of love and care that allows basic human capabilities for physical and emotional intimacy to develop and flourish? First, the marriage initiative provides opportunities for traditional couples to exercise their capabilities and excludes same-sex couples, even though these capabilities exist in all individuals. Although well intended, the initiative suggests unwitting hypocrisy, if nothing else. More important, however, many of the economic and social conditions that foster the desire to marry are absent from the lives of those who often shun marriage. Even where this is not the case, Ball and I agree that marriage is an option, not an institution in which individuals should be pressured to participate. If society has a positive obligation to provide opportunities to exercise basic human capabilities, as Ball suggests, these obligations arguably include the economic and social conditions that ground both the ability and the desire to exercise these capabilities. Absent these conditions, we should not be surprised that many eschew this exercise. The opportunity to obtain a free public education, for example, requires free bus transportation for many, before children and their families can view this educational opportunity as a realistic and desirable option.

Finally, the marriage initiative seems oriented more toward the alleviation of social problems or to the recovery of traditional values; it seems less oriented toward accounting for the basic human capabilities for physical and emotional intimacy that all humans share. Like proponents of the new natural law, advocates of the marriage initiative seem to regard marriage as an intrinsic end that individuals and couples should be induced to serve, rather than as a means that can provide some conditions to allow those who choose it to flourish. Ball's moral liberalism emphasizes not only the importance of opportunities to exercise basic human capabilities but also the centrality of choice as one of these capabilities. "A thicker conception of the good than the one held by moral liberalism—one, in other words, that would require making important choices *for* individuals rather than providing the structure and support necessary for those choices to be made by individuals—would be inconsistent with the exercise of human autonomy" (Ball

2003, 88; see 87–88). Although Mill is most often associated with the negative liberty of freedom from interference, his discussion of individuality also implies a necessity for the positive provision of opportunities for choice in one's manner of individual development. "Human nature is not a machine to be built after a model, and set to do exactly the work prescribed for it, but a tree, which requires to grow and develope [*sic*] itself on all sides, according to the tendency of the inward forces which make it a living thing" (Mill 1859, 60; see 56–61). This potential for growth and development suggests not only the existence of basic human capabilities that different individuals exercise differently if left free of interference, but also the requirement that positive opportunities be provided if individuals are to live full human lives.

Although Ball does not discuss religion, I discuss him at length here partly because his conception of moral liberalism, though not metatheoretically neutral, seems capable of transcending arguments about how to negotiate the elusive and in my view unreachable goal of neutrality. More important, Ball's conception also illustrates Koppelman's point that both religion and sexuality can be endorsed as general goods that different individuals may pursue in their own ways. To paraphrase Ball in the context of religious belief, individuals cannot lead fully human lives without opportunities to meet basic needs and exercise basic human capabilities associated with religious belief and practice. We can engage in moral evaluations about the nature of these needs and capabilities without making moral judgments that pressure individuals to engage in particular religious practices or to affiliate with certain religious organizations, just because these are the ones that the majority finds most acceptable. The exercise of these capabilities associated with religious belief and practice requires not only an absence of state interference with religious pursuits, within broad limits, but also the positive creation of conditions for the meaningful exercise of rights to freedom and autonomy associated with religious belief and practice.

The free exercise and establishment clauses of the First Amendment, David Richards suggests, are grounded in different but complementary aspects of equal respect for human moral powers. The free exercise clause protects against state coercion concerning the observance or expression of conscientious beliefs, whereas the establishment clause focuses on "the formation and revision of conscience," protecting "the processes of forming and changing such conceptions" (Richards 1986, 140). In the present context the free exercise clause of the First Amendment equates with noninterference in the formation of intimate relationships, whereas the establishment clause creates positive conditions that enable free exercise of the human capabilities for love and care, free from pressure by the dominant consensus.

More specifically, free exercise also requires ensuring that in the absence of a compelling state interest, the law does not make it more difficult for practitioners of one religion to engage in the free exercise of their beliefs than it makes it for followers of other religions to exercise theirs. Despite the establishment clause, religion is not privatized; its free exercise is protected, sometimes through positive measures. Within broad limits unpopular or minority religions are subject to the same protections as mainstream beliefs. These protections in turn often require positive action on the part of the government, if equal access to the protection of conscientious belief and practice is to be more than a formality. The state must protect the exercise of human capabilities associated with religious belief and practice without taking a moral stand that prefers one type of exercise to another. By maintaining this framework of opportunity, moreover, the government cannot suggest that because humans possess these capabilities, they must therefore exercise them. Agnostics and atheists have the same rights that conventional religious believers enjoy. As Ball says, "Our concern . . . should be with the societal conditions that promote or impede the exercise of basic human capabilities, not with whether individuals choose to exercise them or how they do so, as long as others are not harmed" (Ball 2003, 84).

Although a formal civil institution concerning religion does not exist, unlike the civil institution of marriage, the analogy holds. Protecting the capabilities associated with freedom of religious belief and practice prohibits an establishment of religion. Protecting the capabilities associated with sexual intimacy in a context of love and care is fostered in our society by institutions that recognize, support, and encourage long-term commitment to a shared life—although the nature of these institutions, as Ball suggests, may be open to revision. Because all humans possess these capabilities, providing opportunities for their exercise requires opening marriage to same-sex couples in the area of sexuality, as surely as it requires protecting adherents to minority religions in the area of religious belief and practice. The analogy is perhaps less apt concerning the correctness of privileging some expressions of sexual intimacy over others, as Ball suggests, because we do not privilege some expressions of religious belief over others. We do, however, privilege religious organizations through the tax code, and we grant exemptions to individuals and organizations grounded in their conscientious beliefs. These sorts of policies represent freedom from interference. In another sense, however, their existence constitutes the positive provision of opportunities for the exercise of religious capabilities in ways that favor some religious beliefs and practices, broadly defined, over others.

Conclusion

Like Ball, I suggest that a difference exists between establishing a particular kind of committed relationship with a prescribed content and supporting relationships that account for the human capabilities associated with sexual intimacy in a context of love and care. The self comprises many facets. We are not only rational beings seeking to satisfy our preferences, but also "social beings struggling to make connections, including lasting connections, with one another" (Eskridge 2004, 59). As William N. Eskridge Jr. puts it, the "rational self" of a contract model of relationship is complemented by the "relational self." For Eskridge, state-sponsored marriage "remains, for many people, an institution that valorizes ongoing relationships that have deep significance for society as well as individuals" (59).

We choose our commitments, but we also are defined by them, as Milton C. Regan Jr. suggests. "As a social institution, marriage plays a crucial role in serving as an impersonal source of value that can give meaning to personal choice," thereby providing social validation for our commitments (Regan 2004, 72; see 69–72). Drucilla Cornell adds that because we all need care and support, other forms of relationships should be accorded the public status that marriage now holds, which for Cornell include different forms of family relationships between adults that may or may not include a sexual connection. Although passing judgment on which alternative family relationships should be encouraged and protected is not the purpose of this book, Cornell's vision does accord with Ball's point that more than one type of relationship might be privileged; support for our capabilities for emotional intimacy may be subject to local variation. Overall, this argument "forbids the state to legislate any particular definition of the 'good' family, and thus the only legally protected family" (Cornell 2004, 84; see 83–85). Wendy Brown goes further, arguing that "the more marriage is promoted as the privileged form in which our 'relational sides' are recognized, the more invisible we will render other ways of committing ourselves to the well-being of others" (Brown 2004, 91; see 88–91; Cossman 2004, 94–96). Although Cornell desires state-sponsored status for varied kinds of families, Brown wants no state recognition of any form of kinship.

The United States Constitution declares through the First Amendment that religion is special. Is marriage special? In arguing for the disestablishment of marriage as a civil institution, Tamara Metz says that although marriage "carries a unique expressive value beyond the concrete and delineable benefits attached to it" (Metz 2004, 100), this extra value, which she terms "constitutive recognition," derives from the fact that the state defines and confers marital status on couples. That is, by the very process of defining and conferring this status, the state transforms a relationship between two people and between the couple and the community into something additional: a status bestowed by an ethical authority. Metz views the state as ill suited to the role of ethical authority, because it crowds out what she views as "the most effective sources of ethical authority," religious, cultural, and secular (102; see 100–104). Although the state should retain its role in protecting the vulnerable and their caregivers, she sees no more reason for the state to control marital status than it has to control bar or bat mitzvah status. Metz does however favor a civil union status that protects caregiving relationships; this functionally defined status, depending on its specifics, could include diverse types of families, including polygamous ones.

At present I remain agnostic about the relative benefits of some of these alternative arrangements. As a society, however, we currently possess a widely recognized institution that is capable of supporting a set of important human capabilities: those associated with sexual intimacy in a context of love and care. Already various political entities define and confer alternative statuses such as civil unions and domestic partnerships. I see no reason that marriage cannot continue to be one such status, subject, as Ball suggests, "to criticism, revision, and, when appropriate, expansion as any other institution" (Ball 2003, 120). People believe that the state is an ethical authority, whether or not it should be regarded as such. Chapter 1 explains that although American citizenship may no longer define the distinctive identity that it once did, it retains social and psychological value that many people feel is still crucial to their personal identities. They believe that their citizenship has ethical worth. Similarly, many believe that marriage as such carries ethical worth that alternative institutions presently do not embody. Many argue that this unique expressive value and the belief that public authority is an ethical authority are the results of false consciousness. As long as the definition of relationships that are encouraged and protected may evolve over time, however, I experience no need to dissuade people from their opinions of its value.

Neither the material benefits of marriage nor the civil rights aspect, as Nussbaum terms it, are what divides people, because many who want to deny the label "marriage" to same-sex couples believe that all committed couples should enjoy equal civil rights. Nor does the religious aspect divide people, for although religious groups may be internally divided about the propriety of religious solemnization of same-sex couples' commitments, people do not want either to prohibit religious groups from engaging in such activities or to force them to do so against their wills. Rather, it is the expressive aspect—the public declaration of love and commitment, the one that is called "marriage" and recognized as such by the state—that same-sex couples and their supporters seek. The absence of this expressive aspect is a public expression of civic inequality. Although Nussbaum, like Metz, prefers that the state withdraw from the definition and conferral of the status of marriage and leave the expressive aspect to religious and other private groups, instead offering civil unions to both traditional and same-sex couples, Nussbaum agrees that "as long as the state is in the marrying business, equality concerns require it to offer marriage to same-sex couples" (Nussbaum 2010, 132; see 128–32). For Nussbaum there is indeed a right to marriage, which minimally "means that if the state chooses to offer a particular package of expressive or civil benefits under the name 'marriage,' it must make that package available to all who seek that status" absent a strong public interest in denying it (151). Alternatively "when the state does offer a status that has both civil benefits and expressive dignity, it must offer it with an even hand" (154; see 150–56, 162–63).

Evenhandedness does not alone protect liberty, however, for the government can impose draconian measures that withdraw protection in certain areas from everyone (Nussbaum 2010, 87; see also 72–73, 152–53). Substantive liberty rights that cannot be invaded without due process of law are well summarized in *Meyer v. Nebraska* (262 U.S. 390 [1923]), in which the Supreme Court in 1923 struck down a law criminalizing the teaching of any modern language other than English in any school, public or private. Substantive liberty rights, the court said, include not only freedom from bodily restraint or interference, "but also the right of the individual to contract, to engage in any of the common occupations of life, to acquire useful knowledge, to marry, establish a home and bring up children, to worship God according to the dictates of his own conscience, and generally to enjoy those privileges long recognized at common law as essential to the orderly pursuit of happiness" (399). Concerning religion, Nussbaum concludes that "defending religious liberty requires more than not persecuting people: it also requires making sure that the conditions of liberty are the same for all" (Nussbaum 2010, 83). Similarly, the conditions of liberty must be the same for all concerning the sustenance of long-term commitments. Nussbaum implies three points here that accord with the argument of this book. First, substantive liberty rights exist that the state must in some way protect and facilitate. Second, the state need not do this in a particular manner; but once it offers a policy, all who wish to participate must be included in its embrace. Finally, protection and facilitation may require not only freedom from interference but also positive state action if people are to be truly able to exercise their human capabilities, whether for religious belief and practice or for sexual intimacy in a context of love and care.

Nussbaum succinctly expresses a similarity between religion and sexuality that I emphasize continually in this book. Sex, like religion, "is intimately personal, connected to a sense of life's ultimate significance, and utterly nontrivial. Like religion, it appears to be something in which authenticity, or the involvement of conscience, is central. We understand that it goes to the heart of people's self-definition, their search for identity and self-expression" (Nussbaum 2010, 39; see 36–41). Achieving what she terms a politics of humanity requires equal respect for our fellow citizens, combined with "a serious and sympathetic attempt to imagine what interests they are pursuing" (50; see also 47–51, xv-xvii; Nussbaum 2008, 332–34). We need not necessarily approve of their practices, whether sexual or religious; but we do need to respect the fact that they, like us, are pursuing in diverse ways the search for life's ultimate significance.

This thought resonates with Thomas Bridges's account of narrative imagination. Although one's identity is defined through a particular life narrative, one must develop the "capacity to incorporate into every narratively constructed identity or self a recognition of its own narratively constructed status" (Bridges 1994, 181; see 168–89, 209). That is, narrative imagination recognizes the possibility of others' commitment to ideals different from those to which one is committed. Individuals come to understand both the contingent character of their current desires and the possibility of other objects of desire than those they currently hold. This process in turn may create sympathy for or identification with those whose values and pursuits may otherwise appear alien to us, because we ourselves might hold different values, ideals, and desires under different circumstances. Finally, the deployment of narrative imagination may lead more of us to understand that positive public action is often needed to provide the conditions for the development of our most central human capabilities, including that for sexual intimacy within a context of love and care. Upon reflection then, we must perceive that the moral arguments animating freedom of religious belief and practice extend to sexual orientation and practice. When a policy cannot be grounded in the prevention of harm, public authority must accord equal treatment to all manifestations of religious belief and of sexuality, including civil recognition of same-sex marriage as a public expression of civic equality.

REFERENCES

Cases Cited

Bowers v. Hardwick, 478 U.S. 186 (1986).
Capitol Square v. Pinette, 515 U.S. 753 (1995).
County of Allegheny v. ACLU, 492 U.S. 573 (1989).
Employment Division v. Smith, 404 U.S. 872 (1990).
Epperson v. Arkansas, 393 U.S. 97 (1968).
Everson v. Board of Education, 330 U.S. 1 (1947).
Goodridge v. Department of Public Health, 440 Mass. 309 (2003).
In re Marriage Cases, 43 Cal. 4th 757 (2008).
In re Opinions of the Justices to the Senate, 440 Mass. 1201 (2004).
Kerrigan v. Commissioner of Public Health, 289 Conn. 135 (2008).
Lawrence v. Texas, 539 U.S. 558 (2003).
Lee v. Weisman, 505 U.S. 577 (1992).
Lemon v. Kurtzman, 403 U.S. 602 (1971).
Loving v. Virginia, 388 U.S. 1 (1967).
Lynch v. Donnelly, 465 U.S. 668 (1984).
McCreary County v. ACLU of Kentucky, 125 S. Ct. 2722 (2005).
Meyer v. Nebraska, 262 U.S. 390 (1923).
Miron v. Trudel, 2 S.C.R. 418 (Canada 1995).
Perez v. Sharpe, 32 Cal. 2d 711, 198 P.2d 17 (1948).
Perry v. Schwarzenegger, 704 F.Supp.2d 921 (Cal. 2010).
Planned Parenthood of Southeastern Pa. v. Casey, 505 U.S. 833 (1992).
Pleasant Grove City v. Summum, 129 S. Ct. 1125 (2009).
Reynolds v. United States, 98 U.S. 145 (1879).
Roe v. Wade, 410 U.S. 113 (1973).
Romer v. Evans, 517 U.S. 620 (1996).
Rosenberger v. Rector, 515 U.S. 819 (1995).
Rust v. Sullivan, 500 U.S. 173 (1991).
Sherbert v. Verner, 374 U.S. 398 (1963).

Thomas v. Review Board, 450 U.S. 707 (1981).
Thornton v. Calder, 105 S. Ct. 2914 (1985).
Turner v. Safley, 482 U.S. 78 (1987).
United States v. Seeger, 380 U.S. 163 (1965).
United States v. Virginia, 518 U.S. 515 (1996).
Van Orden v. Perry, 125 S. Ct. 2854 (2005).
Varnum v. Brien, 763 N.W.2d 862 (Iowa 2009).
Wallace v. Jaffree, 472 U.S. 38 (1985).
Welsh v. United States, 398 U.S. 333 (1970).
Zablocki v. Redhail, 434 U.S. 374 (1978).
Zorach v. Clauson, 343 U.S. 306 (1952).

Works Cited

Abegg, Edmund. 2006. "The Magic of Marriage: Comments on Gill." Paper delivered at the biennial meeting of the American Section, International Association for Philosophy of Law and Social Philosophy, St. Louis, MO, November 2–5.

Almanzar, Yolanne. 2008. "Florida Gay Adoption Ban Is Ruled Unconstitutional." *New York Times*, November 26.

Americans United. 2009. "Supreme Court Ruling in Utah Religious Symbols Case Unlikely to Be Final Word, Says Americans United." Accessed March 2. www.au.org.

Audi, Robert. 1997. "Liberal Democracy and the Place of Religion in Politics." In Audi and Wolterstorff, *Religion in the Public Square*, 1–66.

———. 2000. *Religious Commitment and Secular Reason*. New York: Cambridge University Press.

Audi, Robert, and Nicholas Wolterstorff. 1997. *Religion in the Public Square: The Place of Religious Conscience in Political Debate*. Lanham, MD: Rowman & Littlefield.

Babst, Gordon Albert. 1997. "Community, Rights Talk, and the Communitarian Dissent in *Bowers v. Hardwick*." In Phelan, *Playing with Fire*, 139–72.

———. 2002. *Liberal Constitutionalism, Marriage, and Sexual Orientation: A Contemporary Case for Dis-Establishment*. New York: Peter Lang.

———. 2009. "Consuming Its Own? Heteronormativity *contra* Human Plurality." In Babst, Gill, and Pierceson, *Moral Argument*, 183–203.

Babst, Gordon A., Emily R. Gill, and Jason Pierceson, eds. 2009. *Moral Argument, Religion, and Same-Sex Marriage: Advancing the Public Good.* Lanham, MD: Lexington Books of Rowman & Littlefield.

Badgett, M. V. Lee. 2004. "Will Providing Marriage Rights to Same-Sex Couples Undermine Heterosexual Couples? Evidence from Scandinavia and the Netherlands." Discussion paper, July.

Ball, Carlos. 2003. *The Morality of Gay Rights: An Exploration in Political Philosophy.* New York: Routledge.

————. 2009. "Against Neutrality in the Legal Recognition of Intimate Relationships." In Babst, Gill, and Pierceson, *Moral Argument*, 75–94.

Bamforth, Nicholas, and David A. J. Richards. 2008. *Patriarchal Religion, Sexuality, and Gender: A Critique of New Natural Law.* New York: Cambridge University Press.

Banerjee, Neela. 2008. "Southern Baptists Back a Shift on Climate Change." *New York Times*, March 10.

Barry, Brian. 2001. *Culture and Equality: An Egalitarian Critique of Multiculturalism.* Cambridge, MA: Harvard University Press.

Belkin, Lisa. 2009. "What's Good for the Kids." *New York Times Magazine* (November 8), 9, 11.

Blankenhorn, David. 2007. *The Future of Marriage.* New York: Encounter Books.

Blankenhorn, David, and Jonathan Rauch. 2009. "A Reconciliation on Gay Marriage." *New York Times*, February 22.

Blumenthal, Ralph. 2008. "Texas Loses Court Ruling over Taking Children." *New York Times*, May 30.

Boling, Patricia. 1996. *Privacy and the Politics of Intimate Life.* Ithaca, NY: Cornell University Press.

Boyadzhiev, Marinelle. 2009. Letter to the editor. *New York Times*, February 25.

Bridges, Thomas. 1994. *The Culture of Citizenship: Inventing Postmodern Civic Culture.* Albany: State University of New York Press.

Broder, David. 2002. "Should Government Promote Marriage?" *Peoria (IL) Journal Star*, April 3.

Brown, Robbie. 2008. "Antipathy toward Obama Seen as Helping Arkansas Limit Adoption." *New York Times*, November 9.

Brown, Wendy. 2004. "After Marriage." In Shanley, *Just Marriage*, 87–92.

————. 2006. *Regulating Aversion: Tolerance in the Age of Identity and Empire.* Princeton, NJ: Princeton University Press.

Brudney, Daniel. 2005. "On Noncoercive Establishment." *Political Theory* 33 (December): 812–39.

Burack, Cynthia. 2008. *Sin, Sex, and Democracy: Antigay Rhetoric and the Christian Right*. Albany: State University of New York Press.

Burack, Cynthia, and Jyl J. Josephson, eds. 2003. *Fundamental Differences: Feminists Talk Back to Social Conservatives*. Lanham, MD: Rowman & Littlefield.

Caramagno, Thomas C. 2002. *Irreconcilable Differences? Intellectual Stalemate in the Gay Rights Debate*. Westport, CT: Praeger.

Carens, Joseph S. 1987. "Who Belongs? Theoretical and Legal Questions about Birthright Citizenship." Review of *Citizenship without Consent: Illegal Aliens in the American Polity*, by Peter H. Schuck and Rogers M. Smith. *University of Toronto Law Review* 37 (4, Autumn): 413–43.

Carey, Benedict. 2005. "Experts Dispute Bush on Gay-Adoption Issue." *New York Times*, January 29.

Carter, Stephen L. 1993. *The Culture of Disbelief: How American Law and Politics Trivialize Religious Devotion*. New York: Basic Books.

Chait, Jonathan. 2009. "Miss Guided." *New Republic*, June 17, 2.

Cherlin, Andrew J. 2009. *The Marriage Go-Round: The State of Marriage and the Family in America Today*. New York: Knopf.

Citrin, Jack, Amy Lerman, Michael Murakami, and Kathryn Pearson. 2007. "Testing Huntington: Is Hispanic Immigration a Threat to American Identity?" *Perspectives on Politics* 5 (March): 31–48.

Citron, Jo Ann, and Mary Lyndon Shanley. 2005. "Sexuality, Marriage, and Relationships: The Radical Potential of *Lawrence*." In Hirsch, *Future of Gay Rights*, 209–27.

Clemetson, Lynette. 2004. "Both Sides Court Black Churches in the Battle over Gay Marriage." *New York Times*, March 1.

Cookson, Catherine. 2003. "Fighting for Free Exercise from the Trenches: A Case Study of Religious Freedom Issues Faced by Wiccans Practicing in the United States." In *New Religious Movements and Religious Liberty in America*," 2nd ed., edited by Derek H. Davis and Barry Hankins, 135–53. Waco, TX: Baylor University Press.

Coontz, Stephanie. 2005. *Marriage, a History: From Obedience to Intimacy, or How Love Conquered Marriage*. New York: Viking Penguin.

Cornell, Drucilla. 2004. "The Public Supports of Love." In Shanley, *Just Marriage*, 81–86.

Cossman, Brenda. 2004. "Beyond Marriage." In Shanley, *Just Marriage*, 93–98.

Cott, Nancy. 2000. *Public Vows*. Cambridge, MA: Harvard University Press.

Creppell, Ingrid. 1996. "Locke on Toleration: The Transformation of Constraint." *Political Theory* 24 (May): 200–240.

DeLaet, Debra L., and Rachel Paine Caufield. 2006. "Gay Marriage as a Religious Right." Paper presented at the annual meeting of the Midwest Political Science Association, Chicago, IL, April 20–23.

Devlin, Patrick. 2002. "The Enforcement of Morals." In *Political Philosophy: Classic and Contemporary Readings*, edited by Louis J. Pojman, 311–18. New York: McGraw-Hill.

Dionne, E. J. 2008. "Eucharist Wafer 'as a Weapon.'" *Peoria (IL) Journal Star*, June 6.

———. 2009. "'Values' Debate Takes a Back Seat." *Peoria (IL) Journal Star*, June 2.

Dobson, James. 2003. *Focus on the Family* newsletter, September.

———. 2004. *Focus on the Family* newsletter, April.

Donovan, John B. 2009. Letter to the editor. *New York Times*, February 25.

Dworkin, Ronald. 1978. *Taking Rights Seriously*. Cambridge, MA: Harvard University Press.

———. 1985. *A Matter of Principle*. Cambridge, MA: Harvard University Press.

Eckholm, Erik. 2011. "In Suburb, Fight over Silence on Bullying of Gay Students." *New York Times*, September 13.

Eisgruber, Christopher L., and Lawrence G. Sager. 2007. *Religious Freedom and the Constitution*. Cambridge, MA: Harvard University Press.

Elshtain, Jean Bethke. 1982. "Aristotle, the Public-Private Split, and the Case of the Suffragists." In *The Family in Political Theory*, edited by Jean Bethke Elshtain, 50–65. Amherst: University of Massachusetts Press.

Erdos, David O. 2005. "Questions of Tolerance and Fairness." In Hirsch, *Future of Gay Rights*, 15–35.

Eskridge, William N., Jr. 1997. "Beyond Lesbian and Gay 'Families We Choose.'" In Estlund and Nussbaum, *Sex, Preference, and Family*, 277–89.

———. 1999. *Gaylaw: Challenging the Apartheid of the Closet*. Cambridge, MA: Harvard University Press.

———. 2003. "The Same-Sex Marriage Debate and Three Conceptions of Equality." In Wardle et al., *Marriage and Same-Sex Unions*, 167–85.

———. 2004. "The Relational Case for Same-Sex Marriage." In Shanley, *Just Marriage*, 58–62.

Estlund, David M., and Martha C. Nussbaum, eds. 1997. *Sex, Preference, and Family.* New York: Oxford University Press.

Feldblum, Chai R. 2008. "Moral Conflict and Conflicting Liberties." In Laycock, Picarello, and Wilson, *Same-Sex Marriage and Religious Liberty*, 123–56.

———. 2009. "Conclusion: The Moral Values Project: A Call to Moral Action in Politics." In Babst, Gill, and Pierceson, *Moral Argument*, 205–32.

Feldman, Jan. 2003. *Lubavitchers as Citizens: A Paradox of Liberal Democracy.* Ithaca, NY: Cornell University Press.

Feldman, Noah. 2006. *Divided by God: America's Church-State Problem and What We Should Do about It.* New York: Farrar, Straus & Giroux.

Fineman, Martha Albertson. 2004. "Why Marriage?" In Shanley, *Just Marriage*, 46–51.

Frank, Nathaniel. 2004. "Joining the Debate but Missing the Point." *New York Times*, February 24.

———. 2009. *Unfriendly Fire: How the Gay Ban Undermines the Military and Weakens America.* New York: Thomas Dunne Books.

Fraser, Nancy. 1997. *Justice Interruptus: Critical Reflections on the "Postsocialist" Condition.* New York: Routledge.

Furstenburg, Frank. 2002. "What a Good Marriage Can't Do." *New York Times*, August 18.

Galeotti, Anna Elisabetta. 1993. "Citizenship and Equality: The Place for Toleration." *Political Theory* 21 (November): 585–605.

———. 2002. *Toleration as Recognition.* Cambridge, UK: Cambridge University Press.

Gallagher, Maggie. 2003. "Normal Marriage: Two Views." In Wardle et al., *Marriage and Same-Sex Unions*, 13–24.

Galston, William A. 1991. *Liberal Purposes: Goods, Virtues, and Diversity in the Liberal State.* New York: Cambridge University Press.

George, Robert. 2003. "Neutrality, Equality, and 'Same-Sex Marriage.'" In Wardle et al., *Marriage and Same-Sex Unions*, 119–32.

Gerstmann, Evan. 1999. *The Constitutional Underclass: Gays, Lesbians, and the Failure of Class-Based Equal Protection.* Chicago: University of Chicago Press.

———. 2008. *Same-Sex Marriage and the Constitution.* 2nd ed. New York: Cambridge University Press.

Gill, Emily R. 2001. *Becoming Free: Autonomy and Diversity in the Liberal Polity.* Lawrence: University Press of Kansas.

———. 2004. "Religious Organizations, Charitable Choice, and the Limits of Freedom of Conscience." *Perspectives on Politics* 2 (December): 741–55.

———. 2008. "Coercion, Neutrality, and Same-Sex Marriage." In Reidy and Riker, *Coercion and the State*, 115–27.

Goode, Erica. 2001. "A Rainbow of Differences in Gays' Children." *New York Times*, November 17.

———. 2002. "Group Backs Gays Who Seek to Adopt a Partner's Child." *New York Times*, July 1.

Goodman, Ellen. 2002. "More Marriages Will Not Cure Poverty." *Peoria (IL) Journal Star*, March 11.

Greenawalt, Kent. 1995. *Private Consciences and Public Reason*. New York: Oxford University Press.

Gutmann, Amy. 2003. *Identity in Democracy*. Princeton, NJ: Princeton University Press.

Hayek, F. A. 1960. *The Constitution of Liberty*. Chicago: University of Chicago Press.

Henley, Kenneth. 2008. "The Cheshire Cat: Same-Sex Marriage, Religion, and Coercion by Exclusion." In Reidy and Riker, *Coercion and the State*, 129–43.

Hirsch, H. N., ed. 2005a. *The Future of Gay Rights in America*. New York: Routledge.

———. 2005b. "Liberal with a Twist: Queering Marriage." In Hirsch, *Future of Gay Rights*, 285–95.

Honig, Bonnie. 1993. *Political Theory and the Displacement of Politics*. Ithaca, NY: Cornell University Press.

Hull, Kathleen E. 2006. *Same-Sex Marriage: The Cultural Politics of Love and Law*. New York: Cambridge University Press.

Jacobson, Robin. 2006. "Characterizing Consent: Race, Citizenship, and the New Restrictionists." *Political Research Quarterly* 59 (December): 645–54.

Jakobsen, Janet R., and Ann Pellegrini. 2004. *Love the Sin: Sexual Regulation and the Limits of Religious Tolerance*. Boston: Beacon Press.

Jayson, Sharon. 2009. "I Want You to Get Married." *Chicago Sun-Times*, February 24.

Joseph, Elizabeth. 1991. "My Husband's Nine Wives." *New York Times*, May 23.

Josephson, Jyl. 2005. "Citizenship, Same-Sex Marriage, and Feminist Critiques of Marriage." *Perspectives on Politics* 3 (June): 269–84.

Kautz, Steven. 1993. "Liberalism and the Idea of Toleration." *American Journal of Political Science* 37 (May): 610–32.

———. 1995. *Liberalism and Community*. Ithaca, NY: Cornell University Press.

Kirkpatrick, David D. 2004. "Gay-Marriage Fight Finds Ambivalence from Evangelicals." *New York Times*, February 29.

Kmiec, Douglas. 2008. "Same-Sex Marriage and the Coming Antidiscrimination Campaigns against Religion." In Laycock, Picarello, and Wilson, *Same-Sex Marriage and Religious Liberty*, 103–21.

Kohm, Lynne Marie. 2003. "Marriage by Design." In Wardle et al., *Marriage and Same-Sex Unions*, 81–90.

Koppelman, Andrew. 1988. "The Miscegenation Analogy: Sodomy Laws as Sex Discrimination." *Yale Law Journal* 98 (1, November): 145–64.

———. 1994. "Why Discrimination against Lesbians and Gay Men Is Sex Discrimination." *New York University Law Review* 69: 197–287.

———. 1998. "Sexual and Religious Pluralism." In Olyan and Nussbaum, *Sexual Orientation and Human Rights*, 215–33.

———. 2005. "The Rule of *Lawrence*." In Hirsch, *Future of Gay Rights*, 151–68.

Kosman, L. A. 1980. "Being Properly Affected: Virtues and Feelings in Aristotle's Ethics." In *Essays on Aristotle's Ethics*, edited by Amélie Oksenberg Rorty, 103–16. Berkeley: University of California Press.

Kurtz, Stanley. 2004. "Deathblow to Marriage." *National Review Online*. http://old.nationalreview.com/kurtz/kurtz200402050842.asp.

Kymlicka, Will. 1991. *Liberalism, Community and Culture*. Oxford, UK: Clarendon Press.

———. 1995. *Multicultural Citizenship: A Liberal Theory of Minority Rights*. Oxford, UK: Clarendon Press.

Laycock, Douglas. 2008. Afterword. In Laycock, Picarello, and Wilson, *Same-Sex Marriage and Religious Liberty*, 189–207.

Laycock, Douglas, Anthony R. Picarello Jr., and Robin Fretwell Wilson, eds. 2008. *Same-Sex Marriage and Religious Liberty: Emerging Conflicts*. Lanham, MD: Becket Fund for Religious Liberty/Rowman & Littlefield.

Lehr, Valerie. 1999. *Queer Family Values: Debunking the Myth of the Nuclear Family*. Philadelphia, PA: Temple University Press.

———. 2003. "'Family Values': Social Conservative Power in Diverse Rhetorics." In Burack and Josephson, *Fundamental Differences*, 127–42.

———. 2009. "Supporting Queer Youth: A New Vision of Child, Family, and State." In Babst, Gill, and Pierceson, *Moral Argument*, 161–81.

Liptak, Adam. 2008a. "From Tiny Sect, a Weighty Issue for the Justices." *New York Times*, November 11.

———. 2008b. "Justices Grapple with Question of Church Monument as Free Speech." *New York Times*, November 12.

Locke, John. 1689. *A Letter Concerning Toleration.* Edited by James H. Tully. Indianapolis: Hackett Publishing Company, 1983.

Luker, Kristin. 1984. *Abortion and the Politics of Motherhood.* Berkeley: University of California Press.

Lund, William R. 1993. "Communitarian Politics and the Problem of Equality." *Political Research Quarterly* 43 (September): 577–600.

Luo, Michael, and Laurie Goodstein. 2007. "Emphasis Shifts for New Breed of Evangelicals." *New York Times*, May 21.

Lyall, Sarah. 2002. "With the Blessing of Society, Europeans Opt Not to Marry." *New York Times*, March 24.

Macedo, Stephen. 1990. *Liberal Virtues: Citizenship, Virtue, and Community in Liberal Constitutionalism.* Oxford, UK: Clarendon Press.

———. 1995. "Homosexuality and the Conservative Mind." *Georgetown Law Journal* 84 (2): 261–300.

———. 1997. "Sexuality and Liberty: Making Room for Nature and Tradition?" In Estlund and Nussbaum, *Sex, Preference, and Family*, 86–101.

———. 2000. "In Defense of Liberal Public Reason: Are Slavery and Abortion Hard Cases?" In *Natural Law and Public Reason*, edited by Robert P. George and Christopher Wolfe, 1–49. Washington, DC: Georgetown University Press.

———. 2001. "Against the Old Sexual Morality of the New Natural Law." In *Natural Law, Liberalism, and Morality*, edited by Robert P. George, 27–48. New York: Oxford University Press.

MacIntyre, Alasdair. 1981. *After Virtue.* Notre Dame, IN: University of Notre Dame Press.

Marcosson, Samuel A. 1998. "*Romer* and the Limits of Legitimacy: Stripping Opponents of Gay and Lesbian Rights of Their 'First Line of Defense' in the Same-Sex Marriage Fight." *Journal of Contemporary Law* 24 (2): 217–54.

———. 2009. "The Special Status of Religion under the First Amendment . . . and What It Means for Gay Rights and Antidiscrimination Laws." In Babst, Gill, and Pierceson, *Moral Argument*, 135–60.

Marquardt, Elizabeth. 2009. Letter to the editor. *New York Times*, February 25.

McCabe, David. 1998. "Outline for a Defense of an Unreconstructed Liberalism." *Journal of Social Philosophy* 29 (Spring): 63–80.

McClure, Kirstie. 1990. "Difference, Diversity, and the Limits of Toleration." *Political Theory* 18 (August): 361–91.

McConnell, Michael W. 1992. "Religious Freedom at a Crossroads." *University of Chicago Law Review* 59 (Winter): 115–94.

———. 1998. "What Would It Mean to Have a 'First Amendment' for Sexual Orientation?" In Olyan and Nussbaum, *Sexual Orientation and Human Rights*, 234–60.

———. 2000. "Believers as Equal Citizens." In Rosenblum, *Obligations of Citizenship and Demands of Faith*, 90–110.

Mehta, Pratap Bhanu. 1997. Review of *Isaiah Berlin*, by John Gray. *American Political Science Review* 91 (September): 722–23.

Mellinkoff, Albert. 2001. Letter to the editor. *New York Times*, July 24.

Metz, Tamara. 2004. "Why We Should Disestablish Marriage." In Shanley, *Just Marriage*, 99–105.

———. 2010. *Untying the Knot: Marriage, the State, and the Case for Their Divorce*. Princeton, NJ: Princeton University Press.

Mill, John Stuart. 1859. *On Liberty*. In *On Liberty and Other Writings*, edited by Stefan Collini, 1–115. New York: Cambridge University Press.

———. 1869. *The Subjection of Women*. In *On Liberty and Other Writings*, edited by Stefan Collini, 117–217. New York: Cambridge University Press.

Moruzzi, Norma Claire. 1994. "A Problem with Headscarves: Complexities of Political and Social Identity." *Political Theory* 22 (November): 653–72.

Murphy, Andrew R. 2001. *Conscience and Community: Revisiting Toleration and Religious Dissent in Early Modern England and America*. University Park, PA: Pennsylvania State University Press.

Neal, Patrick. 1997. *Liberalism and Its Discontents*. New York: New York University Press.

New York Times. 2004. Editorial. "Heartless Marriage Plans." January 17.

———. 2006. "Court Overturns Arkansas Ban on Same-Sex Foster Parents." June 30.

———. 2008. Editorial. "A Case of Religious Discrimination." November 12.

———. 2009a. "The Best Interest of the Child." January 6.

———. 2009b. Editorial. "The Nativists Are Restless." February 1.

———. 2010a. Editorial. "A Child's Best Interest." April 22.

———. 2010b. "Victory for Families." September 24.

Nussbaum, Martha C. 1997. "Constructing Love, Desire, and Care." In Estlund and Nussbaum, *Sex, Preference, and Family*, 17–43.

———. 2000. "Religion and Women's Equality: The Case of India." In Rosenblum, *Citizenship and Demands of Faith*, 334–402.

———. 2008. *Liberty of Conscience: In Defense of America's Tradition of Religious Equality*. New York: Basic Books.

———. 2010. *From Disgust to Humanity: Sexual Orientation and Constitutional Law*. New York: Oxford University Press.

Okin, Susan Moller. 1989. *Justice, Gender, and the Family*. New York: Basic Books.

———. 1997. "Sexual Orientation and Gender: Dichotomizing Difference." In Estlund and Nussbaum, *Sex, Preference, and Family*, 44–59.

Olyan, Saul M., and Martha C. Nussbaum, eds. 1998. *Sexual Orientation and Human Rights in American Religious Discourse*. New York: Oxford University Press.

Pateman, Carole. 1988. *The Sexual Contract*. Stanford, CA: Stanford University Press.

Perry, Michael. 1997. *Religion in Politics: Constitutional and Moral Perspectives*. New York: Oxford University Press.

Phelan, Shane, ed. 1997. *Playing with Fire: Queer Politics, Queer Theories*. New York: Routledge.

———. 2001. *Sexual Strangers: Gays, Lesbians, and Dilemmas of Citizenship*. Philadelphia: Temple University Press.

Pierceson, Jason. 2005. *Courts, Liberalism, and Rights: Gay Law and Politics in the United States and Canada*. Philadelphia: Temple University Press.

———. 2009. "Same-Sex Marriage and the American Political Tradition." In Babst, Gill, and Pierceson, *Moral Argument*, 119–34.

Pinello, Daniel. 2006. *America's Struggle for Same-Sex Marriage*. New York: Cambridge University Press.

Polikoff, Nancy D. 2008. *Beyond (Straight and Gay) Marriage: Valuing All Families under the Law*. Boston: Beacon Press.

Posner, Richard A. 1997. "The Economic Approach to Homosexuality." In Estlund and Nussbaum, *Sex, Preference, and Family*, 173–91.

Putnam, Michelle. 2009. Letter to the editor. *New York Times*, February 25.

Rauch, Jonathan. 2005. *Gay Marriage: Why It Is Good for Gays, Good for Straights, and Good for America*. New York: Owl Books.

Regan, Milton C., Jr. 2004. "Beyond Justice and Commitment." In Shanley, *Just Marriage*, 57–74.

Reid, Charles J., Jr. 2008. "Marriage: Its Relationship to Religion, Law, and the State." In Laycock, Picarello, and Wilson, *Same-Sex Marriage and Religious Liberty*, 157–88.

Reidy, David A., and Walter J. Riker, eds. 2008. *Coercion and the State*. Dordrecht, The Netherlands: Springer.

Richards, Cindy. 2001. "Study on Tolerance Offers Hate-mongers an Opening." *Chicago Sun-Times*, June 20.

Richards, David A. J. 1986. *Toleration and the Constitution*. New York: Oxford University Press.

———. 1998. *Women, Gays, and the Constitution*. Chicago: University of Chicago Press.

———. 1999. *Identity and the Case for Gay Rights: Race, Gender, and Religion as Analogies*. Chicago: University of Chicago Press.

———. 2005. *The Case for Gay Rights: From* Bowers *to* Lawrence *and Beyond*. Lawrence: University Press of Kansas.

———. 2009. *The Sodomy Cases:* Bowers v. Hardwick *and* Lawrence v. Texas. Lawrence: University Press of Kansas.

Rollins, Joe. 2005. "*Lawrence*, Privacy, and the Marital Bedroom: A Few Telltale Signs of Ironic Worry." In Hirsch, *Future of Gay Rights*, 169–83.

Rosen, Jeffrey. 1995. "Disoriented." *New Republic*, October 23, 24–26.

Rosenblum, Nancy L. 1997. "Democratic Sex, *Reynolds v. United States*, Sexual Relations, and Community." In Estlund and Nussbaum, *Sex, Preference, and Family*, 63–85.

———. 2000a. "Introduction: Pluralism, Integralism, and Political Theories of Religious Accommodation." In Rosenblum, *Obligations of Citizenship and Demands of Faith*, 3–31.

———, ed. 2000b. *Obligations of Citizenship and Demands of Faith: Religious Accommodation in Pluralist Democracies*. Princeton, NJ: Princeton University Press.

Sandel, Michael J. 1982. *Liberalism and the Limits of Justice*. New York: Cambridge University Press.

———. 1987. "Freedom of Conscience or Freedom of Choice?" In *Articles of Faith, Articles of Peace: The Religious Liberty Clauses and the American Public Philosophy*, edited by James Davison Hunter and Os Guiness, 74–92. Washington, DC: Brookings Institution Press.

———. 1996. *Democracy's Discontent: America in Search of a Public Philosophy*. Cambridge, MA: Belknap Press of Harvard University Press.

Savage, Dan. 2008. "Anti-Gay, Anti-Family." *New York Times*, November 12.

Scanlon, T. M. 1996. "The Difficulty of Tolerance." In *Toleration: An Elusive Virtue*, edited by David Heyd, 226–39. Princeton, NJ: Princeton University Press.

Schuck, Peter H., and Rogers M. Smith. 1985. *Citizenship without Consent: Illegal Aliens in the American Polity*. New Haven, CT: Yale University Press.

Selznick, Philip. 1989. "Dworkin's Unfinished Task." *California Law Review* 77 (3, May): 505–13.

Shanley, Mary Lyndon. 2004a. Afterword. In Shanley, *Just Marriage*, 109–16.

———, ed. 2004b. *Just Marriage*. New York: Oxford University Press.

———. 2004c. "Just Marriage: On the Public Importance of Private Unions." In Shanley, *Just Marriage*, 3–30.

Smith, Anna Marie. 1997. "The Centering of Right-Wing Extremism through the Construction of an 'Inclusionary' Homophobia and Racism." In Phelan, *Playing with Fire*, 113–38.

———. 2005. "The Continuing Triumph of Neo-Conservatism in American Constitutional Law." In Hirsch, *Future of Gay Rights*, 185–207.

———. 2007. *Welfare Reform and Sexual Regulation*. New York: Cambridge University Press.

Smith, Rogers M. 2009. "Beyond Sovereignty and Uniformity: The Challenges for Equal Citizenship in the Twenty-First Century." *Harvard Law Review* 122 (3, January): 907–36.

Snyder, Claire. 2006. *Gay Marriage and Democracy: Equality for All*. Lanham, MD: Rowman & Littlefield.

Spinner, Jeff. 1994. *The Boundaries of Citizenship: Race, Ethnicity, and Nationality in the Liberal State*. Baltimore: Johns Hopkins University Press.

Spinner-Halev, Jeff. 2000. *Surviving Diversity: Religion and Democratic Citizenship*. Baltimore: Johns Hopkins University Press.

Spiro, Peter J. 2008. *Beyond Citizenship: American Identity after Globalization*. New York: Oxford University Press.

Stacey, Judith, and Timothy J. Biblarz. 2005. "(How) Does the Sexual Orientation of Parents Matter?" In Burack and Josephson, *Fundamental Differences*, 27–64.

Stein, Edward. 1999. *The Mismeasurement of Desire: The Science, Theory, and Ethics of Sexual Orientation*. New York: Oxford University Press.

Steinberg, Neil. 2007. "Opening Shot." *Chicago Sun-Times*, May 12.

Steinfels, Peter. 2004. "Voters Say Values Matter, But It's Important to Find Out What Reality Is Behind This Convenient Catchall." *New York Times*, November 6.

Stern, Marc D. 2008. "Same-Sex Marriage and the Churches." In Laycock, Picarello, and Wilson, eds., *Same-Sex Marriage and Religious Liberty*, 1–57.

Stith, Richard. 2004. "Keep Friendship Unregulated." *Notre Dame Journal of Law, Ethics, and Public Policy* 18 (1): 263–71.

Strasser, Mark. 2002. *On Same-Sex Marriage, Civil Unions, and the Rule of Law: Constitutional Interpretation at the Crossroads*. Westport, CT: Praeger.

Struening, Karen. 1996. "Privacy and Sexuality in a Society Divided over Moral Culture." *Political Research Quarterly* 49 (September): 502–23.

———. 2009. "Looking for Liberty and Defining Marriage in Three Same-Sex Marriage Cases." In Babst, Gill, and Pierceson, eds., *Moral Argument*, 19–49. Lanham, MD: Lexington Books of Rowman & Littlefield.

Strum, Philippa. 2002. *Women in the Barracks: The VMI Case and Equal Rights*. Lawrence: University Press of Kansas.

Sullivan, Andrew. 1996. *Virtually Normal: An Argument about Homosexuality*. New York: Vintage.

———. 2001. "Unveiled." *New Republic*, August 13, 7.

Sullum, Jacob. 2008. "A Lesson in Public vs. Private Discrimination." *Chicago Sun-Times*, December 4.

Sunstein, Cass R. 1997. "Homosexuality and the Constitution." In Estlund and Nussbaum, *Sex, Preference, and Family*, 208–26.

Talbot, Margaret. 2010. "A Risky Proposal." *New Yorker*, January 18, 40–51.

Taylor, Charles. 1999. "Cross-Purposes: The Liberal-Communitarian Debate." In *Liberalism and the Moral Life*, edited by Nancy L. Rosenblum, 159–82. Cambridge, MA: Harvard University Press.

Tronto, Joan C. 2004. "Marriage: Love or Care?" In Shanley, *Just Marriage*, 46–51.

Turley, Jonathan. 2008. "An Unholy Union: Same-Sex Marriage and the Use of Governmental Programs to Penalize Religious Groups with Unpopular Practices." In Laycock, Picarello, and Wilson, eds., *Same-Sex Marriage and Religious Liberty*, 59–76.

Turner, Jack. 2008. "Awakening to Race: Ralph Ellison and Democratic Individuality." *Political Theory* 36 (October): 655–82.

Underkuffler-Freund, Laura. 1995. "The Separation of the Religious and the Secular: A Foundational Challenge to First Amendment Theory." *William and Mary Law Review* 36 (Winter): 837–988.

Walker, Graham. 2000. "Illusory Pluralism, Inexorable Establishment." In Rosenblum, *Obligations of Citizenship and Demands of Faith*, 111–26.

Wardle, Lynn D. 2003. "Marriage, Relationships, Same-Sex Unions, and the Right of Intimate Association." In Wardle et al., *Marriage and Same-Sex Unions*, 190–202.

Wardle, Lynn D., Mark Strasser, William C. Duncan, and David Orgon Coolidge, eds. 2003. *Marriage and Same-Sex Unions: A Debate*. Westport, CT: Praeger.

Warnke, Georgia. 2007. *After Identity: Rethinking Race, Sex, and Gender*. New York: Cambridge University Press.

Warren, Mark E. 1996. "What Should We Expect from More Democracy?" *Political Theory* (May): 241–70.

Weithman, Paul J. 1997. "Natural Law, Morality, and Sexual Complementarity." In Estlund and Nussbaum, *Sex, Preference, and Family*, 227–46.

Wilkins, Richard G. 2003. "The Constitutionality of Legal Preferences for Heterosexual Marriage." In Wardle et al., *Marriage and Same-Sex Unions*, 227–40.

Will, George. 2006. "New Term for Voters Simply Has No Value." *Chicago Sun-Times*, May 18.

Wolterstorff, Nicholas. 1997a. "Audi on Religion, Politics, and Liberal Democracy." In Audi and Wolterstorff, *Religion in the Public Square*, 145–65.

———. 1997b. "The Role of Religion in Decision and Discussion of Political Issues." In Audi and Wolterstorff, *Religion in the Public Square*, 67–120.

Yoshino, Kenji. 2007. *Covering: The Hidden Assault on Our Civil Rights*. New York: Random House.

INDEX